D0922287

Get the eBook FREE!

(PDF, ePub, Kindle, and liveBook all included)

We believe that once you buy a book from us, you should be able to read it in any format we have available. To get electronic versions of this book at no additional cost to you, purchase and then register this book at the Manning website.

Go to https://www.manning.com/freebook and follow the instructions to complete your pBook registration.

That's it!
Thanks from Manning!

Elm in Action

RICHARD FELDMAN

MANNING
SHELTER ISLAND

For online information and ordering of this and other Manning books, please visit
www.manning.com. The publisher offers discounts on this book when ordered in quantity.
For more information, please contact

    Special Sales Department
    Manning Publications Co.
    20 Baldwin Road
    PO Box 761
    Shelter Island, NY 11964
    Email: orders@manning.com

Manning Publications Co.	Acquisitions editor: Mike Stephens
20 Baldwin Road	Development editor: Elesha Hyde
PO Box 761	Senior technical development editor: Al Scherer
Shelter Island, NY 11964	Technical development editor: Marius Butuc
	Review editor: Aleksandar Dragosavljević
	Production editor: Anthony Calcara
	Copy editor: Sharon Wilkey
	Proofreader: Katie Tennant
	Technical proofreader: Mathias Polligkeit
	Typesetter and cover designer: Marija Tudor

ISBN 9781617294044
Printed in the United States of America

To Mom and Dad,
who have given me more love and wisdom
than I could ever return

brief contents

v

contents

preface

Shortly after I gave my first conference talk about Elm, I got an email from Manning Publications. It said Manning was interested in publishing a book on Elm, and asked if I had time for a phone call with a guy named Mike to talk about Elm and maybe recommend some potential authors. I hopped on the call and gave Mike a few names. Then—I couldn't help myself—I launched into a stream of unsolicited advice about how I thought this hypothetical book should be done.

From start to finish, the book should be about building things. The world is bursting at the seams with books on typed pure functional programming that focus on theory first, second, and third, and then get to "Hello World" around chapter 7. Elm is part of that family of languages, but Elm is for building things! A great Elm book, I told Mike, should have the reader building an interactive application by chapter 3 at the latest.

Having both taught and participated in my fair share of Elm workshops, I didn't stop there. "The book should introduce types only after the reader has built something. That's really important! Otherwise, what happens is . . . " Pretty soon I was gesturing with my free hand as I paced alone around my apartment.

At some point, I realized I was describing the book I wished I'd had back when I first set out to learn functional programming. By the end of the call, I wanted that book to exist so badly, I volunteered to write it. This, I assume, was the desired outcome of the "Hey, could you recommend another author to us?" call. If so, then well played!

When I got that first email, most of my time with Elm had still been as a happy hobbyist. I'd spent less than a year with it at work—using it "in anger," as the saying goes. I knew Elm as a fun language, and my coworkers were loving it so far, but it remained to be seen how the language would fare in the long run, especially in the pressure cooker of a small startup with ambitious goals.

Now that I can reflect on the four years since our company first started using Elm, our decision to adopt it was without a doubt the most positive technical change I've seen any team make in my entire career. Over the years, I've heard other companies tell similar stories about their experience with Elm—in blog posts, conference talks, and sometimes enthusiastically in person.

Fast-forward a few years—and 10 Elm conferences—from that first phone call, and *Elm in Action* now exists! It has become the book I excitedly described on that call: the book I wished I'd had as a beginner. If you want to build things for web browsers, and you want them to be both reliable and delightful to maintain, then you're the person I had in mind when writing this book. I hope you enjoy exploring this wonderful language as much as I have!

acknowledgments

I wrote this book at a pace that could charitably be described as "glacial," so first and foremost I'd like to acknowledge the patient folks at Manning who supported me through all the written and rewritten (and, let's be honest, sometimes rewritten another time or two) chapters—in particular, Elesha Hyde, my editor, who claims not to be a programmer but who has repeatedly spotted bugs in my code examples, and Marius Butuc, who reviewed every snippet of source code and uncovered more mistakes than I'd prefer to count. Much love to my patient wife, Kristy, for putting up with all my late nights spent writing this thing!

It goes without saying that this book would not exist without Evan Czaplicki, since he created Elm. More than that, though, this book wouldn't have turned out nearly as well as it did without his involvement and feedback on the early drafts. Thank you so much, Evan! Further thanks go to Brian Hicks, Luke Westby, Robin Heggelund Hansen, MEAP readers who commented on Manning's liveBook discussion forum, and to everyone else who gave detailed feedback on early chapter drafts. It made a huge difference to me.

I've learned from many people over the years, and I want to acknowledge a few who taught me things I needed to know to write this book. In particular, thanks go to Aditya "Deech" Siram for setting me on the path to learn typed functional programming, to Al Adams for teaching me I can bite off more than I can chew and get it down anyway, and to Amy Weiss—both for introducing me to the depth of prose and for, in 2005, looking me in my novice eye and exclaiming, "You're a writer!" Lastly, thanks again to Evan Czaplicki for . . . I'm not sure how I could put into words all the things you've taught me about programming, so maybe I should have paid closer attention in Amy Weiss's class.

I'd also like to thank all the book's formal reviewers, including Amit Lamba, Andy Kirsch, Bryce Darling, Damian Esteban, Daniel Carl, Daut Morina, Giovanni Ornaghi, Jake Romer, Jeff Smith, Jeffrey "jf" Lim, Jose Samonte, Kariem Ali, Keith Donaldson, Kent Spillner, Kumar Unnikrishnan, Lance Halvorsen, Mathias Polligkeit, Matt Audesse, Peter Hampton, Rob Bazinet, Tahir Awan, Thomas Ballinger, and Ubaldo Pescatore.

Finally, I'd like to thank the incredible friends and colleagues who have shaped the course of my life, including but by no means limited to Jack Stover, Rob Owen, Paul Bender, Tom "T Money" Mooney, Zac Hill, Josh Leven, Michael "Glass" Glass, Jeff Scheur, Marcos "Dui" Toledo, and my amazing sister, Janet Feldman. I love you all.

about this book

Elm in Action teaches you how to build applications using the Elm programming language. It starts with an introduction to the language's basic syntax and semantics, then moves on to building the beginnings of a photo-sharing application. In each of the following chapters, you build on that application—adding features, improving code quality, and writing tests—and learn more about Elm in the process. By the end of the final chapter, you'll have scratch-built a complete single-page application with routing, tests, client-server communication, and JavaScript interoperation.

Who should read this book

This book is written for people who know at least one programming language. This means, for example, that the book does not explain what a function is, or what if does. That said, the book does not expect you to have prior experience with types, functional programming, or any particular language syntax.

You don't need to be a web programmer to learn Elm through this book. However, because Elm runs in the browser, in many places the book assumes you have some high-level familiarity with web concepts such as browsers, servers, HTTP, HTML, CSS, and JavaScript. If you are unfamiliar with these, you may find yourself glossing over a paragraph or diagram here and there, but by the end of the book, you can still expect to understand Elm almost as well as someone who was familiar with those technologies going in.

An exception to this rule is chapter 5, which is about how Elm code can interoperate with JavaScript code. Understanding some parts of that chapter naturally requires an understanding of JavaScript, but even that chapter contains only a few small snippets of JS code. Even if you don't know JS, you may still be able to generally follow what the JS code is doing in the context of the chapter.

How this book is organized: a roadmap

Elm in Action is divided into three parts and eight chapters. The first three chapters cover the basics; by the end of them, you will have learned the core concepts of the language and will have built a small Elm application. The next three chapters cover intermediate topics that come up in more fully featured Elm projects. The final two are about techniques that let you build larger and more advanced Elm applications.

- *Chapter 1*—"Welcome to Elm" covers the basic syntax and concepts of the language. It teaches you to "speak Elm" but not yet to do much with it.
- *Chapter 2*—"Your first Elm application" introduces the Elm Architecture, which is the foundation on which all Elm applications are built. By the end of the chapter, you'll have used the Elm Architecture to build a working application.
- *Chapter 3*—"Compiler as assistant" covers Elm's compiler and type system and shows how you can use it to make the application you built in chapter 2 easier to maintain.
- *Chapter 4*—"Talking to servers" shows how to use JSON decoders and commands to communicate between your application and a web server.
- *Chapter 5*—"Talking to JavaScript" introduces subscriptions over the course of adding some JavaScript interoperation to your application.
- *Chapter 6*—"Testing" shows how to use `elm-test`'s unit-testing and fuzz-testing features to make your application more reliable through automated tests.
- *Chapter 7*—"Data modeling" details recursive data modeling techniques, which give you the ability to build a wider variety of applications.
- *Chapter 8*—"Single-page applications" brings all the code from the previous chapters together, connecting your application's two separate pages through a single-page application architecture, including handling routing and sharing code between pages.

Each chapter builds on concepts introduced in the ones before it, so the book is designed to be read in normal chapter order rather than jumping around. Every line of code in the application is introduced in one chapter or another, so if you do decide to skip around, it might help to look at the code listings at www.manning.com /books/elm-in-action to see where the application's code base stands at the beginning of that chapter.

About the code

This book contains many examples of source code in numbered listings and in line with normal text. In both cases, source code is formatted in a `fixed-width font like this` to separate it from ordinary text. Sometimes code is also **in bold** to highlight code that has changed from previous steps in the chapter, such as when a new feature adds to an existing line of code.

In many cases, the original source code has been reformatted; we've added line breaks and reworked indentation to accommodate the available page space in the book. Code annotations accompany many of the listings, highlighting important concepts.

The code listings in each chapter fall into two categories: independent examples related to a particular concept, and code changes for the application whose development begins in chapter 2 and continues through chapter 8.

The complete source code for the application is available online on the Manning website at www.manning.com/books/elm-in-action and on GitHub at github.com /rtfeldman/elm-in-action. The end of each chapter also includes a final listing indicating where any changes to the application ended up, including annotations that comment on relevant details. The independent code examples (the ones unrelated to the application) are not included in the online repository.

The book was developed with Elm version 0.19.1, which is available for free and runs on Windows, macOS, and Linux. Appendix A has instructions on how to install Elm, as well as some supplemental free tools used in chapters 6 and 8.

liveBook discussion forum

Purchase of *Elm in Action* includes free access to a private web forum run by Manning Publications where you can make comments about the book, ask technical questions, and receive help from the author and from other users. To access the forum, go to https://livebook.manning.com/#!/book/elm-in-action/discussion. You can learn more about Manning's forums and the rules of conduct at https://livebook.manning .com/#!/discussion.

Manning's commitment to our readers is to provide a venue where a meaningful dialogue between individual readers and between readers and the author can take place. It is not a commitment to any specific amount of participation on the part of the author, whose contribution to the forum remains voluntary (and unpaid). We suggest you try asking him some challenging questions lest his interest stray! The forum and the archives of previous discussions will be accessible from the publisher's website as long as the book is in print.

Other online resources

The following are additional Elm resources:

- guide.elm-lang.org—The official Elm guide is a fantastic resource that will always be an up-to-date language reference whenever a new version of Elm is released.
- github.com/rtfeldman/elm-spa-example—This code repository contains a sizeable (roughly 4,000 lines of code) single-page application the author wrote in Elm as an example of good practices as he sees them. It can give you a sense of what a larger Elm application than the one you'll build over the course of this book might look like.
- frontendmasters.com/courses/elm—The author recorded both an "Introduction to Elm" and an "Advanced Elm" video workshop course for Frontend

Masters. The Introduction course covers topics similar to those in this book, but with different examples and exercises. The Advanced course is intended for people who have spent a few months with Elm, so you might find it a nice next step if you've finished this book and are looking for more advanced topics.

about the author

Richard has spent 24 years programming, almost half of them professionally. Most of his career has been as a web programmer, where he has often found himself pushing the browser to its limit in the pursuit of ambitious user interfaces. He first used Java-Script before jQuery came out, was among the earliest contributors to React after it was open sourced, and started writing Elm before it had a core team.

Today Richard is a member of the Elm core team, is a frequent conference speaker on the topic of Elm, and is the organizer of the Philadelphia Elm Meetup. He is also an instructor for Frontend Masters, where he teaches an "Introduction to Elm" as well as an "Advanced Elm" course. He maintains several widely used open source Elm projects, including elm-test, elm-css, elm-spa-example, and elm-json-decode-pipeline.

Some have said he's "into Elm," but he's not sure where they got that wild idea.

about the cover illustration

Turkey/Ottoman Empire collection

The illustration of the woman on the cover of *Elm in Action* is titled "An Egyptian Arab." The illustration is taken from a collection of costumes of the Ottoman Empire published on January 1, 1802, by William Miller of Old Bond Street, London. The title page is missing from the collection, and we have been unable to track it down to date. The book's table of contents identifies the figures in both English and French, and each illustration bears the names of two artists who worked on it, both of whom would no doubt be surprised to find their art gracing the front cover of a computer programming book ... 200 years later.

The collection was purchased by a Manning editor at an antiquarian flea market in the "Garage" on West 26th Street in Manhattan. The seller was an American based in Ankara, Turkey, and the transaction took place just as he was packing up his stand for the day. The Manning editor didn't have on his person the substantial amount of cash that was required for the purchase, and a credit card and check were both politely turned down. With the seller flying back to Ankara that evening, the situation was getting hopeless. What was the solution? It turned out to be nothing more than an old-fashioned verbal agreement sealed with a handshake. The seller simply proposed that the money be transferred to him by wire, and the editor walked out with the bank information on a piece of paper and the portfolio of images under his arm. Needless to say, we transferred the funds the next day, and we remain grateful and impressed by this unknown person's trust in one of us. It recalls something that might have happened a long time ago.

We at Manning celebrate the inventiveness, the initiative, and, yes, the fun of the computer business with book covers based on the rich diversity of regional life of two centuries ago, brought back to life by the pictures from this collection.

Part 1

Getting started

The first three chapters cover the fundamentals of building a user interface in Elm. By the end of chapter 3, you'll have built a basic Elm application from scratch, having learned how to read and write Elm syntax, use The Elm Architecture to build interactive user interfaces, and leverage Elm's compiler to get strong guarantees about your code.

Chapter 1 introduces the basics of Elm syntax and some basic operations. It focuses on small, self-contained examples and shows you how to run them. It sets the stage for chapter 2, where you begin by rendering a single page in the browser, and then make it interactive using The Elm Architecture.

Finally, chapter 3 builds on the application you wrote in chapter 2. You'll extend it by adding some documentation and new functionality, learning some helpful techniques that will come in handy throughout the rest of the book. Once you complete chapter 3, you'll know enough to be able to build a basic Elm project on your own

Welcome to Elm

Back in 2014, I set out to rewrite a side project and ended up with a new favorite programming language. Not only was the rewritten code faster, more reliable, and easier to maintain, but writing it was the most fun I'd had in over a decade of writing code. Ever since that project, I've been hooked on Elm.

The rewrite in question was a writing application I'd built even longer ago, in 2011. Having tried out several writing apps over the course of writing a novel, and being satisfied with none, I decided to scratch my own itch and build my dream writing app. I called it Dreamwriter.

For those keeping score: yes, I was indeed writing code in order to write prose better.

Things went well at first. I built the basic web app, started using it, and iterated on the design. Months later I'd written over fifty thousand words in Dreamwriter. If I'd been satisfied with that early design, the story might have ended there. However, users always want a better experience—and when the user and the developer are the same person, further iteration is inevitable.

The more I revised Dreamwriter, the more difficult it became to maintain. I'd spend hours trying to reproduce bugs that knocked me out of my writing groove. At some point, the copy and paste functions stopped working, and I found myself resorting to the browser's developer tools whenever I needed to move paragraphs around.

Right around when I'd decided to scrap my unreliable code base and do a full rewrite, a blog post crossed my radar. After reading it, I knew three things:

- The Elm programming language compiled to JavaScript, just like Babel or TypeScript. (I already had a compile step in my build script, so this was familiar territory.)
- Elm used the same rendering approach as React.js—which I had recently grown to love—except Elm had rendering benchmarks that outperformed React's!
- Elm's compiler would catch a lot of the errors I'd been seeing before they could harm me in production. I did not yet know just how many it would catch.

I'd never built anything with a functional programming language like Elm before, but I decided to take the plunge. I didn't really know what I was doing, but the compiler's helpful error messages kept picking me up whenever I stumbled. Eventually, I got the revised version up and running, and began to refactor.

The refactoring experience blew me away. I revised the Elm-powered Dreamwriter gleefully, even recklessly—and no matter how dramatic my changes, the compiler always had my back. It would point out whatever corner cases I'd missed, and I'd go through and fix them. As soon as the code compiled, lo and behold, everything worked again. I felt *invincible*.

I related my Elm experience to my coworkers at NoRedInk, and they were curious but understandably cautious. How could we find out if the team liked it without taking a big risk? A full rewrite may have been fine for Dreamwriter, but it would have been irresponsible to attempt that for our company's entire frontend.

So we introduced Elm gently, by rewriting just one portion of one production feature in Elm. It went well, so we did a bit more. And then more.

Today our frontend programmers code almost exclusively in Elm, and our team has never been happier. Our test suites are smaller, yet our product is more reliable. Our feature set has grown more complex, yet refactoring remains delightful. We swap stories with other companies using Elm about how long our production code has run without throwing a runtime exception. In this book, we'll explore all of these benefits.

After learning some basics, we'll begin building an Elm single-page web application called *Photo Groove*. Building it will involve learning concepts that apply to any Elm application, not just single-page apps—concepts like rendering, state management, testing, talking to servers, interoperating with JavaScript, and performance optimization.

We'll build this application the way teams typically do: ship a basic version that works, but has minimal features and some technical debt. As we advance through the chapters, we'll expand and refactor our code, adding features and paying off technical debt as we learn more about Elm. By the end of the book, we will have transformed our application into a more featureful product, with a more maintainable code base, than the one we initially shipped.

With any luck, we'll have a lot of fun doing it. Welcome to Elm!

1.1 How Elm fits in

Elm can be used either as a replacement for in-browser JavaScript code or as a complement to it. You write some .elm files, run them through Elm's compiler, and end up with plain old .js files that the browser runs as it normally would. If you have separate stylesheets that you use alongside JavaScript, they'll work the same way alongside Elm.

Figure 1.1 illustrates this process.

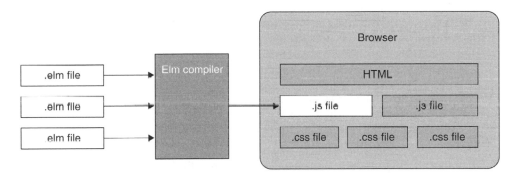

Figure 1.1 Elm files are compiled to plain old JavaScript files.

The appropriate Elm-to-JavaScript ratio can vary by project. Some projects may want primarily JavaScript and only a touch of Elm for business logic or rendering. Others may want a great deal of Elm but just a pinch of JavaScript to leverage its larger ecosystem. No single answer applies to every project.

What distinguishes Elm from the many flavors of JavaScript is *reliability*. Handwritten JavaScript code is notoriously prone to runtime crashes like "undefined is not a function." TypeScript has improved on this, but there are enough loopholes and escape hatches in its design that the surrounding ecosystem is often regarded with caution.

In contrast, Elm programmers consistently describe the *confidence* Elm's compiler inspires in them. Elm applications have a reputation for never throwing runtime exceptions in practice! This reliability extends to the entire Elm package ecosystem, which is built around a small set of simple primitives like expressions, immutable values, and managed effects—all verified by the compiler.

Elm's compiler also has a reputation for user-friendliness. Not only does it infer the types of entire programs without requiring the handwritten type annotations that many languages do—in chapter 2 we'll build an entire application, and then in chapter 3 we'll see how to add optional annotations to it—but when the compiler does find problems, it reports them with such clarity that it has made a name for itself even among legendary programmers.

> *That should be an inspiration for every error message.*
>   —John Carmack, after seeing one of Elm's compiler errors

Having this level of compiler assistance makes Elm code dramatically easier to refactor and debug, especially as code bases grow larger. There is an up-front cost to learning and adopting Elm, but you reap more and more maintainability benefits the longer the project remains in active development.

> **TIP** Most teams that use Elm in production say they used a "planting the seed" approach. Instead of waiting for a big project where they could build everything in Elm from the ground up, they rewrote a small part of their existing JavaScript or TypeScript code base in Elm. This was low-risk and could be rolled back if things did not go as planned, but having that small seed planted in production meant they could grow their Elm code at a comfortable pace from then on.

Although Elm is in many ways a simpler language than JavaScript, it's also much younger. This means Elm has fewer off-the-shelf solutions available for any given problem. Elm code can interoperate with JavaScript code to piggyback the larger JavaScript library ecosystem, but Elm's design differs enough from JavaScript's that incorporating JavaScript libraries takes effort.

Balancing these trade-offs depends on the specifics of a given project. Let's say you're on a team where people are comfortable with JavaScript or TypeScript, but are new to Elm. Here are some projects I expect would benefit from the team learning and using Elm:

- Feature-rich web applications whose code bases are large or will grow large
- Individual features that will be revised and maintained over an extended period of time
- Projects where most functionality comes from in-house code, not off-the-shelf libraries

In contrast, I might choose a more familiar language and toolset for projects like these:

- Time-crunched projects where learning a language is unrealistic given the deadline
- Projects that will consist primarily of gluing together off-the-shelf components
- Quick proof-of-concept prototypes that will not be maintained long-term

We'll explore these trade-offs in more detail throughout the course of the book.

1.2 Expressions

To get our feet wet with Elm, let's tap into one of the most universal traits across the animal kingdom: the innate desire to *play*. Researchers have developed many theories as to why we play, including to learn, to practice, to experiment, and, of course, for the pure fun of it.

These researchers could get some high-quality data by observing a member of the *homo sapiens programmerus* species in its natural environment for play—the read-eval-print loop, or REPL. You'll be using Elm's REPL to play as you take your first steps as an Elm programmer.

1.2.1 Using elm repl

The Elm Platform includes a nice REPL called elm repl, so if you have not installed the Elm Platform yet, head over to appendix A to get hooked up.

Once you're ready, enter elm repl at the terminal. You should see this prompt:

```
---- Elm 0.19.1 ------------------------------------------------------
Say :help for help and :exit to exit!
--------------------------------------------------------------- >
```

Alexander Graham Bell invented the telephone over a century ago. There was no customary greeting back then, so Bell suggested one: lift the receiver and bellow out a rousing "Ahoy!" Thomas Edison later proposed the alternative "Hello," which stuck, and today programmers everywhere append "World" as the customary way to greet a new programming language.

Let's spice things up a bit, shall we? Enter this at the prompt:

```
> "Ahoy, World!"
```

You should see this response from elm repl:

```
"Ahoy, World!" : String
```

Congratulations—you are now an Elm programmer!

> **NOTE** To focus on the basics, for the rest of this chapter I'll omit the type annotations that elm repl prints. For example, the previous code snippet would have omitted the : String portion of "Ahoy, World!" : String. We'll get into these annotations in chapter 3.

If you're the curious sort, by all means feel free to play as we continue. Enter things that occur to you and see what happens! Whenever you encounter an error you don't understand yet, picture yourself as a tiger cub building intuition for physics through experimentation: adorable for now, but powerful in time.

1.2.2 *Building expressions*

Let's rebuild our `"Ahoy, World!"` greeting from two parts and then play around from there. Try entering these into `elm repl`.

Listing 1.1   Combining strings

```
> "Ahoy, World!"
"Ahoy, World!"

> "Ahoy, " ++ "World!"
"Ahoy, World!"

> "Pi is " ++ String.fromFloat pi ++ " (give or take)"  ◁───┐
"Pi is 3.141592653589793 (give or take)"
```

> **String.fromFloat is a standalone function, not a method associated with a particular object. We will cover it later.**

In Elm, we use the `++` operator to combine strings, instead of the `+` operator JavaScript uses. At this point, you may be wondering: does Elm even have a `+` operator? What about the other arithmetic operators? Let's find out by experimenting in `elm repl`!

Listing 1.2   Arithmetic expressions

```
> 1234 + 103
1337

> 12345 - (5191 * -15)        ◁───┐  Nests expressions
90210                              │  via parentheses

> 2 ^ 11
2048

> 49 / 10
4.9
                                    Integer division
> 49 // 10        ◁───┐            (decimals get truncated)
4
```

Sure enough, Elm has both a `++` and a `+` operator. They're used for different things:

- The `++` operator is for appending. Using it on a number is an error.
- The `+` operator is for addition. It can be used *only* on numbers.

You'll see this preference for *being explicit* often in Elm. If two operations are sufficiently different—in this case, adding and appending—Elm implements them separately, so each implementation can *do one thing well.*

STRINGS AND CHARACTERS

Elm also distinguishes between *strings* and their individual UTF-8 *characters*. Double quotes in Elm represent string literals, just as in JavaScript, but single quotes in Elm represent character literals. Table 1.1 shows a few examples of strings and characters.

Table 1.1 Strings and characters

Elm literal	Result
"a"	A string with a length of 1.
'a'	A single character.
"abc"	A string with a length of 3.
'abc'	*Error*: Character literals must contain exactly one character.
""	An empty string.
' '	*Error*: Character literals must contain exactly one character.

COMMENTS

There are two ways to write comments in Elm:

- Use -- for single-line comments (like // in JavaScript).
- Use {- to begin a multiline comment, and -} to end it (like /* and */ in JS).

Let's see these in action!

Listing 1.3 Characters, comments, and named values

```
> 'a'  -- This is a single-line comment. It will be ignored.    ◁      JavaScript
'a'                                                                     comment: //

> "a"  {- This comment could span multiple lines. -}    ◁───┐   JavaScript
"a"                                                            comment: /* ... */

> milesPerHour = 88          ◁────┐   JavaScript: const
88                                    milesPerHour = 88;

> milesPerHour
88
```

ASSIGNING NAMES TO VALUES

In the last two lines of code in the preceding listing, we did something new: we assigned the name milesPerHour to the value 88.

NOTE Normally, once we assign a name to a value, that name cannot be reassigned later to a different value in the same scope. Assignment in Elm works like JavaScript's const keyword, as opposed to var or let. The only exception to this is in elm repl, where you can override a previous assignment for convenience.

There are a few things to keep in mind when assigning names to values:

- The name must begin with a lowercase letter. After that, it can be a mix of letters, numbers, and underscores.

- By convention, all letters should be in one uninterrupted sequence. For example, `map4` is a reasonable name, but `map4ever` is not, as the sequence of letters is interrupted by the `4`.
- Because of the previous two rules, you should never use `snake_case` or `SCREAMING_SNAKE_CASE` to name values. Use `camelCase` instead.
- If you absolutely must know whether the compiler will accept `some_raD __TH1NG___` as a valid name, remember: what happens in `elm repl` stays in `elm repl`.

ASSIGNING NAMES TO EXPRESSIONS

You can assign names not only to literal values, but also to expressions.

DEFINITION   An *expression* is anything that evaluates to a single value.

Table 1.2 lists some expressions we've seen so far.

Table 1.2   Examples of Elm expressions

Expression	Evaluates to
`"Ahoy, " ++ "World!"`	`"Ahoy, World!"`
`2 ^ 11`	`2048`
`pi`	`3.141592653589793`
`42`	`42`

NOTE   Since an expression is anything that evaluates to a value, literal values like `"Ahoy, World!"` and `42` are expressions too—just expressions that have already been fully evaluated.

Expressions are the basic building block of Elm applications. This is different from JavaScript, which offers many features as statements instead of expressions.

Consider these two lines of JavaScript code:

```
label = (num > 0) ? "positive" : "negative"  // ternary expression
label = if (num > 0) { "positive" } else { "negative" }  // if-statement
```

The first line is a ternary *expression*. As an expression, it evaluates to a value, and JavaScript happily assigns that value to `label`.

The second line is an *if-statement*, and since statements do not evaluate to values, trying to assign it to `label` yields a syntax error.

This distinction does not exist in Elm, as Elm programs express logic by using expressions only. As such, Elm has *if-expressions* instead of if-statements. As you will see in chapter 2, every Elm application is essentially one big expression built up from many smaller ones!

1.2.3 *Booleans and conditionals*

There aren't many Boolean values out there—just the two, really—and working with them in Elm is similar to working with them in JavaScript. There are a few differences, though:

- You write `True` and `False` instead of `true` and `false`.
- You write `/=` instead of `!==`.
- To negate values, you use Elm's `not` function instead of JavaScript's `!` prefix.

Let's try them out!

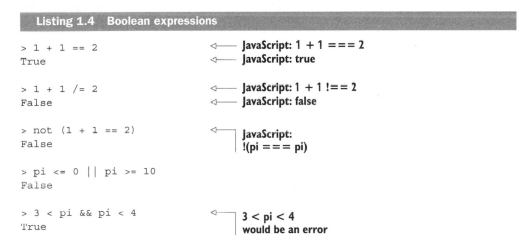

Listing 1.4 Boolean expressions

```
> 1 + 1 == 2          ⟵── JavaScript: 1 + 1 === 2
True                  ⟵── JavaScript: true

> 1 + 1 /= 2          ⟵── JavaScript: 1 + 1 !== 2
False                 ⟵── JavaScript: false

> not (1 + 1 == 2)    ⟵┐ JavaScript:
False                   │ !(pi === pi)

> pi <= 0 || pi >= 10
False

> 3 < pi && pi < 4    ⟵┐ 3 < pi < 4
True                    │ would be an error
```

Now let's say it's a lovely afternoon at the North Pole, and we're in Santa's workshop writing a bit of user interface (UI) logic to display how many elves are currently on vacation. The quick-and-dirty approach would be to add the string `" elves"` after the number of vacationing elves, but then when the count is 1, we'd display `"1 elves"`, and we're better than that.

Let's polish our user experience with the if-expression shown in figure 1.2.

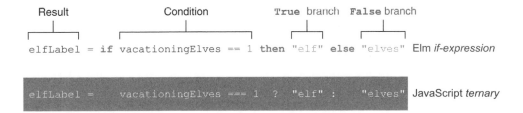

```
  Result              Condition          True branch  False branch

elfLabel = if vacationingElves == 1 then "elf" else "elves"   Elm if-expression

elfLabel =     vacationingElves === 1 ? "elf" :     "elves"   JavaScript ternary
```

Figure 1.2 Comparing an Elm if-expression to a JavaScript ternary

Like JavaScript ternaries, Elm if-expressions require three ingredients:

- A condition
- A branch to evaluate if the condition passes
- A branch to evaluate otherwise

Each ingredient must be an expression, and the whole if-expression evaluates to the result of whichever branch got evaluated. You'll get an error if any of these three ingredients is missing, so make sure to specify an `else` branch every time!

> **NOTE** JavaScript has a concept of "truthiness," where conditionals can be values other than `true` and `false`. Elm doesn't have truthiness. Conditions can be either `True` or `False`, and that's it. Life is simpler this way.

Now let's say we modified our pluralization conditional to include a third case:

- If we have one Elf, evaluate to `"elf"`.
- Otherwise, if we have a positive number of elves, evaluate to `"elves"`.
- Otherwise, we must have a negative number of elves, so evaluate to `"anti-elves"`.

In JavaScript, you may have used `else if` to continue branching conditionals like this. It's common to use `else if` for the same purpose in Elm, but it's worth noting that `else if` in Elm is nothing more than a stylish way to combine the concepts we learned a moment ago. Check it out!

Listing 1.5 Using `else if`

```
if elfCount == 1 then
  "elf"
else
  (if elfCount >= 0 then "elves" else "anti-elves")
```
Uses an if-expression inside else

```
if elfCount == 1 then
  "elf"
else (if elfCount >= 0 then
  "elves"
else
  "anti-elves")
```
Rearranges some whitespace

```
if elfCount == 1 then
  "elf"
else if elfCount >= 0 then
  "elves"
else
  "anti-elves"
```
Drops the parentheses

This works because the `else` branch of an if-expression must be an expression, and it just so happens that if-expressions themselves are expressions. As shown in figure 1.3,

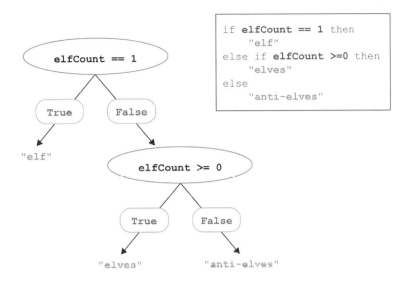

```
if elfCount == 1 then
    "elf"
else if elfCount >=0 then
    "elves"
else
    "anti-elves"
```

Figure 1.3 The **else-if** technique: use an if-expression as the **else** branch of another if-expression.

all it takes is putting an if-expression after another one's else, and voilà! Additional branching achieved.

Nesting expressions is a recurring theme in Elm, and you'll see plenty more recipes like else if throughout the book.

Chapter 3 will add a powerful new conditional to our expression toolbox, one that has no analogue in JavaScript: the *case-expression*.

1.3 Functions

Earlier we wrote this expression:

```
elfLabel = if vacationingElves == 1 then "elf" else "elves"
```

Suppose it turns out that a general-purpose singular/plural labeler would be really useful, and we want to reuse similar logic across the code base at Santa's workshop. Search results might want to display "1 result" and "2 results" as appropriate, for example. We can write a *function* to make this pluralization logic easily reusable.

DEFINITION Elm *functions* represent reusable logic. They are not objects. They have no fields, no prototypes, and no ability to store state. All they do is accept values as arguments and then return a value.

If you thought expressions would be a recurring theme in Elm, wait 'til you see functions!

1.3.1   *Defining functions*

Let's define our first function: isPositive. It will take a number and then do the following:

- Return True if the number is greater than zero
- Return False otherwise

We can define isPositive in elm repl and try it out right away.

Listing 1.6   Defining a function

```
> isPositive num = num > 0
<function>
```
← JavaScript: function isPositive(num) { return num > 0; }

```
> isPositive 2
True
```
← JavaScript: isPositive(2)

```
> (isPositive 2)
True
```
← JavaScript: (isPositive(2))

```
> isPositive (2 - 10)
False
```
← JavaScript: isPositive(2 - 10)

As you can see, in Elm we put the function parameter name before the = sign. We also don't surround the function body with { }. And did you notice the return keyword is nowhere to be seen? That's because Elm doesn't have one! In Elm, a function body is a single expression, and since an expression evaluates to a single value, Elm uses that value as the function's return value. This means all Elm functions return values!

For our isPositive function, the expression num > 0 serves as the function's body and provides its return value.

Refactoring out an early return

In JavaScript, return is often used to exit a function early. This is harmless when used responsibly, but can lead to unpleasant surprises when used in the middle of large functions. Elm does not support these unpleasant surprises, because it has no return keyword.

Let's refactor the early return out of this JavaScript function:

```
function capitalize(str) {
    if (!str) {
        return str;              ← Early return
    }

    return str[0].toUpperCase() + str.slice(1);
}
```

Without making any other changes, we can refactor this early return into a ternary:

```
function capitalize(str) {
    return !str ? str : str[0].toUpperCase() + str.slice(1);
}
```

Poof! There it goes. Since JavaScript's ternaries are structurally similar to Elm's if-expressions, this code is now much more straightforward to rewrite in Elm. More-convoluted JavaScript functions may require more steps than this, but it is always possible to untangle them into plain old conditionals.

Removing an early `return` is one of many quick refactors you can do to ease the transition from legacy JavaScript to Elm, and we'll look at more of them throughout the book. When doing these, do not worry if the intermediate JavaScript code looks ugly! It's intended to be a stepping-stone to nicer Elm code, not something to be maintained long-term.

Let's use what you just learned to generalize our previous elf-labeling expression into a reusable `pluralize` function. Our function this time will have a longer definition than last time, so let's use multiple lines to give it some breathing room. In `elm repl`, you can enter multiple lines by pressing Enter to insert a line break as normal. If you do, you'll need to press Enter twice when you're finished entering everything.

NOTE Indent with spaces only! Tab characters are syntax errors in Elm.

Listing 1.7 Using multiple REPL lines

```
> pluralize singular plural count =
|     if count == 1 then singular else plural          Don't forget to press Enter
<function>                                             twice when you're done.

> pluralize "elf" "elves" 3          No commas
"elves"                              between arguments!

> pluralize "elf" "elves" (round 0.9)          (round 0.9)
"elf"                                          returns 1.
```

When passing multiple arguments to an Elm function, separate the arguments with whitespace and not commas. That last line of code is an example of passing the result of one function call, namely `round 0.9`, as an argument to another function. Think about what would happen if we did not put parentheses around `(round 0.9)` —how many arguments would we then be passing to `pluralize`?

1.3.2 Importing functions

So far, we've used only basic operators and functions we wrote ourselves. Now let's expand our repertoire of functions by using one from an external module.

DEFINITION A *module* is a named collection of Elm functions and other values.

The `String` module is a core module that ships with Elm. Additional modules can be obtained from Elm's official package repository, copying and pasting code from elsewhere, or through a back-alley rendezvous with a shadowy figure known as Dr. Deciduous. Chapter 4 covers the former, but neither the author nor Manning Publications endorses obtaining Elm modules through a shadowy back-alley rendezvous.

Let's import the `String` module and try out some of its functions.

```
> String.toLower "Why don't you make TEN louder?"
"why don't you make ten louder?"

> String.toUpper "These go to eleven."
"THESE GO TO ELEVEN."

> String.fromFloat 44.1
"44.1"

> String.fromInt 531
"531"
```

The `String.fromFloat` and `String.fromInt` functions convert *floats* (numbers that may be fractions) and *integers* (numbers that may not be fractions) to strings.

In JavaScript, both are handled by the catchall `toString` method, whereas Elm generally uses separate functions to convert between different types of values. This way, Elm can (and will) give an error if you accidentally call `String.fromFloat` on a function instead of a number, rather than cheerfully displaying gibberish to a very confused user who was expecting to see their account balance.

USING FUNCTIONS FROM THE STRING MODULE

Observant readers may note a striking resemblance between Elm's `String.toUpper` function and the `toUpperCase()` method one finds on JavaScript strings. This is the first example of a pattern we will encounter many times!

JavaScript has several ways of organizing string-related functionality: fields on a string, methods on a string, or methods on the `String` global itself.

In contrast, Elm strings have neither fields nor methods. As detailed in table 1.3, the `String` module houses the standard set of string-related features, and exposes them in the form of plain old functions like `toLower` and `toUpper`.

Table 1.3 String functionality comparison

JavaScript	Elm
`"storm".length`	`String.length "storm"`
`"dredge".toUpperCase()`	`String.toUpper "dredge"`
`String.fromCharCode(someChar)`	`String.fromChar someChar`

This organizational pattern is consistent not only within the `String` module, but also across Elm. Want a function related to sets? Look no further than the functions in the `Set` module. Debugging functions? Hit up the `Debug` module.

Methods are never the answer in Elm; over here it's all vanilla functions, all the time.

> **TIP** Complete documentation for String, Set, Debug, and other tasty modules can be found in the elm/core section of the https://package.elm-lang.org website.

You'll learn more about modules in the coming chapters, including how to write your own!

USING STRING.FILTER TO FILTER OUT CHARACTERS

Another useful function in the String module is filter. It lets us filter out unwanted characters from a string, such as non-numeric digits from a phone number.

To do this, we'll pass filter a function that specifies which characters to keep. The function will take a single character as an argument and return True if we should keep that character, or False if we should chuck it. Figure 1.4 illustrates using String.filter to remove dashes from a US telephone number.

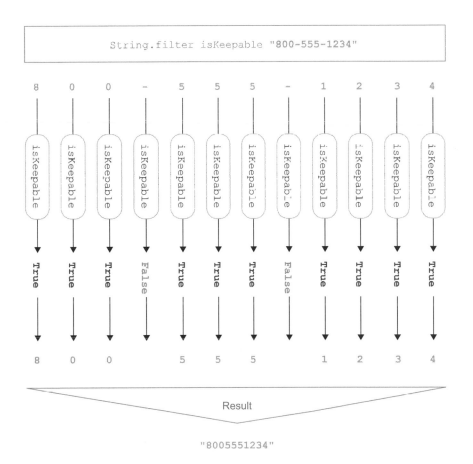

Figure 1.4   Using String.filter to remove dashes from a US phone number

Elm functions are first-class values that can be passed around just like any other value. This lets us provide `filter` with the function it expects by defining that function and then passing it in as a plain old argument.

Listing 1.9   Filtering with a named function

```
> isKeepable character = character /= '-'
<function>

> isKeepable 'z'
True

> isKeepable '-'
False

> String.filter isKeepable "800-555-1234"
"8005551234"
```

A function describing which characters to keep

Passing our function to String.filter

This code normalizes these telephone numbers splendidly. Alexander Graham Bell would be proud!

`String.filter` is one of the *higher-order functions* (functions that accept other functions as arguments) that Elm uses to implement customizable logic like this.

1.3.3   *Creating scope with let-expressions*

Let's say we find ourselves removing dashes from phone numbers so often that we want to make a reusable function for the operation. We can do that with our trusty `isKeepable` function:

```
withoutDashes str = String.filter isKeepable str
```

This works, but in a larger Elm program, it might be annoying having `isKeepable` in the global scope like this. After all, its implementation is useful only to `without-Dashes`. Can we avoid globally reserving such a nicely self-documenting name?

Absolutely! We can scope `isKeepable` to the implementation of `withoutDashes` by using a *let-expression*.

DEFINITION   A *let-expression* adds locally scoped named values to an expression.

Figure 1.5 shows how to implement `withoutDashes` by using a single let-expression.

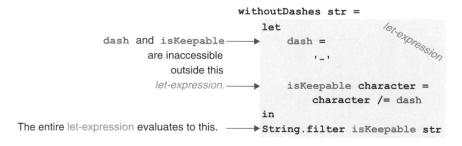

Figure 1.5   Anatomy of the wild let-expression

The code in figure 1.5 does very nearly the same thing as entering the following in
elm repl:

```
> dash = '-'
> isKeepable character = character /= dash
> withoutDashes str = String.filter isKeepable str
```

In both versions, the implementation of withoutDashes boils down to
String.filter isKeepable str. The only difference between the two is the
scope of dash and isKeepable:

- In the elm repl version, dash and isKeepable are in the global scope.
- In figure 1.5, dash and isKeepable are scoped locally to the let-expression.

You can mentally replace any let-expression with the part after its in keyword—in this
case, String.filter isKeepable str. All the named values between let and in
are intermediate values that are no longer in scope once the expression after in gets
evaluated.

> **NOTE** The indentation you see in figure 1.5 is no accident! In a multiline
> let-expression, the let and in keywords must be at the same indentation
> level, and all other lines in the let-expression must be indented further than
> they are.

Anywhere you'd write a normal expression, you can swap in a let-expression instead.
Because of this, you don't need to learn anything new to define locally scoped named
values inside function bodies, branches of if-expressions, or anyplace else.

Wherever you want some local scope, reach for a refreshing let-expression!

1.3.4 Anonymous functions

Anonymous functions work like named functions, except they don't have a name. The
following listing compares named and anonymous functions in JavaScript and in Elm.

Listing 1.10 Named and anonymous functions

```
function area(w, h) { return w * h; }          ◁———  JavaScript
                                                      named function
function(w, h) { return w * h; }          ◁———  JavaScript
                                                anonymous function
area w h = w * h          ◁———  Elm named
                                function
\w h -> w * h     ◁———  Elm anonymous
                        function
```

Elm's anonymous functions differ from named functions in three ways:

- They have no names.
- They begin with a \ symbol.
- Their parameters are followed by a -> symbol instead of an = symbol.

Once defined, anonymous functions and named functions work the same way; you can always use one in place of the other. For example, the following do exactly the same thing:

```
isKeepable char = char /= '-'
isKeepable = \char -> char /= '-'
```

Let's use an anonymous function to call `String.filter` in one line instead of two, and then see if we can improve the business logic! For example, we can try using `Char.isDigit` to cast a wider net, filtering out any nondigit characters instead of just dashes.

Listing 1.11   Filtering with anonymous functions

```
> String.filter (\char -> char /= '-') "800-555-1234"
"8005551234"

> String.filter (\char -> char /= '-') "(800) 555-1234"    ◁──┐ Our simple filter
"(800) 5551234"                                                └ fell short here.

> String.filter (\char -> Char.isDigit char) "(800) 555-1234"    ◁──┐ Much
"8005551234"                                                         └ better!

> String.filter Char.isDigit "(800) 555-1234"    ◁──┐ Refactor of previous
"8005551234"                                         └ approach
```

Anonymous functions are often used with higher-order functions like `String.filter`.

1.3.5   *Operators*

So far, we've seen functions such as `String.filter`, as well as operators such as `++`, `-`, and `==`. How do operators and functions relate?

As it turns out, Elm's operators *are* functions! There are a few things that distinguish operators from normal functions:

- Operators must always accept exactly two arguments—no more, no fewer.
- Normal functions have names that begin with a letter. You typically call them by writing the name of the function followed by its arguments. This is *prefix-style* calling.
- Operators have names that contain neither letters nor numbers. You typically call them by writing the first argument, followed by the operator, followed by the second argument. This is *infix-style* calling.
- Wrapping an operator in parentheses treats it as a normal function—prefix-style calling and all! Figure 1.6 illustrates calling the `(-)` operator in both infix style and prefix style.

Figure 1.6   Calling the - operator in both infix style and prefix style

Let's play with some operators in `elm repl`.

Listing 1.12 Showing that operators are functions

```
> (/)
<function>

> divideBy = (/)
<function>

> 7 / 2
3.5

> (/) 7 2
3.5

> divideBy 7 2
3.5
```

7 / 2 ◁— **Infix-style calling**

(/) 7 2 ◁— **Prefix-style calling**

OPERATOR PRECEDENCE

Try entering an expression involving both arithmetic operators and `(==)` into `elm repl`:

```
> 3 + 4 == 8 - 1
True : Bool
```

Now consider how we'd rewrite this expression in prefix style:

```
> (==) ((+) 3 4) ((-) 8 1)
True : Bool
```

Notice anything about the order in which these operators appear?

- Reading the *infix-style* expression from left to right, we see +, then ==, and finally -.
- The *prefix-style* expression has a different order: first we see ==, then +, and finally -.

How come? They get reordered because `(==)`, `(+)`, and `(-)` have different *precedence* values, illustrated in figure 1.7.

> **DEFINITION** In any expression containing multiple operators, the operators with higher *precedence* get evaluated before those with lower precedence. This applies only to *infix-style* calls, as all *prefix-style* calls implicitly have the same precedence.

There isn't much formal documentation on operators' relative precedence values, but operators that appear in many programming languages (such as the `(==)`, `(+)`, and `(-)` operators) tend to work similarly in Elm as they do everywhere else.

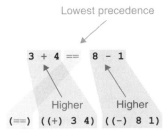

Figure 1.7 `(==)` gets evaluated after `(+)` and `(-)` because it has lower precedence.

NORMAL FUNCTION CALLS HAVE TOP PRECEDENCE

Here are two ways to write the same thing:

```
> negate 1 + negate 5
-6

> (negate 1) + (negate 5)
-6
```

These two are equivalent because plain function calls have higher precedence than any operator. This means anytime you want to pass the results of two plain function calls to an operator, you won't need to add any parentheses! You'll still get the result you wanted.

OPERATOR ASSOCIATIVITY

Besides precedence, the other factor that determines evaluation order for operators called in *infix style* is whether the operators are *left-associative*, *right-associative*, or *nonassociative*. Every operator is one of these.

An easy way to think about operator associativity is in terms of where the implied parentheses go, as shown in table 1.4. Infix expressions involving left-associative operators, such as arithmetic operators, have implied parentheses that cluster on the left.

Table 1.4   **Implied parentheses for the (-) operator**

Parentheses shown	Expression	Result
None	10 - 6 - 3	1
Assuming *left-associative*	((10 - 6) - 3)	1
Assuming *right-associative*	(10 - (6 - 3))	7

If (-) were right-associative, 10 - 6 - 3 would have parentheses clustering on the right, meaning it would evaluate to (10 - (6 - 3)) and the undesirable result of 10 - 6 - 3 == 7. Good thing arithmetic operators are left-associative!

Nonassociative operators cannot be chained together. For example, foo == bar == baz does not result in clustered parentheses; it results in an error!

1.4   Collections

Elm's most basic *collections* are lists, records, and tuples. Each has varying degrees of similarity to JavaScript's arrays and objects, but one way in which they differ from JavaScript collections is that Elm collections are always *immutable*.

> **DEFINITION**   An *immutable* value cannot be modified in any way once created.

This is in contrast to JavaScript, where some values (like strings and numbers) are immutable, but collections (like arrays and objects) can be mutated.

1.4.1 Lists

An Elm *list* has many similarities to a JavaScript array:

- You can create one with a square bracket literal; for example, ["one fish", "two fish"].
- You can ask for its first element.
- You can ask for its length.
- You can iterate over its elements in various ways.

An Elm list does have some differences, though:

- It is immutable.
- It has no fields or methods. You work with it by using functions from the List module.
- Because it is a *linked list*, you can ask for its first element, but not for other individual elements. (If you need to ask for elements at various positions, you can first convert from an Elm List to an Elm Array. We'll discuss Elm arrays in chapter 3.)
- All elements in an Elm list must have a consistent type. For example, it can be a "list of numbers" or a "list of strings," but not a "list where strings and numbers intermingle." (Making a list containing both strings and numbers involves first creating wrapper elements for them, using a feature called *custom types* that we'll cover in chapter 3.)

Although Elm supports both (immutable) lists and (also immutable) arrays, Elm lists are much more commonly used in practice. Table 1.5 shows some examples of how Elm lists and JavaScript arrays differ.

Table 1.5 Contrasting JavaScript arrays and Elm lists

JavaScript array	Elm list
[1, 2, 3].length	List.length [1, 2, 3]
["one fish", "two fish"][0]	List.head ["one fish", "two fish"]
["one fish", "two fish"][1]	No arbitrary position-based element access.
[1, 2].concat([3, 4])	[1, 2] ++ [3, 4]
[1, 2].push(3)	Cannot be modified; use, for example, append instead.
[1, "Paper", 3]	All elements in a list must have a consistent type.

Let's focus on that last one. Why must all elements in an Elm list have a consistent type?

To understand how this requirement benefits us, let's delve into the List.filter function, which works like the String.filter function we used earlier.

We saw earlier that `String.filter` takes a function that returns `True` when the given character should be kept, and `False` when it should be dropped. `List.filter` differs only in that the function you provide doesn't necessarily receive characters—instead, it receives elements from the list, whatever they may be.

Let's see that in action. Quick! To `elm repl`!

Listing 1.13   Filtering lists

```
> List.filter (\char -> char /= '-') [ 'Z', '-', 'Z' ]       ⟵ Same function we passed
['Z','Z']                                                       to String.filter earlier

> List.filter (\str -> str /= "-") [ "ZZ", "-", "Top" ]      ⟵ Strings instead
["ZZ","Top"]                                                    of characters

> List.filter Char.isDigit [ '7', '-', '9' ]                 ⟵ Works just as with
['7','9']                                                       String.filter

> List.filter (\num -> num > 0) [ -2, -1, 0, 1, 2 ]          ⟵ Keeps only the
[1,2]                                                           positive numbers
```

Here's how we would rewrite that last line of code in JavaScript:

```
[ -2, -1, 0, 1, 2 ].filter(function(num) { return num > 0; })
```

This looks straightforward enough, but JavaScript arrays permit inconsistent element types. Without looking it up, can you guess what happens if we change it to the following?

```
[ -2, "0", "one", 1, "+02", "(3)" ].filter(function(num) { return num > 0; })
```

Will it crash? Will it happily return numbers? What about strings? It's a bit of a head-scratcher.

Because Elm requires consistent element types, this is a no-brainer: in Elm it would be an error. Even better, it would be an error at build time—meaning you can rest easy knowing that whatever surprises would result from executing this code will not inflict pain on your users. Requiring consistent element types means all lists in Elm guarantee this level of predictability.

By the way, the preceding `filter()` call returns `[ 1, "+02" ]`. (Like, *duh*, right?)

1.4.2   Records

We've now seen how JavaScript's mutable arrays resemble Elm's immutable lists. In a similar vein, JavaScript's mutable objects resemble Elm's immutable *records*.

DEFINITION   A *record* is a collection of named fields, each with an associated value.

Array and list literals in the two languages are syntactically identical. But whereas JavaScript object literals use `:` to separate fields and values, Elm record literals use `=` instead. Let's get a sense of some of their other differences in table 1.6.

Table 1.6 Comparing JavaScript objects and Elm records

JavaScript object	Elm record
`{ name: "Li", cats: 2 }`	`{ name = "Li", cats = 2 }`
`({ name: "Li", cats: 2 }).cats`	`({ name = "Li", cats = 2 }).cats`
`({ name: "Li", cats: 2 })["cats"]`	Fields can be accessed only directly, using a dot.
`({ name: "Li", cats: 2 }).cats = 3`	Cannot be modified. (New cat? New record!)
`{ NAME: "Li", CATS: 2 }`	Field names can't start with uppercase letters.
`({ name: "Li", cats: 2 }).__proto__`	No prepackaged fields, only the ones you define.
`Object.keys({ name: "Li", cats: 5 })`	No listing of field names is available on demand.
`Object.prototype`	Records have no concept of inheritance.

Wow—compared to objects, records sure don't do much! It's like all they do is sit around holding onto the data we gave them. (Yep.) Personally, I've found Elm's records a welcome reprieve from the intricacies of JavaScript's `this` keyword.

RECORD UPDATES

Record updates let us concisely obtain a new record by copying the old one and changing only the specified values. (Because records are immutable, Elm will reuse values from the existing record to save time and memory, rather than copying *everything*.)

Let's use this technique to represent someone obtaining an extra cat, going from `{ name = "Li", cats = 2 }` to `{ name = "Li", cats = 3 }` by way of a record update.

Listing 1.14 Record updates

```
> catLover = { name = "Li", cats = 2 }
{ name = "Li", cats = 2 }

> catLover
{ name = "Li", cats = 2 }

> withThirdCat = { catLover | cats = 3 }     ⟵ Record update syntax
{ name = "Li", cats = 3 }

> withThirdCat
{ name = "Li", cats = 3 }

> catLover                                    Original record unmodified!
{ name = "Li", cats = 2 }

> { catLover | cats = 88, name = "LORD OF CATS" }   ⟵ Updates multiple fields (order doesn't matter)
{ name = "LORD OF CATS", cats = 88 }
```

Record updates let us represent this incremental evolution without mutating our records or re-creating them from scratch. In chapter 2, we'll represent our application state with a record, and use record updates to make changes based on user interaction.

1.4.3   *Tuples*

Lists let us represent collections of *varying size*, whose elements share a *consistent type*. Records let us represent collections of *fixed fields*—that is, fields that cannot be added or removed at runtime—but the values corresponding to those fields may have *varied types*.

   Tuples introduce no new capabilities to this mix, as there is nothing a tuple can do that a record can't. Compared to records, though, what tuples bring to the party is conciseness.

> **DEFINITION**   A *tuple* is a record-like value whose fields are accessed by position rather than by name.

In other words, tuples are for when you want a record but don't want to bother naming its fields. They are often used for things like key-value pairs, where writing out { key = "foo", value = "bar" } would add verbosity but not much clarity. Let's try some out!

Listing 1.15   Using tuples

```
> ( "Tech", 9 )
("Tech",9)

> Tuple.first ( "Tech", 9 )        ←——  Returns first element (works
"Tech"                                   only on two-element tuples)

> Tuple.second ( "Tech", 9 )       ←——  Returns second element (works
9                                        only on two-element tuples)
```

You can use the Tuple.first and Tuple.second functions only on tuples that contain two elements. If they have three elements, you can use *tuple destructuring* to extract their values.

> **DEFINITION** *Tuple destructuring* extracts the values inside a tuple and assigns them to names in the current scope.

Let's use tuple destructuring to implement a function that takes a tuple of three elements.

Listing 1.16   Tuple destructuring

```
> multiply3d ( x, y, z ) = x * y * z    ←——  Destructuring a tuple into
<function>                                    three named values: x, y, and z

> multiply3d ( 6, 7, 2 )
84
```

```
> multiply2d someTuple = let ( x, y ) = someTuple in x * y
<function>
```

Destructuring a tuple inside a let-expression

As demonstrated here, once you have named the values inside the tuple, you can use them just as you would any other named value.

> **TIP** Mind the difference between a tuple and a parenthetical function call! (foo, bar) is a tuple, whereas (foo bar) is a call to the foo function, passing bar as an argument. A simple mnemonic to remember the difference is "comma means tuple."

Table 1.7 compares the feature sets of lists, records, and tuples.

Table 1.7 Comparing lists, records, and tuples

List	Record	Tuple
Can add or remove elements at runtime	Cannot add or remove fields at runtime	Cannot add or remove elements at runtime
Can iterate over	Cannot iterate over	Cannot iterate over
No names	Named fields	No names
Immutable	Immutable	Immutable

Because any tuple can be represented using a record instead, Elm does not support tuples of more than three elements. For those situations, it's better to use a record! When you need only two or three elements, though, choose tuples or records based on whichever would yield more readable code; their performance characteristics are equivalent.

Summary

We're off to a fantastic start! First, we discussed some of the toughest problems web programmers face: crashing is too easy in JavaScript, and maintenance is too error-prone even with a boost from TypeScript. Then, you learned how Elm addresses these problems, with a design that prioritizes maintainability and a helpful compiler that catches would-be runtime exceptions before they can cause user pain. From there, you dove in and wrote your first Elm code in elm repl.

Here is a brief review of things we covered along the way:

- The ++ operator combines strings, whereas the + operator is for addition only.
- Double quotes refer to strings. Single quotes refer to individual UTF-8 characters.
- Let-expressions introduce scoped named values to an expression.
- There is no concept of "truthiness" in Elm, just True and False.
- if foo /= bar then "different" else "same" is an *if-expression*. Like Java-Script ternaries, if-expressions require an else branch and always evaluate to a value.

- Lists like [3, 1, 4] are immutable. Their elements must share a consistent type.
- List.filter (\num -> num > 0) numbersList returns a list containing all the positive numbers in the original numbersList.
- catLover = { name = "Li", cats = 2 } assigns a record to the name catLover. Once assigned, names cannot be reassigned.
- { catLover | cats = 3 } returns a new record that is the same as the cat-Lover record, except the cats value is now 3.
- (foo, bar) destructures a tuple such as (2, 3). In this example, foo would be 2, and bar would be 3.

Table 1.8 summarizes some of the differences between JavaScript and Elm.

Table 1.8   Differences between JavaScript and Elm

JavaScript	Elm
`// This is an inline comment`	`-- This is an inline comment`
`/* This is a block comment */`	`{- This is a block comment -}`
`true && false`	`True && False`
`"Ahoy, " + "World!"`	`"Ahoy, " ++ "World!"`
`"A spade" === "A spade"`	`"A spade" == "A spade"`
`"Calvin" !== "Hobbes"`	`"Calvin" /= "Hobbes"`
`Math.pow(2, 11)`	`2 ^ 11`
`Math.trunc(-49 / 10)`	`-49 // 10`
`n > 0 ? "positive" : "not"`	`if n > 0 then "positive" else "not"`
`nums.filter(function(n) { ... })`	`List.filter (\n -> n > 0) nums`
`function pluralize(s, p, c) { ... }`	`pluralize singular plural count = ...`

You also learned about several differences between plain functions and operators, as shown in table 1.9.

Table 1.9   Differences between plain functions and operators

Function	How to identify one	Calling style	Examples
Plain	Name begins with a letter	Prefix style	`negate, not, pluralize`
Operator	Name has no letters or numbers	Infix style	`(++), (*), (==)`

In chapter 2, we'll expand on what you've learned here to create a working Elm application. Let's go build something!

Your first Elm application

Elm applications are built to last. They have a reputation for being scalable, easy to refactor, and difficult to crash unexpectedly. Because JavaScript applications have . . . well . . . a different reputation, it stands to reason that Elm must be doing things differently. And so it is!

Whereas each line of code in a JavaScript application could result in a change or effect—like "update that text!" or "send this to the server!"—the code in an Elm application builds up a *description* of what the program should do in response to various inputs. Elm's compiler translates this description into the appropriate JavaScript code for the browser to run at the appropriate times, and the end user may have no idea Elm was involved at all.

In this chapter, you'll build your first Elm application: *Photo Groove,* a simple photo-browsing web app where users select thumbnails to view larger versions.

We'll create a user interface by using declarative rendering, and manage state by using The Elm Architecture. By the end of the chapter, we will have a fully functioning application—and a code base we can build on for the rest of the book!

2.1   Rendering a page

Since the very early days of the web, browsers have been translating HTML markup into a Document Object Model (or DOM, for short) that represents the structure of the current page. The DOM consists of *DOM nodes*, and it's only by changing these nodes that web applications can modify the current page on the fly.

In this chapter, we'll work with the two most common types of DOM nodes:

- *Elements*—These have a `tagName` (such as `"button"` or `"img"`), and may have child DOM nodes.
- *Text nodes*—These have a `textContent` property instead of a `tagName`, and are childless.

As figure 2.1 shows, elements and text nodes can freely intermingle inside the DOM.

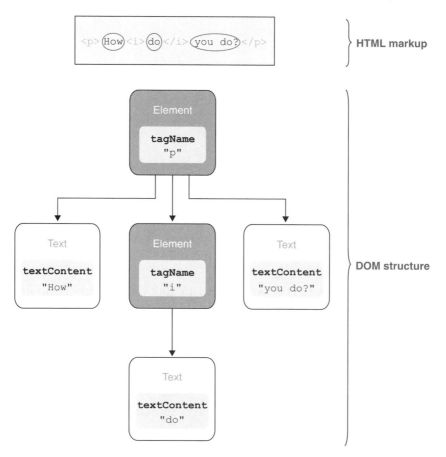

Figure 2.1   Intermingling element DOM nodes and text nodes

Here we've pulled back the curtain on the markup `<p>How <i>do</i> you do?</p>` to see that despite its two element tags—namely, `<p>` and `<i>`—we are actually working with five DOM nodes here! The other three are not elements, but rather text nodes.

2.1.1 *Describing a page using the Html module*

When describing how a page looks in Elm, we don't write markup. Instead, we call functions to create representations of DOM nodes. The most flexible of these functions is called `node`, and as figure 2.2 shows, its arguments line up neatly with the analogous markup.

HTML markup (`<button class="funky" id="submitter">Submit</button>`

                            Type   Attributes   Child nodes

Elm function calls (`node "button" [ class "funky", id "submitter" ] [ text "Submit" ]`

                                             Nested function calls

Figure 2.2 Representing a button using HTML markup (top) and Elm's node function (bottom)

This line of Elm code contains four function calls. Can you spot them?

- A call to the `node` function, passing three arguments: the string `"button"`, a list of attributes, and a list of child nodes
- A call to the `class` function, passing `"funky"`
- A call to the `id` function, passing `"submitter"`
- A call to the `text` function, passing `"Submit"`

These are plain old Elm functions. Each returns a representation of a portion of the DOM: a `button` element, a text node, and some `class` and `id` attributes. You can call these functions anytime you like, and pass their return values to other functions as usual.

In Elm, we usually refer to a "virtual DOM node" as "`Html`" for short. This name comes from the `Html` module, which provides a variety of intuitively named functions that let you avoid calling `node` directly. For example, the `Html` module's `img` function is shorthand for calling `node` and passing `"img"` as the first argument. The following two lines are equivalent:

```
node "img" [ src "logo.png" ] []
     img  [ src "logo.png" ] []
```

It's best practice to use functions like `img` as much as possible, and to fall back on `node` only when no alternative is available. (For example, you may notice that there is no equivalent of the `img` function for the deprecated `<blink>` element. I'm not saying you should call `node "blink" [] [ text "<BLINK> LIVES AGAIN" ]`, but I'm not *not* saying that, either.)

RENDERING A PAGE

Let's use what you've learned to render your first page with Elm! For the rest of this chapter, we'll be building the Photo Groove application. Eventually, we'll add features like applying filters and viewing larger versions, but first we need to render a basic page labeled "Photo Groove" across the top, with some thumbnail images below.

Because our output is visual this time, `elm repl` won't get us very far. Instead, let's kick things off with our first .elm file:

1 Make a new directory called PhotoGroove and open it in a terminal.
2 Run `elm init` and enter `y` when prompted. This will create a file called elm.json, which Elm needs to build our project. If you're curious about elm.json, take a look at appendix B.
3 `elm init` will have created a directory called src. Create a file called Photo-Groove.elm inside this src directory.

Now that our file structure is set up, enter the following into the src/Photo-Groove.elm file.

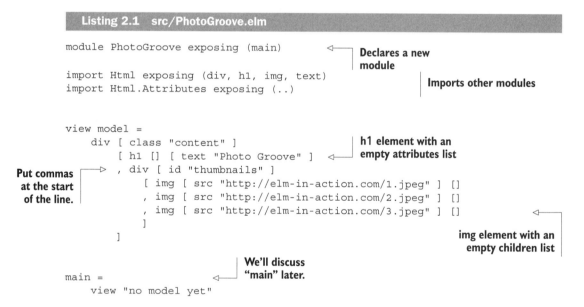

Listing 2.1   src/PhotoGroove.elm

```
module PhotoGroove exposing (main)          ◁──┐ Declares a new
                                                │ module
import Html exposing (div, h1, img, text)
import Html.Attributes exposing (..)            Imports other modules


view model =
    div [ class "content" ]
        [ h1 [] [ text "Photo Groove" ]    ◁── h1 element with an
                                               empty attributes list
        , div [ id "thumbnails" ]
            [ img [ src "http://elm-in-action.com/1.jpeg" ] []
            , img [ src "http://elm-in-action.com/2.jpeg" ] []
            , img [ src "http://elm-in-action.com/3.jpeg" ] []   ◁──┐
            ]                                                        │
        ]                                    img element with an
                                             empty children list

main =                          ◁──┐ We'll discuss
    view "no model yet"             "main" later.
```

Put commas at the start of the line.

DECLARING THE PHOTOGROOVE MODULE

By writing `module PhotoGroove exposing (main)` at the top of our Photo-Groove.elm file, we define a new module. This means future modules in our project will be able to import this `PhotoGroove` module just as they would the `String` or `Html` modules; for example, like so:

```
import PhotoGroove exposing (main)
```

Because we wrote `exposing (main)` after `module PhotoGroove`, we are exposing only one of our two top-level values—`main` but not `view`—for other modules to import.

This means another module that imported `PhotoGroove` would get an error if it tried to access PhotoGroove.view. Only exposed values can be accessed by other modules. As a general rule, it's best for our modules to expose as little as possible.

Why commas in front?

When writing a multiline literal in JavaScript, the usual convention is to put commas at the end of each line. Consider the following code:

```
rules = [
    rule("Do not talk about Sandwich Club."),
    rule("Do NOT talk about Sandwich Club.")
    rule("No eating in the common area.")
]
```

Did you spot the mistake? A comma is missing after the second call to `rule`, meaning this is not syntactically valid JavaScript. Running this code will result in a `SyntaxError`.

Now consider the equivalent Elm code, with the same missing comma:

```
rules = [
    rule "Do not talk about Sandwich Club.",
    rule "Do NOT talk about Sandwich Club."
    rule "No eating in the common area."
]
```

The mistake is just as easy to overlook, but harder to fix because this is syntactically valid Elm code—but not the code you intended to write!

The missing comma means the preceding code is essentially equivalent to the following:

```
rules = [
    (rule "Do not..."),
    (rule "Do NOT..." rule "No eating...")
]
```

Instead of calling `rule` three times, each time with one argument, here the second call to `rule` is receiving three arguments—and there is no third call. Instead of the syntax error JavaScript gave you, you'll get a seemingly nonsensical error about functions being called with the wrong number of arguments.

Now try to make this mistake when writing in a commas-first style:

```
rules =
    [ rule "Do not talk about Sandwich Club."
      rule "Do NOT talk about Sandwich Club."
    , rule "No eating in the common area."
    ]
```

This style makes it blindingly obvious that a comma is missing. Now we don't even need to compile our code to identify the problem!

It may feel different at first, but the commas-first style gives you one less potential error to worry about once you get used to it.

Now that we have our `PhotoGroove` module, it's time to see what it looks like in a browser. Still inside the same directory as the one where we ran `elm init`, run this:

```
elm reactor
```

This will start up a local server running at http://localhost:8000 that can compile and serve our Elm files. Open http://localhost:8000/src/PhotoGroove.elm in your browser, and you should see the results of the compiled PhotoGroove.elm file. The page should look like the screenshot in figure 2.3.

Photo Groove

Figure 2.3   Viewing http://localhost:8000/src/PhotoGroove.elm

Congratulations! You've rendered your first user interface in Elm. Figure 2.4 shows the DOM structure of the interface we just rendered.

Notice how the functions that create elements—in this case, `div`, `h1`, and `img`—take exactly two arguments in all cases:

- *A list of attributes*—If an element has no attributes, we pass `[]` like so:

  ```
  h1 [] [ text "Photo Groove" ]
  ```

- *A list of child DOM nodes*—If an element has no children, we pass `[]` like so:

  ```
  img [ src "1.jpeg" ] []
  ```

If an element has neither attributes nor children? In that case, we pass `[]` `[]` like this:

```
br [] []
```

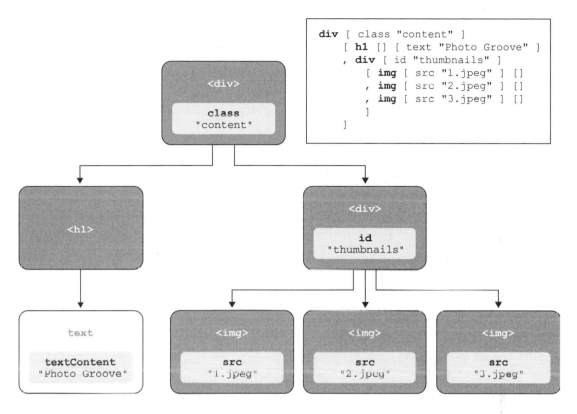

Figure 2.4   The DOM structure of our first Elm user interface

This two-argument pattern is consistent throughout the Html module, and it's worth following if you ever decide to make a custom element of your own by using the node function. We'll see more of the node function in chapter 5.

IMPORTING UNQUALIFIED VALUES WITH EXPOSING

We've now used several functions from the Html module, but we wrote them in a style different from that of chapter 1. Back then, we wrote functions like String.filter in a *qualified* style—that is, we included the String module's name right there in the function call. With the Html module's functions, we used an *unqualified* style—we wrote div instead of Html.div, we wrote h1 instead of Html.h1, and so forth.

We could do this because we used exposing when we imported the Html module:

```
import Html exposing (div, h1, img, text)
```

This line of code both imports the Html module so we can use its contents, and brings Html.div, Html.h1, Html.img, and Html.text into the global scope. That lets us refer to them as div, h1, img, and text without the prefix of Html.

We could have achieved essentially the same result by assigning them names directly:

```
import Html

div = Html.div
h1 = Html.h1
img = Html.img
text = Html.text
```

However, since this pile of code can be replaced by a single line—import Html exposing (div, h1, img, text)—it's normal to use exposing for this purpose instead.

EXPOSING EVERYTHING WITH (..)

When we imported the Html module, we listed exactly which values we wanted to expose: div, h1, img, and text. For the Html.Attributes module, we wrote this instead:

```
import Html.Attributes exposing (..)
```

Using exposing (..) means "expose everything," which lets us use every value in the Html.Attributes module in an unqualified style. Let's change our first import to use exposing (..) instead:

```
import Html exposing (..)
```

Now we won't need to extend the list of div, h1, img, and text whenever we want to use a new element type. Everything the Html module has to offer is now in our global scope.

Why is the qualified style the better default choice?

In chapter 1, we wrote out String.toUpper and List.filter, instead of toUpper and filter. Here we're doing the opposite, writing img and div instead of Html.img and Html.div.

This raises the question: when is it a good idea to use the qualified style (with the module name prefixed) over the unqualified style? The unqualified style is more concise, so why not use exposing (..) every time?

Unqualified imports have two primary downsides. One is that unqualified names can become ambiguous. Try this in elm repl:

```
> import String exposing (..)
> import List exposing (..)
> reverse
```

You'll get an error saying that reverse is ambiguous. After importing and exposing both String.reverse and List.reverse, it's no longer clear which of the two you meant. (In cases like this, you can still use the qualified style to resolve the ambiguity, so if you now put `String.reverse` or `List.reverse` into `elm repl`, they will still work as usual.)

Unqualified imports are also less self-documenting. Suppose you come across code that says `partition foo bar`, and you've never seen `partition` before. Naturally, you wonder: "How can I find out what `partition` does? Is it defined in this file?" You search through the file and can't find it, so it must come from an `import`. You scroll up to the imports and discover a long list of `exposing (..)` declarations. Argh! `partition` could be in any of those!

This could take a while. . . .

Suppose instead you see the code `List.partition foo bar`. You want to know what `List.partition` does, so you bring up the documentation for the `List` module on https://package.elm-lang.org. You learn about `List.partition`, then get on with your day.

Scenarios like this are why it's best practice to write things in a *qualified* way by default.

Still, sometimes there's a good reason to prefer the unqualified style—for example, unqualified `Html` functions are designed to resemble HTML markup. In these cases, it's best to limit yourself to one `exposing (..)` (or perhaps one "family" of them, such as `Html` and `Html.Attributes`) per file. This way, if you encounter an unfamiliar function of mysterious origin, you'll have the fewest modules to hunt through to find its documentation.

2.1.2 Building a project

Now that we have something on the screen, let's add some styles!

> **TIP** There are many ways to style a web page, each with its own trade-offs. The two most popular Elm-specific choices are `rtfeldman/elm-css`, a package for writing CSS directly in Elm, and the groundbreaking `mdgriffith/elm-ui`, which provides a way to style pages without writing CSS at all. Comparing styling alternatives is outside the scope of this book, but both of these can be found at https://package.elm-lang.org.

We could style our page by using a separate Elm package, or by writing inline CSS styles using the `Html.Attributes.style` attribute, but instead we're going to organize things by writing our CSS declarations in a separate .css file.

The only way to get multiple files involved in the same web page is to give a browser some HTML markup, so our first step in the process of styling our application will be to create a .html file.

Let's create a file named index.html in the same directory as our elm.json file (the one where we ran `elm init` back in section 2.1.1) and put the following content inside it.

Listing 2.2   index.html

```html
<!doctype html>
<html>
    <head>
        <style>
            body { background-color: rgb(44, 44, 44); color: white; }
            img { border: 1px solid white; margin: 5px; }
            .large { width: 500px; float: right; }
            .selected { margin: 0; border: 6px solid #60b5cc; }
            .content { margin: 40px auto; width: 960px; }
            #thumbnails { width: 440px; float: left; }
            h1 { font-family: Verdana; color: #60b5cc; }
        </style>
    </head>

    <body>
        <div id="app"></div>          ⟵  Our Elm application
                                          will render into this div.

        <script src="app.js"></script>        ⟵  PhotoGroove.elm will
        <script>                                  get compiled into app.js.
            Elm.PhotoGroove.init({node: document.getElementById("app")});  ⟵
        </script>
    </body>                                   The Elm object
</html>                                        comes from app.js
```

The markup we put in this file covers things like these:

- The standard `<!doctype>`, `<html>`, and `<body>` tags
- Whatever `<head>` inclusions we need—styles, metadata, `<title>`, and so on
- Importing a file called app.js, which we will have Elm's compiler generate in a moment

The line `Elm.PhotoGroove.init({node: document.getElementById ("app")});` starts our Elm code running in the `<div id="app"></div>` element we included in index.html.

COMPILING TO JAVASCRIPT

Next, it's time to compile our Elm code into JavaScript. Run this in the terminal:

```
elm make src/PhotoGroove.elm --output app.js
```

This will compile our PhotoGroove.elm file into the JavaScript file the browser will read. (That generated JavaScript file will be called app.js, because we passed `--output app.js` to `elm make`.) Now our HTML file has a compiled app.js file to load up.

THE ELM RUNTIME AND MAIN

When Elm compiles our code into JavaScript, it includes an extra bit of JavaScript known as the *Elm Runtime*. The Elm Runtime is behind-the-scenes code that quietly handles things like the following:

- Adding and removing event listeners for any events our code depends on
- Efficiently scheduling tasks like HTTP requests and DOM updates
- Storing and managing application state

When we called `Elm.PhotoGroove.init` from index.html, we told the Elm Runtime to use the top-level `main` value in the `PhotoGroove` module as the application's entry point. If we did not have a module called `PhotoGroove`, or if it did not define a top-level value named `main`, we'd receive an error.

This means when the browser runs our compiled code, `view "no model yet"` will be the first line of code executed, because that's what we assigned to `main`. If we renamed the `PhotoGroove` module to `CubeDraft`, we'd have to call `Elm.Cube-Draft.init` instead, but otherwise everything would still work. If the `CubeDraft` module did not define a value named `main`, however, the application would not start. There's no renaming `main`!

If you open index.html in a browser, you should see the application displaying as it does in figure 2.5. Fantastic! Next, we'll make it interactive.

Figure 2.5   Rendering the application

2.2 *Handling user input with The Elm Architecture*

So far, we haven't had much data flowing through our application. Okay, we haven't had *any*—all we did was generate some `Html` and render it. That will soon change, as we're about to start handling user input! This brings us to a common question that every growing application faces sooner or later: how will we keep data flow manageable as our code base grows?

JavaScript offers a staggering selection of data flow architectures to choose from, but Elm has just one. It's called *The Elm Architecture*, and the Elm Runtime is optimized for applications that follow it. We'll learn about The Elm Architecture as we add interactivity to Photo Groove.

Figure 2.6 shows a preview of the architecture we'll be building toward in this chapter. Don't worry if this does not make sense yet! We'll get there, one step at a time.

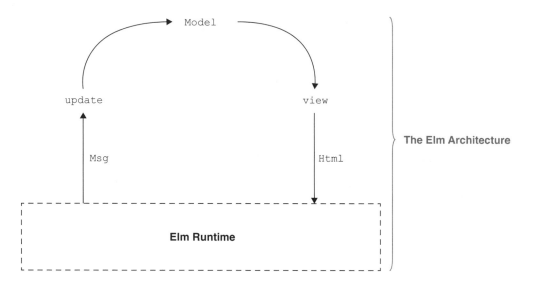

Figure 2.6   The Elm Runtime uses The Elm Architecture to manage data flow.

Let's begin where data flow naturally begins in an application: with the application's *state*.

2.2.1 *Representing application state with a model*

Back in the Wild West days of the web, it was common to store application state primarily in the DOM itself. Is that menu expanded or collapsed? Check whether one of its DOM nodes has `class="expanded"` or `class="collapsed"`. Need to know what value a user has selected in a drop-down menu? Query it out of the DOM at the last possible instant.

This approach turned out not to scale very well, especially as applications grew more complex. Today it's common practice to store application state completely outside the DOM, and to propagate changes from that independent state over to the DOM as necessary. This is how we do it in The Elm Architecture.

DECLARING A MODEL

We're going to store our application state separately from the DOM, and we'll refer to that state as our *model*.

> **DEFINITION** The *model* represents the state of an Elm application.

Remember how earlier we wrote this code?

```
main =
    view "no model yet"
```

Let's replace that code with the contents of the following listing.

Listing 2.3 Adding a model

```
initialModel =
    [ { url = "1.jpeg" }
    , { url = "2.jpeg" }
    , { url = "3.jpeg" }
    ]
```
We'll add more fields beyond url later.

```
main =
    view initialModel
```
Passes our new initialModel record to view

Excellent! Now we have an initial model to work with. So far, it contains a list of photos, each of which is represented by a record containing a `url` string.

WRITING A VIEW FUNCTION

Next, we'll render a thumbnail for each photo in our list. At the top level of a typical Elm application is a single *view function*, which accepts our current model as an argument and then returns some `Html`. The Elm Runtime takes the `Html` returned by this view function and alters the page's actual DOM to match it.

By pure coincidence, we've already written just such a view function—it's the function we had the foresight to name `view`. Unfortunately, our current `view` implementation ignores the `model` argument it receives, which means changing our model won't result in a change visible to the end user. Let's fix that! `view` should base its return value on its `model` argument.

It'll be easier to do this if we first write a separate `viewThumbnail` *helper function*, which renders a single thumbnail as `Html`.

> **DEFINITION** A *helper function* helps another function do its job. Here, the `viewThumbnail` helper function will help `view` do its job.

Let's replace our `view` implementation with the code in the following listing.

Listing 2.4   Splitting out `viewThumbnail`

```
urlPrefix =
    "http://elm-in-action.com/"
```
We'll prepend this to strings like "1.jpeg".

```
view model =
    div [ class "content" ]
        [ h1 [] [ text "Photo Groove" ]
        , div [ id "thumbnails" ] []
        ]


viewThumbnail thumb =
    img [ src (urlPrefix ++ thumb.url) ] []
```
Prepend urlPrefix to get a complete URL like "http://elm-in-action.com/1.jpeg".

Figure 2.7 illustrates how our current `model` and `view` connect to the Elm Runtime.

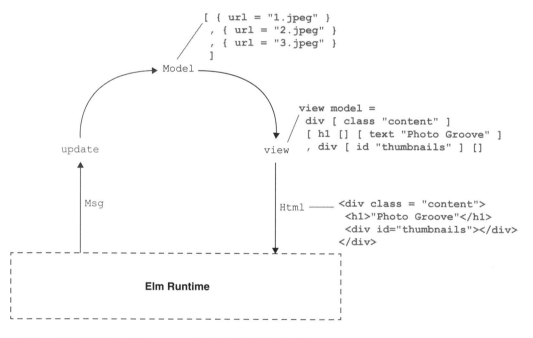

Figure 2.7   Model and view connecting with the Elm Runtime

Next, we'll iterate over our list of photo records and call `viewThumbnail` on each one, in order to translate it from a dusty old record to a vibrant and inspiring `img`. Fortunately, the `List.map` function does exactly this!

USING LIST.MAP

List.map is another *higher-order* function similar to the List.filter function we used in chapter 1. We pass List.map a translation function and a list, and it runs that translation function on each value in the list. Once that's done, List.map returns a new list containing the translated values. Take a look at figure 2.8 to see List.map do its thing for viewThumbnail.

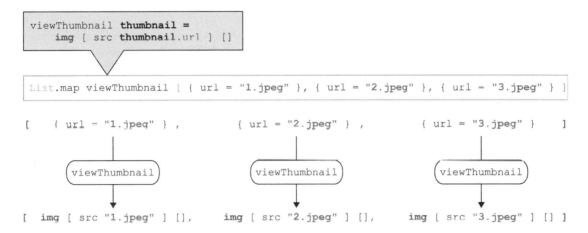

Figure 2.8   Using List.map to transform photo records into img nodes

Because div is a plain Elm function that accepts two lists as arguments—first a list of attributes, followed by a list of child nodes—we can swap out our entire hardcoded list of child img nodes with a single call to List.map! Let's do that now:

```
view model =
    div [ class "content" ]
        [ h1 [] [ text "Photo Groove" ]
        , div [ id "thumbnails" ] (List.map viewThumbnail model)
        ]

viewThumbnail thumb =
    img [ src (urlPrefix ++ thumb.url) ] []
```

If you run elm make src/PhotoGroove.elm --output app.js again to recompile this code, you should see the same result as before. The difference is that now we have a more flexible internal representation, setting us up to add interactivity in a way that was impossible before we connected model and view.

EXPANDING THE MODEL

Now let's add a feature: when the user clicks a thumbnail, it will become selected—indicated by a blue border surrounding it—and we'll display a larger version of it beside the thumbnails.

To do this, we first need to store which thumbnail is selected. That means we'll want to convert our model from a list to a record, so we can store both the list of photos and the current `selectedUrl` value at the same time.

Listing 2.5   Converting the model to a record

```
initialModel =
    { photos =
        [ { url = "1.jpeg" }
        , { url = "2.jpeg" }
        , { url = "3.jpeg" }
        ]
    , selectedUrl = "1.jpeg"        ◁——  Selects the first
    }                                     photo by default
```

Next, let's update `viewThumbnail` to display the blue border for the selected thumbnail. That's easier said than done! `viewThumbnail` accepts only one argument—`thumbnail`—so it has no way to access the model. That, in turn, means it can't possibly know the current value of `selectedUrl`—but without knowing which thumbnail is selected, how can it know whether to return a selected or unselected `img`? It can't! We'll have to pass that information along from `view` to `viewThumbnail`.

Let's rectify this situation by passing `selectedUrl` into `viewThumbnail` as an additional argument. Armed with that knowledge, `viewThumbnail` can situationally return an `img` with the `"selected"` class—which our CSS has already styled to display with a blue border—if the `url` of the given `thumbnail` matches `selectedUrl`:

```
viewThumbnail selectedUrl thumb =
    if selectedUrl == thumb.url then
        img
            [ src (urlPrefix ++ thumb.url)
            , class "selected"
            ]
            []

    else
        img
            [ src (urlPrefix ++ thumb.url) ]
            []
```

Comparing our `then` and `else` cases, we see quite a bit of code duplication. The only thing different about them is whether `class "selected"` is present. Can we trim down this code?

Absolutely! We can use the `Html.classList` function. It builds a `class` attribute by using a list of tuples. Each tuple contains, first, the desired class name, and, second, a Boolean indicating whether to include the class in the final class string.

Let's refactor the preceding code to the following, which does the same thing:

```
viewThumbnail selectedUrl thumb =
    img
        [ src (urlPrefix ++ thumb.url)
```

```
        , classList [ ( "selected", selectedUrl == thumb.url ) ]
        ]
        []
```

Now all that remains is to pass in `selectedUrl`, which we can do with an anonymous function. While we're at it, let's also add another `img` to display a larger version of the selected photo.

Listing 2.6   Rendering a selected thumbnail via an anonymous function

```
view model =
    div [ class "content" ]
        [ h1 [] [ text "Photo Groove" ]
        , div [ id "thumbnails" ]
            (List.map
                (\photo -> viewThumbnail model.selectedUrl photo)
                model.photos
            )
        , img                                    Displays a larger version
            [ class "large"                      of the selected photo
            , src (urlPrefix ++ "large/" ++ model.selectedUrl)
            ]
            []
        ]
```

If you recompile with the same `elm make` command as before, the result should now look like figure 2.9. Looking good!

Figure 2.9   Rendering a larger version alongside the selected thumbnail

REPLACING ANONYMOUS FUNCTIONS WITH PARTIAL APPLICATION

Although the way we've written this works, it's not quite idiomatic Elm code. The idiomatic style would be to remove the anonymous function like so:

```
Before: List.map (\photo -> viewThumbnail model.selectedUrl photo)
    model.photos
After:  List.map         (viewThumbnail model.selectedUrl)
    model.photos
```

Whoa! Does the revised version still work? Do these two lines somehow do the same thing? It totally does, and they totally do! This is because calling `viewThumbnail` without passing all of its arguments is an example of *partially applying* a function.

> **DEFINITION** *Partially applying* a function means passing it some of its arguments—but not all of them—and getting back a new function that will accept the remaining arguments and finish the job.

When we called `viewThumbnail model.selectedUrl photo`, we provided `view-Thumbnail` with both of the arguments it needed to return some `Html`. If we call it without that second `photo` argument, what we get back is not `Html`, but rather a function—specifically, a function that accepts the missing `photo` argument and *then* returns some `Html`.

Let's think about how this would look in JavaScript, where functions don't support partial application by default. If we'd written `viewThumbnail` in JavaScript, and wanted it to support partial application, it would have had to look like this:

```
function viewThumbnail(selectedUrl) {
    return function(thumb) {
        if (selectedUrl === thumb.url) {
            // Render a selected thumbnail here
        } else {
            // Render a non-selected thumbnail here
        }
    };
}
```

Functions that can be partially applied, such as the one in this JavaScript code, are known as *curried functions*.

> **DEFINITION** A *curried function* is a function that can be partially applied.

All Elm functions are curried. That's why when we call (`viewThumbnail model.selectedUrl`), we end up partially applying `viewThumbnail`, not getting an `undefined` argument or an error.

In contrast, JavaScript functions are not curried by default. They are instead *tupled*, which is to say they expect a complete "tuple" of arguments. (In this case, *tuple* refers to "a fixed-length sequence of elements," not specifically one of Elm's tuple values.)

Elm and JavaScript both support either curried or tupled functions. The difference is in which they choose as the default:

- In JavaScript, functions are tupled by default. If you'd like them to support partial application, you can first curry them by hand—as we did in our JavaScript `viewThumbnail` implementation in the preceding code.
- In Elm, functions are curried by default. If you'd like to partially apply them, go right ahead. They're already set up for it. If you'd like a tupled function, write a curried function that accepts a single tuple as its argument, and then destructure that tuple.

Table 2.1 shows how to define and use both curried and tupled functions in either language.

Table 2.1　Curried functions and tupled functions in Elm and JavaScript

	Elm	JavaScript

Curried function	`splitA separator str =`
	`    String.split separator str`
		`function splitA(sep) {`
		`  return function(str) {`
		`    return str.split(sep);`
		`  }`
		`}`

Tupled function	`splitB ( separator, str ) =`
	`    String.split separator str`
		`function splitB(sep, str) {`
		`  return str.split(sep);`
		`}`

Total application	`splitB ( "-", "867-5309" )`	`splitB("-", "867-5309")`
Total application	`splitA    "-"   "867-5309"`	`splitA("-")("867-5309")`
Partial application	`splitA    "-"`	`splitA("-")`

We can use our newfound powers of partial application to make `view` more concise. We now know we can replace our anonymous function with a partial application of `viewThumbnail`:

Before: `List.map (\photo -> viewThumbnail model.selectedUrl photo) model.photos`
After: `List.map       (viewThumbnail model.selectedUrl) model.photos`

> **TIP** In Elm, an anonymous function like `(\foo -> bar baz foo)` can always be rewritten as `(bar baz)` by itself. Keep an eye out for this pattern; it comes up surprisingly often.

Here's how our updated `view` function should look.

Listing 2.7   Rendering a selected thumbnail via a partial application

```
view model =
    div [ class "content" ]
        [ h1 [] [ text "Photo Groove" ]
        , div [ id "thumbnails" ]
            (List.map (viewThumbnail model.selectedUrl) model.photos)
        , img
            [ class "large"
            , src (urlPrefix ++ "large/" ++ model.selectedUrl)
            ]
            []
        ]
```

**Partially applies
viewThumbnail with
model.selectedUrl**

Because all Elm functions are curried, it's common to give a function more information by adding an argument to the *front* of its arguments list. For example, when `viewThumbnail` needed access to `selectedUrl`, we made this change:

```
Before: List.map  viewThumbnail                      model.photos
After:  List.map (viewThumbnail model.selectedUrl) model.photos
```

Fortunately, we added the new `selectedUrl` argument to the front. This let us pass it in using partial application instead of an anonymous function. This is a common technique in Elm code.

> **NOTE**   *Currying* is named after acclaimed logician Haskell Brooks Curry. The Haskell programming language is also named after him. Whether the Brooks Brothers clothing company is named after his middle name is left as an exercise for the reader.

2.2.2   *Handling events with messages and updates*

Now that we can properly render which thumbnail is selected, we need to change the appropriate part of the model whenever the user clicks a different thumbnail. If we were writing JavaScript, we might implement this logic by attaching an event listener to each thumbnail like so:

```
thumbnail.addEventListener("click", function() { model.selectedUrl = url; });
```

Elm wires up event handlers a bit differently. Similarly to the way we wrote a `view` function that translated our current `model` into a desired DOM structure, we're now going to write an `update` function that translates *messages* into our desired `model`.

> **DEFINITION**   A *message* is a value used to pass information from one part of the system to another.

When the user clicks a thumbnail, a message will be sent to an `update` function, as illustrated in figure 2.10.

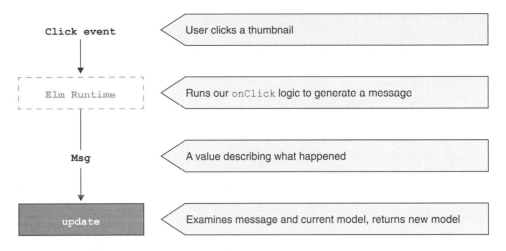

Figure 2.10 Handling the event when a user clicks a thumbnail

The message should describe *what happened*—for example, "the user clicked a photo"—but the format of our message is entirely up to us. We could represent it as a string, or a list, or a number, or anything else we please. Here's a message implemented as a record:

```
{ description = "ClickedPhoto", data = "2.jpeg" }
```

This record is a message that conveys the following: "The user clicked the 2.jpeg photo." It will be up to our update function to decide what to do with this information. In general, when update receives a message, it will do the following:

1 Look at the message it received
2 Look at our current model
3 Use these two values to determine a new model, and then return it

We can implement our "select photo" logic by adding this update function right above main:

```
update msg model =
    if msg.description == "ClickedPhoto" then
        { model | selectedUrl = msg.data }

    else
        model
```

Notice that if we receive an unrecognized message, we return the original model unchanged. This is important! Whatever else happens, the update function must always return a new model, even if it happens to be the same as the old model.

ADDING ONCLICK TO VIEWTHUMBNAIL

We can declare that a `ClickedPhoto` message should be sent to `update` whenever the user clicks a thumbnail, by adding an `onClick` attribute to `viewThumbnail`. To do this, we'll first need to import the `Html.Events` module, since that's where `onClick` lives.

Our imports now look like this:

```
import Html exposing (..)
import Html.Attributes exposing (..)
import Html.Events exposing (onClick)
```

Now that we've imported `onClick`, let's introduce it to `viewThumbnail` like so:

```
viewThumbnail selectedUrl thumb =
    img
        [ src (urlPrefix ++ thumb.url)
        , classList [ ( "selected", selectedUrl == thumb.url ) ]
        , onClick { description = "ClickedPhoto", data = thumb.url }
        ]
        []
```

The Elm Runtime takes care of managing event listeners behind the scenes, so this one-line addition is the only change we need to make to our view. We're ready to see this in action!

THE MODEL-VIEW-UPDATE LOOP

To wire our Elm Application together, we're going to change `main = view model` to the following, which incorporates `update` according to how we've set things up so far. First, we'll add one final import to the top of our imports list:

```
import Browser
```

This module gives us access to the `Browser.sandbox` function, which we can use to describe an interactive Elm application like so:

```
main =
    Browser.sandbox
        { init = initialModel
        , view = view
        , update = update
        }
```

The `Browser.sandbox` function takes a record with three fields:

- `model`—A value that can be anything you please
- `view`—A function that takes a model and returns an `Html` node
- `update`—A function that takes a message and a model, and returns a new model

It uses these arguments to return a description of a program, which the Elm Runtime sets in motion when the application starts up. Before we got the Browser module involved, main could render only static views. Browser.sandbox lets us specify how to react to user input. Figure 2.11 shows how data flows through our revised application.

Notice that view builds fresh Html values after every update. That might sound like a lot of performance overhead, but in practice, it's almost always a performance *benefit!*

This is because Elm doesn't actually re-create the entire DOM structure of the page every time. Instead, it compares the Html it got this time to the Html it got last time and updates only the parts of the page that are different between the two requested representations.

This approach to *virtual DOM* rendering, popularized by the JavaScript library React, has several benefits over manually altering individual parts of the DOM:

- Updates are batched to avoid expensive repaints and layout reflows.
- Application state is far less likely to get out of sync with the page.
- Replaying application state changes effectively replays user interface changes.

Let's compile once more with elm make src/PhotoGroove.elm --output app.js. If you open index.html, you should now be able to click a thumbnail to select it. You

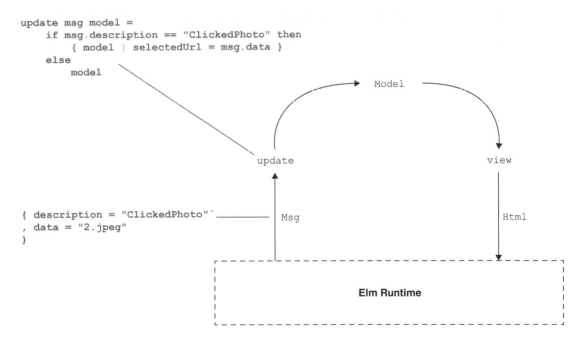

Figure 2.11   Data flowing from the start of the program through the Model-View-Update loop

Figure 2.12   Our final Photo Groove application

can tell it worked by the outline that appears around the selected photo, like the one in figure 2.12. Huzzah!

At this point, we've also worked our way through the complete Elm Architecture diagram from the beginning of section 2.2. Figure 2.13 shows where things ended up.

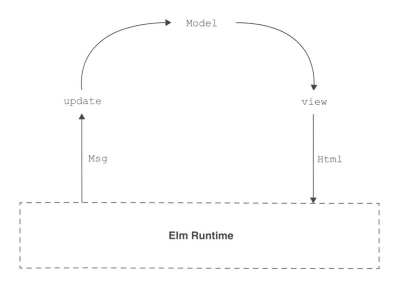

Figure 2.13   Our final
Elm Architecture setup

Congratulations on a job well done!

Summary

In this chapter, you learned three ways to handle interactions, each of which differs from the JavaScript way of handling the same. Table 2.2 summarizes these differences.

Table 2.2 Handling interactions in JavaScript compared to Elm

Interaction	JavaScript approach	Elm approach
Changing the DOM	Directly alter DOM nodes	Return some `Html` from a view function
Reacting to user input	Attach a listener to an element	Specify a message to send to `update`
Changing application state	Alter an object in place	Return a new model in `update`

We covered many other concepts in the course of building our first Elm application, including the following:

- A model represents our application state.
- A view function takes a model and returns a list of `Html` nodes.
- User events such as clicks get translated into message values.
- Messages get run through the `update` function to produce a new model.
- After an `update`, the new model is sent to the view function to determine the new DOM.
- `Browser.sandbox` wires together `model`, `view`, and `update`.
- `List.map` is a higher-order function that translates one list into another.
- All Elm functions are curried, which means they can be partially applied.

Here's the complete src/PhotoGroove.elm file we ended up with.

Listing 2.8 PhotoGroove.elm with a complete Model-View-Update in place

```
module PhotoGroove exposing (main)        ◁——┐ The name of
                                              │ our module
import Browser
import Html exposing (..)                  The other modules
import Html.Attributes exposing (..)       we're importing
import Html.Events exposing (onClick)


urlPrefix =
    "http://elm-in-action.com/"

                                    ┌─ The view function takes the current
view model =                   ◁——┘  model and returns some HTML.
    div [ class "content" ]
```

```
            [ h1 [] [ text "Photo Groove" ]
            , div [ id "thumbnails" ]
                (List.map (viewThumbnail model.selectedUrl) model.photos)
            , img
                [ class "large"
                , src (urlPrefix ++ "large/" ++ model.selectedUrl)
                ]
                []
            ]
```

viewThumbnail is partially applied here.

```
viewThumbnail selectedUrl thumb =
    img
        [ src (urlPrefix ++ thumb.url)
        , classList [ ( "selected", selectedUrl == thumb.url ) ]
        , onClick { description = "ClickedPhoto", data = thumb.url }
        ]
        []
```

When the user clicks, this message is sent to update.

```
initialModel =
    { photos =
        [ { url = "1.jpeg" }
        , { url = "2.jpeg" }
        , { url = "3.jpeg" }
        ]
    , selectedUrl = "1.jpeg"
    }
```

```
update msg model =
    if msg.description == "ClickedPhoto" then
        { model | selectedUrl = msg.data }

    else
        model
```

Changes the selected URL to the photo the user clicked

```
main =
    Browser.sandbox
        { init = initialModel
        , view = view
        , update = update
        }
```

Browser.sandbox describes our complete application.

In the next chapter, we'll get into ways to improve the application we've made so far, both adding features and refactoring to make it easier to maintain. Onward!

Compiler as assistant 3

This chapter covers

- Documenting guarantees with type annotations
- Implementing multiway conditionals with case-expressions
- Storing flexible data with custom types
- Using `Array` and `Maybe` for positional element access
- Generating random numbers by using commands

In chapter 2, we built your first Elm application. It doesn't do much yet, but it has potential! So far, it displays thumbnails of three photos, and lets users click one to view a larger version.

We showed it to our manager, who was thrilled with what we made: "Wow, this is looking *incredible*. The part where you click the thumbnail and it shows the bigger version? Just brilliant. I'm going to get some more team members working with you on this."

Nice! Quite a vote of confidence. Sure, we have no tests or documentation to help get these new teammates up to speed, but there's no time like the present to clean up our code.

Our manager also has a couple of feature requests: "Let's give users the ability to choose between viewing small, medium, or large thumbnails. Also, for this next version, I want to kick the fun factor into overdrive. Let's add a button that says *Surprise Me!*, and when you click it, it selects one of the photos—*at random*."

We resist the urge to tell our manager, "Whoa there, that might be too much fun," and instead review the tasks we've just received:

- Improve code quality to help new team members get up to speed.
- Let users choose between small, medium, and large thumbnails.
- Add a Surprise Me! button that randomly selects a photo.

Improving code quality *while* adding new features is often a tall order—even more so because these particular features involve aspects of Elm you have not yet encountered. Fortunately, we have an assistant to help us out: Elm's compiler.

In this chapter, you'll learn how the compiler can help you improve documentation, refactor without introducing regressions, and accomplish both while introducing new features. Let's get to it!

3.1 Documenting guarantees with type annotations

One of the quickest ways we can make our code nicer for incoming teammates is to add comments that document what our code does. Although comments are simple and flexible, they're also notoriously unreliable. Sometimes they're written inaccurately. Other times they start out accurate but become inaccurate as the code base changes out from under them.

> *Code never lies. Comments sometimes do.*
> —Ron Jeffries

Elm gives us access to a permanently trustworthy form of documentation: type annotations.

3.1.1 Adding optional type annotations

In chapter 2, we assigned the constant `urlPrefix` to `"http://elm-in-action .com"`. Let's edit our PhotoGroove.elm file to add a type annotation on top of that `urlPrefix` assignment, as shown in figure 3.1.

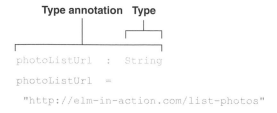

Figure 3.1   Adding a type annotation to `urlPrefix`

This annotation is saying, "urlPrefix is a String," and it's not kidding around with that. Elm's compiler will check our entire code base to verify this claim. If it finds even one incidence where urlPrefix is not used as a String, it will give us an error at compile time. This means if our code compiles, we can be certain urlPrefix is a String absolutely everywhere it's used!

This guarantee is even more useful for annotated functions. When teammates are new to the code base, being able to reliably tell at a glance what a function expects and what it returns can be an incredible time saver.

ANNOTATING FUNCTIONS

We can annotate functions by writing -> between their arguments and return values:

```
isEmpty : String -> Bool
isEmpty str = str == ""
```

This annotation says, "isEmpty takes a String and returns a Bool." Bool refers to one of those True or False Boolean values that we can use as the condition of an if-expression.

ANNOTATING RECORDS

Record annotations use : instead of = but otherwise look about the same as record values:

```
selectPhoto : { description : String, data : String }
selectPhoto = { description = "ClickedPhoto", data = "1.jpeg" }
```

This annotation says, "selectPhoto is a record with a description field and a data field, and each of those fields is a String." We can add a similar annotation to our initialModel:

```
initialModel =
    { photos = [ { url = "1.jpeg" }, { url = "2.jpeg" }, { url = "3.jpeg" } ]
    , selectedUrl = "1.jpeg"
    }
```

Ah, but this record has a list in it! How do we annotate lists?

ANNOTATING LISTS

In chapter 1, you learned that all elements in an Elm list must have a consistent type. This is reflected in their type annotations. For example, Elm represents a list of strings with the type annotation List String, and a list of Booleans with the type annotation List Bool. Let's play around with some lists to see their type annotations in elm repl.

Listing 3.1 Annotating lists

```
> [ "funk", "soul" ]                                    A list of
["funk","soul"] : List String                           strings

> [ [ "thanks", "for" ], [ "all", "the", "fish" ] ]          A list of lists
[["thanks","for"],["all","the", "fish"]] : List (List String)   of strings
```

```
> [ { url = "1.jpeg" }, { url = "2.jpeg" } ]
[{ url = "1.jpeg" },{ url = "2.jpeg" }] : List { url : String }
```

◁——┐ **A list of**
    records

Notice anything about the structure of that last example? It looks just like the list of photos in our model. This means we can use it to write an annotation for our model. Let's do that:

```
initialModel : { photos : List { url : String }, selectedUrl : String }
initialModel =
    ...
```

Model annotations are among the most helpful forms of documentation for new teammates, because they concisely (and reliably!) describe the structure of our entire application state.

3.1.2 *Annotating functions with type variables*

Functions, records, and lists served us well in chapter 2, but implementing the Surprise Me! button will involve a collection we haven't used before.

LISTS AND ARRAYS

Chapter 1 mentioned that Elm supports arrays as well as lists. Both are sequential collections of varying length, whose elements share a consistent type. However, arrays and lists differ in a few ways:

- Lists can be created with square bracket literals, whereas arrays have no literal syntax in Elm. We always create arrays by calling functions.
- Lists perform better in typical Elm use cases. This makes them the standard choice for representing a sequence of values, in contrast to JavaScript (where arrays are standard).
- Arrays are better for arbitrary positional access. That means it's quick and easy to say, "Give me the third element in this array." Lists have no first-class way to do this.

Randomly choosing a photo involves arbitrary positional access. As such, we've found ourselves in exactly the sort of situation where an array will serve us better than a list.

ARRAY.FROMLIST

The most common way to obtain an array is by calling `Array.fromList` on an existing list. Table 3.1 shows the results of a few calls to `Array.fromList`.

Table 3.1 Translating a list into an array by using `Array.fromList`

Expression	Result
`Array.fromList [ 2, 4, 6 ]`	Array containing three elements: 2, 4, and 6
`Array.fromList [ "foo" ]`	Array containing one element: `"foo"`
`Array.fromList []`	Array containing zero elements

TYPE VARIABLES

How would we write a type annotation for `Array.fromList`? It's a bit different from the functions we've annotated so far, as it returns a different type depending on what you pass it. Table 3.2 shows some examples of the types of values it can return.

Table 3.2 `Array.fromList`'s return type depends on its input

Given one of these	`Array.fromList` returns one of these
List Float	Array Float
List String	Array String
List { url : String }	Array { url : String }

Notice the pattern? Whatever type of list we pass in, that's what type of array we get out. We can capture this pattern in a type annotation like so:

```
fromList : List elementType -> Array elementType
```

In this annotation, `elementType` is a *type variable*.

> **DEFINITION** A *type variable* represents more than one possible type. Type variables have lowercase names, making them easy to differentiate from *concrete types* like `String`, which are always capitalized.

When you call `Array.fromList`, passing a list, the type variable `elementType` gets replaced by that list's element type. Table 3.3 shows this process in action.

Table 3.3 Replacing `Array.fromList`'s type variable

When we pass this in . . .	. . . `elementType` becomes . . .	. . . and we get this back
List Float	Float	Array Float
List String	String	Array String
List { url : String }	{ url : String }	Array { url : String }

CHOOSING NAMES FOR TYPE VARIABLES

When annotating `fromList`, we can choose a different name for its type variable besides `elementType`. Because a type variable serves as a placeholder for a concrete type like `String` or `List Int`, it can have just about any name, so long as it's lowercase and we use it consistently. For example, we could annotate `Array.fromList` in any of the following ways:

- `List elementType -> Array elementType`
- `List foo          -> Array foo`
- `List a            -> Array a`

In contrast, *none* of the following would work as annotations for `Array.fromList`:

- `List elementType -> Array blah`
- `List foo         -> Array bar`
- `List a           -> Array b`

These three annotations are saying, "`Array.fromList` takes a list containing elements of one type and returns an array that potentially contains elements of another type."

That just ain't so! `Array.fromList` can return only an array whose elements have the same type as the list it receives. Its type annotation must reflect that, by having the same type variable for both the `List` it accepts and the `Array` it returns.

> **NOTE**   Elm has three type variable names that have special meanings—`number`, `appendable`, and `comparable`—which we'll dive into later. For now, avoid choosing any of those as your type variable names.

By the way, you'll often encounter type variables in documentation with single-letter names like `a`, `b`, `c`, and so on. (For example, the official documentation for `Array.fromList` annotates it as `List a -> Array a`.) You are by no means obliged to do the same. Feel free to use the most self-descriptive names you can think of for your own type variables.

CREATING AN ARRAY OF PHOTOS

Because we want to access our photos by position, we'll be using `Array.fromList` on our `model.photos` list to translate it into an array. Let's add this code below our `initialModel` definition in PhotoGroove.elm:

```
photoArray : Array { url : String }
photoArray =
    Array.fromList initialModel.photos
```

If we tried to compile this right now, we'd get an error because we have not imported the `Array` module. Let's add it to the top of our imports list:

```
import Array exposing (Array)
```

Nice. Let's verify that our code still compiles by running `elm make src/Photo-Groove.elm --output app.js` once more before proceeding.

> #### Exposing imported types
>
> Notice how we wrote `exposing (Array)` there? If we'd written `import Array` without the `exposing (Array)` part, we'd need to refer to the `Array` type in a qualified style, like so:
>
> ```
> photoArray : Array.Array { url : String }
> ```
>
> `Array.Array` refers to "the `Array` type from the `Array` module," just as `Array.fromList` refers to "the `fromList` function from the `Array` module." Kinda verbose, right?

> By writing `exposing (Array)` after `import Array,` we get to skip the `Array.` prefix and use the more concise annotation:
>
> `photoArray : Array { url : String }`
>
> Lovely!

3.1.3 Reusing annotations with type aliases

Now that we've created `photoArray`, we can see that our annotations for `initialModel` and `photoArray` have a bit of code duplication going on: they both include `{ url : String }`:

```
initialModel : { photos : List { url : String }, selectedUrl : String }
photoArray : Array { url : String }
```

We can replace this duplication with shared code by using a type alias.

> **DEFINITION** A *type alias* assigns a name to a type. Anywhere you would refer to that type, you can substitute this name instead.

Let's create a type alias called `Photo`, and then use that in place of `{ url : String }`.

Listing 3.2 Creating a type alias called `Photo`

```
type alias Photo =                   "Whenever I say Photo,
    { url : String }                 I mean { url : String }"

initialModel : { photos : List Photo, selectedUrl : String }
initialModel =
    ...

photoArray : Array Photo
photoArray =
    Array.fromList initialModel.photos
```

This makes our `initialModel` annotation not only more concise, but also easier to maintain! Now if we add a new field to our `Photo` record, we can change the type alias in one place instead of having to hunt down several individual annotations.

ANNOTATING INITIALMODEL BY USING A TYPE ALIAS

Since `initialModel`, `view`, and `update` all involve our model record, let's add a type alias for `Model` as well, and then revise `initialModel`'s type annotation to use it:

```
type alias Model =
    { photos : List Photo
    , selectedUrl : String
    }

initialModel : Model
```

That takes care of `initialModel`. What about `view`?

HTML'S TYPE VARIABLE

We know view takes a Model and returns Html, but we can't just write "view returns Html" and call it a day. This is because, just like List and Array, the Html type has a type variable.

Html's type variable reflects the type of message it sends to update in response to events from handlers like onClick. Table 3.4 compares the type variables for List to the ones in Html.

Table 3.4   Comparing type variables for List and Html

Value	Type	Description
["foo"]	List String	List of String elements
[3.14]	List Float	List of Float elements
div [onClick "foo"] []	Html String	Html producing String messages
div [onClick 3.14] []	Html Float	Html producing Float messages
div [onClick { x = 3.3 }] []	Html { x : Float }	Html producing { x : Float } messages

Because our onClick handler produces messages in the form of records that have a description string and a data string, our view function's return type is as follows:

```
Html { description : String, data : String }
```

That's pretty verbose! Even though it won't remove any code duplication yet, it's perfectly fine to introduce a type alias to make view's annotation more concise. Let's add one above view:

```
type alias Msg =
    { description : String, data : String }


view : Model -> Html Msg
```

Excellent! Next, we'll look into annotating view's helper function, viewThumbnail.

3.1.4   *Annotating longer functions*

We've now seen a few type annotations for functions that take a single argument, but none for functions that take multiple arguments. Our viewThumbnail function will be the first.

To learn how to annotate a multi-argument function, let's play around with one that has a simpler return type: the humble padLeft function. padLeft makes sure strings meet a certain minimum length. You give it a minimum length, a *filler character,* and a string. If the string is not at least the given length, padLeft adds filler characters to its left until the string reaches that length.

We can try it out in `elm repl`, because `padLeft` is included in Elm's core `String` module:

```
> String.padLeft 9 '.' "not!"
".....not!" : String

> String.padLeft 2 '.' "not!"
"not!" : String
```

We can see that `String.padLeft` takes three arguments—an `Int`, a `Char`, and a `String`—and then returns another `String`. How can we annotate a function like that?

Believe it or not, you've already seen the answer! It's one of those answers that likes to hide in plain sight.

ANNOTATING A PARTIALLY APPLIED FUNCTION

Let's think back to chapter 2, where you learned that all functions in Elm are *curried*. That means they all support *partial application*—the practice of calling a function without passing all the arguments it requires. If we call `padLeft`, passing only one of its three arguments, the result will be a function that takes the remaining arguments and "finishes the job."

Here's a partial application of `padLeft`. What would the annotation for this be?

```
padNine = String.padLeft 9
```

`padLeft 9` is a partial application, so we know `padNine` must be a function. That's a start!

We also know that `padLeft` takes a `Char` as its next argument after the 9. That gives us enough information to rough out some pseudocode:

```
padNine : Char -> (a function of some sort)
padNine = String.padLeft 9
```

Now let's suppose we gave this `padNine` function the `Char` it wants. Passing a `'.'` character to `padNine` would be the same as passing 9 and then `'.'` to the original `padLeft`, like so:

```
padNineDots = String.padLeft 9 '.'
```

How would we annotate `padNineDots`? Because it gives `padLeft` two of three arguments, only one more argument is needed to finish the job. That last argument is a `String`, so `padNineDots` must *take* a `String` and *return* a `String`. We know how to write that one!

```
padNineDots : String -> String
padNineDots = String.padLeft 9 '.'
```

We now know the following:

- `padNine` takes a `Char` and returns a function (of some type).
- If you pass `padNine` a `Char`, it returns a `String -> String` function.

Putting those two together, our mystery function must be a `String -> String`! That tells us we can annotate `padNine` like so:

```
padNine : Char -> (String -> String)
padNine = String.padLeft 9
```

Now let's unwind our original partial application. If we cease partially applying the 9, we can follow the pattern we saw here to arrive at a valid annotation for the original `padLeft` itself:

```
padLeft : Int -> (Char -> (String -> String))
```

This is a perfectly accurate annotation, but it's a bit heavy on the parentheses, yeah? Fortunately, we can be more concise. Elm's syntax lets us omit the parentheses here, so the following two annotations are equivalent:

```
padNine : Int -> (Char -> (String -> String))
padNine : Int ->  Char ->  String -> String
```

Either style works just as well as the other, but the latter is considered best practice. You can see `elm repl` use this annotation style in the following listing, as we partially apply `String.padLeft` step by step, until it has no more arguments to accept and finally returns a `String`.

Listing 3.3   Multi-argument function annotations

```
> String.padLeft
<function:padLeft> : Int -> Char -> String -> String

> String.padLeft 9
<function> : Char -> String -> String

> String.padLeft 9 '.'
<function> : String -> String

> String.padLeft 9 '.' "not!"
".....not!" : String
```

Notice that each time we partially applied `padLeft`, our annotation got shorter, as shown in table 3.5.

Table 3.5   Type annotations changing as a function gets partially applied

Function	Type annotation
`String.padLeft`	`Int -> Char -> String -> String`
`String.padLeft 9`	`Char -> String -> String`
`String.padLeft 9 '.'`	`String -> String`
`String.padLeft 9 '.' "not!"`	`String`

If you think about it, this means, technically, *every Elm function takes only one argument*. After all, any function that *appears* to take multiple arguments is ultimately calling out to single-argument functions behind the scenes. The fact that Elm lets you omit the parentheses for these nested calls is just a syntactic convenience.

> **TIP** You can now tell your friends that, in chapter 2, you wrote an entire working Elm application in which every function took only a single argument. This sounds like some really hardcore programming unless your friends are familiar with currying.

ANNOTATING VIEWTHUMBNAIL

Armed with this knowledge, we can follow this pattern to annotate `viewThumbnail` like so:

```
viewThumbnail : String -> Photo -> Html Msg
viewThumbnail selectedUrl thumb =
```

> **TIP** Searching for "viewThumbnail :" in your editor is now a quick way to jump to `viewThumbnail`'s definition.

Splendid! Our code is getting easier and easier for teammates to pick up at a glance.

3.2 Using case-expressions and custom types

Now that our documentation situation is looking better, let's shift gears to work on those two new features: the Surprise Me! button and the Thumbnail Size Chooser.

We'll introduce these iteratively, first adding the visual elements with only a token level of interactivity, and then circling back to make them work properly afterward.

3.2.1 Using case-expressions

Let's start by adding the Surprise Me! button to our `view`, right above the thumbnails `div`:

```
, button
    [ onClick { description = "ClickedSurpriseMe", data = "" } ]
    [ text "Surprise Me!" ]
, div [ id "thumbnails" ]
```

Next, let's revise our `update` function to add a quick `else if` branch for our new `"ClickedSurpriseMe"` message, and a shiny new type annotation while we're at it:

```
update : Msg -> Model -> Model
update msg model =
    if msg.description == "ClickedPhoto" then
        { model | selectedUrl = msg.data }

    else if msg.description == "ClickedSurpriseMe" then
        { model | selectedUrl = "2.jpeg" }

    else
        model
```

This implementation always selects the second photo. That's not much of a *surprise,* granted, but we'll get there. For now, let's smooth out that code duplication we just introduced.

REFACTORING AN IF-EXPRESSION INTO A CASE-EXPRESSION

We now have two conditionals that do nothing more than compare `msg.description` to a string. Let's express this more cleanly by rewriting these if-expressions as a *case-expression,* as shown in figure 3.2.

```
case msg.description of
    "ClickedPhoto" ->
        { model | selectedUrl = msg.data }

    "ClickedSurpriseMe" ->
        { model | selectedUrl = "2.jpeg" }

    _ ->
      model
```

```
Equivalent if-expression

if msg.description == "ClickedPhoto" then
    { model | selectedUrl = msg.data }

else if msg.description == "…" then
    { model | selectedUrl = "2.jpeg" }

else
    model
```

Figure 3.2   **Refactoring an if-expression into a case-expression**

Whereas an *if-expression* is a two-way conditional, a *case-expression* is a multiway conditional. It lets us compare something to a wider range of values than just `True` or `False`.

Just as with a JavaScript switch-statement, we begin a case-expression by providing a value that will be run through a series of comparisons. Here we wrote `case msg.description of` because we want to run `msg.description` through these comparisons. Following the `case` are a series of *branches* such as the following:

```
"ClickedPhoto" ->
    { model | selectedUrl = msg.data }
```

This says that if `msg.description` is equal to `"ClickedPhoto"`, then the branch after the `->` will be evaluated, and the entire case-expression will evaluate to that branch's result.

If `msg.description` is not equal to `"ClickedPhoto"`, the next branch (in this case, the `"ClickedSurpriseMe" ->` branch) will be checked in the same way, and so on. Elm has no equivalent of JavaScript's `break` statement, because case-expression branches don't "fall through" like branches in JavaScript's switch-statements do.

Just like if-expressions, case-expressions must always evaluate to a single value, meaning exactly one branch must always be chosen for evaluation. When we're writing if-expressions, we have `else` to ensure that we end up with a value no matter what, whereas in case-expressions, we can use the default branch of `_ ->` for the same purpose.

NOTE In a case-expression, every branch must be indented the same amount—similar to what you saw in chapter 1 with let-expressions. Indentation level is significant only with let-expressions and case-expressions.

Our code is really shaping up! Let's copy the case-expression from figure 3.2 into PhotoGroove.elm, and then run `elm make` once more to recompile it.

TRYING OUT THE SURPRISE ME! BUTTON

Before we open up index.html and view our progress, we have one last change to make. While we've been hard at work on code quality and new functionality, one of our new teammates has been busy improving our stylesheets. Let's edit index.html to make use of their work, by changing its `<head>` to the following:

```
<head>
    <link rel="stylesheet" href="http://elm-in-action.com/styles.css">
</head>
```

Lovely! Now we can open our revised index.html to see the new button in all its glory, as shown in figure 3.3.

Figure 3.3   The new Surprise Me! button

In addition to styling the Surprise Me! button, our helpful teammate went ahead and added styles for the Thumbnail Size Chooser too. How about we introduce some logic to go with those styles?

3.2.2 *Enumerating possibilities with custom types*

Our second feature lets users choose one of three thumbnail sizes: small, medium, or large. The first step toward implementing it will be storing the current `chosenSize` in our model.

In JavaScript, we might represent `chosenSize` as a `String`—perhaps setting it to either `"SMALL"`, `"MEDIUM"`, or `"LARGE"`. But in Elm, we can do better with custom types.

DEFINITION A *custom type* is one you define by specifying the values it can contain.

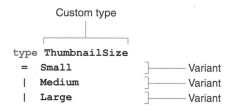

Figure 3.4   Defining an enumeration of values with a custom type called `ThumbnailSize`

One use for a custom type is as an enumeration of values. Figure 3.4 illustrates how we can define a custom type to represent the thumbnail size choices we'll support.

This is saying, "Define a new type called `ThumbnailSize` with three possible values: `Small`, `Medium`, and `Large`." Let's add this code to PhotoGroove.elm, right above `type alias Msg`.

We'll add the definition of `ThumbnailSize` in figure 3.4 to our code, right above `type alias Photo`. We can now define `chosenSize` in one of the following ways:

```
chosenSize : ThumbnailSize
chosenSize = Small

chosenSize : ThumbnailSize
chosenSize = Medium

chosenSize : ThumbnailSize
chosenSize = Large
```

Notice that in each of these examples, the type of `chosenSize` is `ThumbnailSize`. These new values we've created—`Small`, `Medium`, and `Large`—aren't "actually integers under the hood" or "just strings behind the scenes." We really have scratch-built a brand-new type here! Trying to compare a `ThumbnailSize` to a number, string, or any other type (using `==` or any other comparison) will yield an error at build time. This is different from `type alias`, which gives a *name* to an existing type—much as a variable gives a name to an existing value.

These custom type values are also unique. The expression `Medium == Medium` is `True`. But put absolutely any other value (besides `Medium`) on either side of that `==`, and the expression will no longer be `True`. The same can be said of `Small == Small` and `Large == Large`.

> **NOTE**   Boolean values in Elm are capitalized because `Bool` is a custom type. Its definition looks like this: `type Bool = True | False`.

Let's add the `chosenSize` field to our model and initialize it to `Medium` in `initial-Model`:

```
type alias Model =
    { photos : List Photo
    , selectedUrl : String
    , chosenSize : ThumbnailSize
    }

initialModel : Model
initialModel =
```

```
{ photos = ...
, selectedUrl = "1.jpeg"
, chosenSize = Medium
}
```

Great! Next, we'll render some radio buttons to let users change the chosen size.

RENDERING A THUMBNAIL-SIZE RADIO BUTTON

We can use our newfound knowledge of custom types and case-expressions to write a helper function that takes a `ThumbnailSize` and renders a radio button for choosing that size. Let's add the following to PhotoGroove.elm, right below `viewThumbnail`.

Listing 3.4   Rendering a thumbnail-size radio button

```
viewSizeChooser : ThumbnailSize -> Html Msg
viewSizeChooser size =
    label []
        [ input [ type_ "radio", name "size" ] []
        , text (sizeToString size)
        ]


sizeToString : ThumbnailSize -> String
sizeToString size =
    case size of
        Small ->
            "small"          Evaluates to "small"
                             if size == Small

        Medium ->
            "med"            Evaluates to "med"
                             if size == Medium

        Large ->
            "large"          Evaluates to "large"
                             if size == Large
```

NOTE   The underscore in that `type_` attribute is very important! As you've seen, `type` is a reserved keyword in Elm (used to define custom types), which means it can't be used for an `Html` attribute name. The `Html.Attributes` module names the attribute `type_` to work around this.

Notice anything missing from that case-expression? It has no default branch! We accounted for the cases where `size` is `Small`, `Medium`, and `Large`—but what if `size` has another value, such as `null`, `undefined`, or `"halibut"`?

Can't happen! `sizeToString`'s type annotation tells us that `size` is guaranteed to be a `ThumbnailSize`, and a `ThumbnailSize` can be only `Small`, `Medium`, or `Large`. It can't be `null` or `undefined` because those don't exist in Elm, and it can't be `"halibut"` because that's a `String`, not a `ThumbnailSize`.

Elm's compiler knows we've covered every possibility here, so it doesn't require a default branch. In fact, if we tried to add one, the compiler would politely inform us that we'd written unreachable code.

RENDERING THREE RADIO BUTTONS

We can now call this `viewSizeChooser` function three times, passing `Small`, `Medium`, and `Large`, to render the three radio buttons on the page. Let's do that right above `thumbnails`:

```
, h3 [] [ text "Thumbnail Size:" ]
, div [ id "choose-size" ]
    [ viewSizeChooser Small, viewSizeChooser Medium, viewSizeChooser Large ]
, div [ id "thumbnails" ]
    (List.map (viewThumbnail model.selectedUrl) model.photos)
```

Once again we see some code duplication: we're calling the same function (`view-SizeChooser`) on every element in a list. Anytime we're calling the same function on every element in a list, there's a good chance we can make our code cleaner with `List.map`.

This is absolutely one of those times. Let's refactor our `choose-size` element to this:

```
, div [ id "choose-size" ]
    (List.map viewSizeChooser [ Small, Medium, Large ])
```

This refactor not only reduces duplication, but also makes our code more concise.

RENDERING DIFFERENT THUMBNAIL SIZES

Rendering the interface for *choosing* a thumbnail size is great, but it's only half the battle! We still need to actually render our thumbnails differently based on what the user has chosen.

Thanks to our coworker having written a stylesheet for us, we can implement this by adding one of the classes `"small"`, `"med"`, or `"large"` to our `thumbnails` container. Because those classes conveniently correspond to the results of our `size-ToString` function, we can go ahead and replace our current `div [ id "thumbnails" ]` with the following:

```
div [ id "thumbnails", class (sizeToString model.chosenSize) ]
```

> **TIP** It would be best practice to write a separate `sizeToClass` function and use it here in place of `sizeToString`, even if their implementations were identical for the time being. Having separate functions means if someone later changes the text on the radio buttons, our thumbnail classes won't accidentally break.

Let's see how it looks! Because we haven't implemented the radio button logic yet, try changing the `chosenSize` value in `initialModel` to `Large` and then recompile to see how that affects the way the page looks. Then try recompiling again with `Small`, and finally back to `Medium`. You should be able to see a range of thumbnail sizes this way, as shown in figure 3.5.

Figure 3.5 Recompiling with `chosenSize = Small`, `chosenSize = Medium`, **and** `chosenSize = Large`

Cool! Now that we have our interface rendering, it's time to start making the logic work.

3.2.3 Holding data in custom types

Making the Surprise Me! button change our model's `selectedUrl` field to a random photo's `url` means we'll need to access a random photo from our `photoArray`. In JavaScript, we might implement reading a photo from an array as follows:

```
var photos = [ ...maybe there are photos here, but maybe not... ];
var selectedId - photos[2].url;  // Select the third photo
```

What happens if `photos` doesn't have at least three elements? In that case, `photos[2]` would evaluate to `undefined`, and `photos[2].url` would throw an angry runtime exception such as this:

```
Uncaught TypeError: Cannot read property 'url' of undefined
```

Elm avoids this runtime exception by handling this situation differently, in three ways:

- In Elm, you call `Array.get` to get an element in an array; there is no `[2]` accessor.
- `Array.get` never returns `undefined` or `null`, because Elm has neither of these.
- `Array.get` *always* returns a container value called a `Maybe`.

What's a Maybe? Glad you asked!

> **DEFINITION** A `Maybe` is a container like a `List`, except it can hold one element at most.

`Maybe` is implemented as a custom type, but a flavor of custom type you haven't covered yet: one that holds data. Its definition looks like this:

```
type Maybe value
    = Just value
    | Nothing
```

MAYBE VERSUS UNDEFINED

The most common use for `Maybe` is to represent the potential absence of a value. It provides a *container-based* alternative to JavaScript's *drop-in replacements* of `null` and

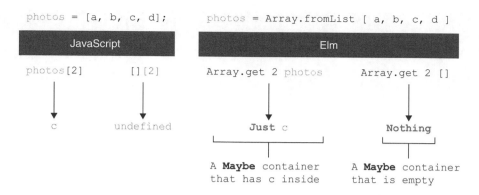

Figure 3.6   Comparing Elm's `Maybe` to JavaScript's `undefined`

`undefined`. Figure 3.6 compares Elm's `Array.get` and `Maybe` to JavaScript's `[2]` and `undefined`.

`Array.get 2 photos` expresses the desire to access the third element of an array called `photos`. However, the `photos` array may have fewer than three elements in it. If the index 2 is outside the bounds of `photos`, then `Array.get 2 photos` will return `Nothing`.

On the other hand, if 2 is inside its bounds, then `Array.get` will return `Just c`— where c is the element at index 2 in the `photos` array.

MAYBE'S TYPE VARIABLE

As we've seen before with `List`, `Array`, and `Html`, the `Maybe` type has a type variable. We chose to name it `value` in the definition we gave for `Maybe`'s custom type earlier:

```
type Maybe value
    = Just value
    | Nothing
```

Just as you can have a `List String` or a `List Photo`, you can also have a `Maybe String` or `Maybe Photo`. The difference is that whereas `List Photo` means "a list of photos," `Maybe Photo` means "either a `Photo` or nothing at all." Put another way, `Maybe` is a container that can hold at most one element.

Now that we know `Just "1.jpeg"` is a `Maybe String`, what is the type of `Just` itself?

"JUST" IS A FUNCTION

Argh, that heading totally gave away the answer. Oh well.

As the heading suggests, whereas `Nothing` is a `Maybe` value, `Just` is a *function* that returns a `Maybe` value. We can confirm this in `elm repl`:

```
> Nothing
Nothing : Maybe a

> Just
<function> : a -> Maybe a
```

```
> Just "dance"
Just ("dance") : Maybe String
```

Chapter 1 noted that when you write a function by hand, its name must be lowercase. Yet here we see that custom type variants (like `Just`) are functions with capitalized names. What makes them so special?

A capital question! The answer is right around the corner.

DESTRUCTURING CUSTOM TYPES

In chapter 1, you learned how to *destructure* tuples to both extract and name their values:

```
multiply3d ( x, y, z ) = x * y * z
```

As it turns out, we can also destructure custom type variants such as `Just` in the branches of case-expressions. This destructuring is what sets variants apart from other functions. Let's use what you've learned about `Array.get` and `Maybe` to add this `getPhotoUrl` function right above our `update` function.

> **Listing 3.5 Selecting a photo by index**

```
getPhotoUrl : Int -> String
getPhotoUrl index =
    case Array.get index photoArray of
        Just photo ->              Destructuring Just and naming
            photo.url              its contained value "photo"

        Nothing ->                 Fall back on "" if there was
            ""                     no photo at that index.
```

Here, `Just photo ->` is saying two things:

- This branch matches a `Maybe` value that was created using the `Just` variant.
- We're extracting the value that was passed to `Just` and naming it `photo`.

> **NOTE** This is where the distinction between capitalized and uncapitalized functions matters. By comparing their capitalizations, Elm's compiler can tell that `Just photo ->` refers to a type variant called `Just` that holds a value we've chosen to name `photo`. If we'd instead written `Just True ->`, the compiler would know we meant "the `Just` variant holding *exactly* the value `True`."

Notice that this case-expression did not need a `_ ->` branch. This is because its branches already cover all possible values of `Maybe`. One branch covers `Nothing`, and the other covers any values created with `Just`. Because `Nothing` and `Just` are the only ways to obtain a `Maybe`, these branches have every possibility covered.

Also notice that because `Array.get` returns a `Maybe`, you can't help but remember to handle the case where `index` is outside the bounds of `photoArray`. This design means that you'll always be doing the minimal amount of coding necessary to handle error cases. You don't need to defensively check whether something is `null` or `undefined`, because Elm's compiler has your back in cases where the value you want might not be available.

3.2.4 *Representing flexible messages with custom types*

We've made so much progress! We've updated our views to render the new interfaces, expanded our model to hold our new `chosenSize` field, and introduced helper functions for `photoArray`. Now it's time to wire all that together with changes to `update`.

Let's start by updating that `chosenSize` field, which currently gets initialized to `Medium` and then never changes. We'll want to update it whenever the user clicks a radio button.

This might seem like the obvious change to make to `viewSizeChooser`:

```
viewSizeChooser : ThumbnailSize -> Html Msg
viewSizeChooser size =
    ...
        onClick { description = "ClickedSize", data = size )
```

There's just one problem: this is a type mismatch! Remember our `type alias` for `Msg`?

```
type alias Msg =
    { description : String, data : String }
```

This says the `data` field of a `Msg` needs to be a `String`, not a `ThumbnailSize`. To preserve backward compatibility with existing code, we need a `Msg` type that can accommodate both `ThumbnailSize` and `String`. One way we could do this would be to add a new field called `size`:

```
type alias Msg =
    { description : String, data : String, size : ThumbnailSize }
```

This solves one problem while creating another. Now our existing `onClick` handler will no longer compile, because it's missing a field. Here's how we wrote it back in chapter 2:

```
onClick { description = "ClickedPhoto", data = thumb.url }
```

Without specifying a value for that new `size` field, this record is no longer a valid `Msg`. We'd need to change it to something like this:

```
onClick { description = "ClickedPhoto", data = thumb.url, size = Small }
```

Yuck. Having to set `size = Small` for a message that doesn't care about `size`? That doesn't smell right. And are we really planning to add a field to every `Msg` in our program whenever we need it to support a new data type? This doesn't seem like it will scale well. Is there a better way?

IMPLEMENTING MSG AS A CUSTOM TYPE

There totally is! Implementing `Msg` as a custom type will work much better. Here's the plan:

1. Replace our `type alias Msg` declaration with a `type Msg` declaration.
2. Revise `update` to use a case-expression that destructures our new custom type.
3. Change our `onClick` handler to pass a type variant instead of a record.

The following listing shows the first two changes: replacing type alias Msg with type Msg, and revising update accordingly. Let's edit PhotoGroove.elm to incorporate these changes.

Listing 3.6 Implementing Msg as a custom type

```
type Msg                          Replaces our earlier              Replaces our
    = ClickedPhoto String         declaration of type alias Msg     ClickedPhoto
    | ClickedSize ThumbnailSize                                     message
    | ClickedSurpriseMe                        Our new message: user
                                               clicked a thumbnail size
update : Msg -> Model -> Model    Replaces our
update msg model =               ClickedSurpriseMe message
    case msg of
        ClickedPhoto url ->                 Previous condition:
            { model | selectedUrl = url }   msg.description == "ClickedPhoto"

        ClickedSurpriseMe ->                Nothing to destructure
            { model | selectedUrl = "2.jpeg" }   for Surprise Me!
```

This change means our onClick handlers now expect type variants instead of records. We'll need to make this change in view:

```
Old: onClick { description = "ClickedSurpriseMe", data = "" }
New: onClick ClickedSurpriseMe
```

Let's also make this change in viewThumbnail:

```
Old: onClick { description = "ClickedPhoto", data = thumb.url }
New: onClick (ClickedPhoto thumb.url)
```

THE MISSING-PATTERNS ERROR

If we recompile, we'll see a type of error we haven't seen before: a *missing-patterns* error:

```
-- MISSING PATTERNS ------------------------------- src/PhotoGroove.elm

This `case` does not have branches for all possibilities.
...
Missing possibilities include:

    ClickedSize _

I would have to crash if I saw one of those. Add branches for them!
```

Oops! The compiler noticed we handled only ClickedPhoto and ClickedSurpriseMe in our update function's case-expression; we never wrote the logic for ClickedSize. Fortunately, that problem will never reach our end users because the compiler *didn't let us forget.*

> **TIP** Anytime you use the default case `_  ->` in a case-expression, you cannot get this error. That is not a good thing! The missing-patterns error is your friend. When you see it, it's often saving you from a bug you would have had to hunt down later. Try to use `_  ->` only as a last resort, so you can benefit from as many missing-pattern safeguards as possible.

Let's add this to our `update` function, right above the `ClickedSurpriseMe` branch:

```
ClickedSize size ->
    { model | chosenSize = size }

ClickedSurpriseMe index ->
    { model | selectedUrl = "2.jpeg" }
```

Finally, we need to add a new `onClick` handler to our radio button in `view-SizeChooser`:

Old: input [type_ "radio", name "size"] []
New: input [type_ "radio", name "size", onClick (ClickedSize size)] []

If we recompile and click the radio buttons, we can now see the thumbnail sizes change.

> **TIP** We could improve user experience in at least two ways here. One way is to make the Medium option display as selected on page load. Another is to use a broader event handler than `onClick`—one that detects whenever the radio state changes, even if it not from a click. Try implementing these improvements sometime for practice.

Using custom types for `Msg` has two major advantages over records:

- The compiler can save us from typos. Before, if we wrote `ClickedPhoti` instead of `ClickedPhoto`, our code would silently fail and we'd have to hunt down the cause. Now, if we write `ClickedPhoti` instead of `ClickedPhoto`, Elm's compiler will give us an error at build time—including the line number of the typo. No bug hunting necessary!
- Each flavor of `Msg` now holds only the minimum amount of data it needs. `ClickedPhoto` holds only a `String`, and `ClickedSize` holds only a `ThumbnailSize`. Best of all, `ClickedSurpriseMe` doesn't need to hold any data at all—and so it doesn't!

To sum up, implementing `Msg` as a custom type has made our code more reliable, more concise, and easier to scale. These advantages make custom types the typical choice for representing messages in production Elm applications, and they're what we will use for the rest of the book. Now all that remains is to introduce random number generation into Surprise Me!

3.3 Generating random numbers with commands

Currently, our Surprise Me! button always selects the second photo, but we want it to select a random photo instead. Here's how we're going to do that:

1 Generate a random integer between 0 and 2. This will be our index.
2 Ask `photoArray` for the photo it's storing at that index.
3 Set our model's `selectedUrl` to be that photo's `url`.

We'll start by generating the random integer.

3.3.1 Describing random values with Random.Generator

In JavaScript, `Math.random()` is the typical starting point for generating random values. Calling `Math.random()` gives you a random `Float` between 0 and 1. To randomly generate an `Int` or a `String`, you manually convert that `Float` into the value you actually want.

In Elm, we start with a `Random.Generator`, which specifies the type of value we want to randomly generate. For example, the `Random.int` function takes a lower bound and an upper bound, and returns a `Random.Generator` that generates a random `Int` between those bounds.

Here's a `Generator` that randomly generates integers between 0 and 2:

```
randomPhotoPicker : Random.Generator Int
randomPhotoPicker =
    Random.int 0 2
```

Notice that the type annotation says `Random.Generator Int`. This means, "We have a `Random.Generator` that produces `Int` values." If we'd used `Random.bool` instead of `Random.int`, it would have returned a `Random.Generator Bool` instead.

GENERATING A RANDOM PHOTO INDEX

Because `randomPhotoPicker` generates random integers between 0 and 2, and `photoArray` has three photos in it, we could use this generator to pick an index within `photoArray` to select. That would work, but it would be brittle because it relies on `photoArray` having exactly three photos.

We can improve it by replacing the hardcoded 2 with (`Array.length photoArray - 1`). Let's add the following after our `getPhotoUrl` declaration:

```
randomPhotoPicker : Random.Generator Int
randomPhotoPicker =
    Random.int 0 (Array.length photoArray - 1)
```

INSTALLING PACKAGE DEPENDENCIES

We also need to add the `Random` module to the end of our imports:

```
import Random
```

This won't quite compile yet, because although we've added `import Random`, the Random module is not among the standard modules that were installed when we ran `elm init` in chapter 2. For `import Random` to work, we first need to install the package that contains the `Random` module.

> **DEFINITION** An Elm *package* is an installable collection of modules.

The `elm install` command downloads and installs packages when you give it the name of the package you want. Package names consist of a username followed by a / and then the package name; in this case, the package we seek is named `elm/random`.

Let's use `elm install` to get some `Random` going. Run this command in the terminal:

```
elm install elm/random
```

You should see something like this:

```
Here is my plan:

  Add:
    elm/random    1.0.0

Would you like me to update your app.js accordingly? [Y/n]:
```

Answer y, and you should shortly see the text `Dependencies ready`.

> **TIP** If you'd like to know more details about package installation, see appendix B. It covers the app.js file, Elm's versioning system, and more.

Now that we've described the random value we want by using a `Random.Generator`, added `import Random` to access the module where `Random.Generator` lives, and used `elm install` to obtain the `elm/random` package that houses that module, our code will compile again. We're ready to generate some random values!

3.3.2   *Introducing commands to The Elm Architecture*

If you call JavaScript's `Math.random()` five times, you'll probably get back five different numbers. Elm functions are more consistent. If you call any Elm function five times with the same arguments, you can expect to get the same return value each time. This is no mere guideline, but a language-level guarantee! Knowing that all Elm functions have this useful property makes bugs easier to track down and reproduce.

Because Elm forbids functions from returning different values when they receive the same arguments, it's not possible to write an inconsistent function like `Math.random` as a plain Elm function. Instead, Elm implements random number generation by using a command.

> **DEFINITION** A *command* is a value that describes an operation for the Elm Runtime to perform. Unlike calling a function, running the same command multiple times can have different results.

When the user clicks the Surprise Me! button, we'll use a command to translate our `Random.Generator Int` into a randomly generated `Int`, which will represent our new selected photo index.

RETURNING COMMANDS FROM UPDATE

Remember how we specified what `onClick` should do in terms of a message that got sent to our `update` function? We didn't say, "Add this click event listener to the DOM right away." We said, "I want this `Msg` to get sent to my `update` function whenever the user clicks here."

Commands work similarly. We don't say, "Generate a random number right this instant." We say, "I want a random number, so please generate one and send it to my `update` function gift-wrapped in a `Msg`." As with `onClick`, we let `update` take it from there—and if we so desire, `update` can return new commands that trigger new calls to `update` when they complete. Figure 3.7 shows how commands flow through The Elm Architecture.

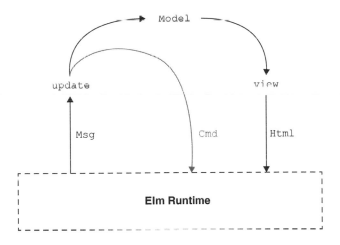

Figure 3.7   How commands flow through The Elm Architecture

Importantly, the addition of commands has not altered the fundamental structure of The Elm Architecture you learned in chapter 2. All of the following still hold true:

- Our `Model` value is still the single source of truth for the application state.
- Our `update` function is still the only way to alter that model.
- Sending a `Msg` to `update` remains the only way for the runtime to tell `update` what happened.

All we've done is give `update` some new powers: the ability to run logic that can have inconsistent results, such as generating a random number. As you will soon see, the key to unlocking these powers is upgrading from `Browser.sandbox` to `Browser.element`.

RUNNING COMMANDS IN RESPONSE TO USER INPUT

We want to generate our random number in response to a click event, so we'll need to alter our `update` function a bit. Specifically, we'll have `update` return a tuple containing not only the new `Model` we want, but also whatever commands we want the Elm Runtime to execute.

Before we edit `update`'s implementation, let's revise its type annotation to guide our work:

```
update : Msg -> Model -> ( Model, Cmd Msg )
```

As you can see, tuple annotations look just like tuple values. (`Model`, `Cmd Msg`) means "a tuple where the first element is a `Model` and the second is a `Cmd Msg`."

> **NOTE**   We write `Cmd Msg` instead of just `Cmd` for the same reason that we write `Html Msg` instead of `Html`. Like `Html`, the `Cmd` type also has a type variable, and for a familiar reason: whenever a `Cmd` finishes, a `Msg` value is what gets sent to `update` for further processing.

Let's revise our `update` implementation to reflect this new reality:

```
update : Msg -> Model -> ( Model, Cmd Msg )
update msg model =
    case msg of
        ClickedPhoto url ->
            ( { model | selectedUrl = url }, Cmd.none )

        ClickedSize size ->
            ( { model | chosenSize = size }, Cmd.none )

        ClickedSurpriseMe ->
            ( { model | selectedUrl = "2.jpeg" }, Cmd.none )
```

A fine start! Next, we'll replace that `Cmd.none` in `ClickedSurpriseMe`'s branch with a command to randomly generate the index of the photo we want to select.

3.3.3   *Generating random values with Random.generate*

The `Random.generate` function returns a command that generates random values wrapped up in messages. It's just what the doctor ordered here! `Random.generate` takes two arguments:

- A `Random.Generator`, which specifies the type of random value we want
- A function that can wrap the resulting random value in one of our `Msg` values

The `randomPhotoPicker` we created earlier will do nicely for `Random.Generator`, so all we're missing is a way to wrap these randomly generated integers in a `Msg`. We can introduce one by adding a new variant to `Msg` and a new branch to `update`:

```
type Msg
    = ClickedPhoto String
    | GotSelectedIndex Int
    ...
```

```
update : Msg -> Model -> ( Model, Cmd Msg )
update msg model =
    case msg of
        GotSelectedIndex ->
            ( { model | selectedUrl = getPhotoUrl index }, Cmd.none )

        ...
```

Great! Next, we'll get `Random.generate` to produce one of these `GotSelected-Index` messages.

CALLING RANDOM.GENERATE

When a user clicks the Surprise Me! button, the `ClickedSurpriseMe ->` branch of our `update` function's case-expression runs. Currently, that returns a `Cmd.none`, but now we want it to return a different command: one that generates a random `Int` and sends it back to `update` wrapped in a `GotSelectedIndex`. We'll obtain this command by calling `Random.generate`. Earlier we noted that `Random.generate` needs two ingredients:

- A `Random.Generator`, which specifies the type of random value we want. (We'll use `randomPhotoPicker`, our `Random.Generator Int`, for this.)
- A function that can wrap the resulting random value in one of our `Msg` values. (We'll use our `GotSelectedIndex` variant for this, since it's a function that returns a `Msg`.)

Let's revise our `ClickedSurpriseMe` branch to return an unchanged model, and to call `Random.generate` instead of returning `Cmd.none`:

```
ClickedSurpriseMe ->
    ( model, Random.generate GotSelectedIndex randomPhotoPicker )
```

Figure 3.8 illustrates how this would cause data to flow through our application, assuming the Elm Runtime randomly generated a 2 after the user clicked our Surprise Me! button.

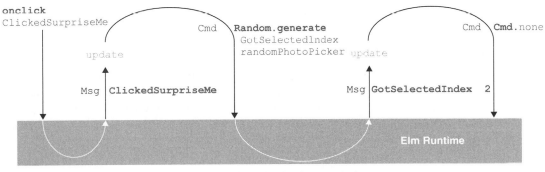

Figure 3.8 Data flowing through our application, assuming the Elm Runtime randomly generated a 2

TIP   Because update returns a tuple of a new Model and a command, it's possible for the same update branch to change the Model and to run a command as well. In such a case, first Model would change, then view would get run on the new Model to update the page, and finally the command would run.

Calling Random.generate GotSelectedIndex randomPhotoPicker returns a command that does the following:

1 Randomly generates an Int between 0 and 2, because that's the type of random value randomPhotoPicker specified it should generate
2 Takes that randomly generated Int, passes it to GotSelectedIndex (which is an Int -> Msg function), and runs the resulting Msg through update

We could write a type annotation for Random.generate like so:

```
generate : (randomValue -> msg) -> Random.Generator randomValue -> Cmd msg
```

NOTE   Capitalization is important! There is a big difference between Msg and msg here. A function that returns Msg returns an instance of the exact Msg custom type we defined in PhotoGroove.elm. In contrast, msg is a type variable. A function that returns msg could return anything at all!

Table 3.6 shows how the expressions involved in our call to Random.generate relate to the parameters and type variables in this annotation.

Table 3.6   Types involved in calling Random.generate

Expression	Type	Type in original annotation
GotSelectedIndex	(Int -> Msg)	(randomValue -> msg)
randomPhotoPicker	Random.Generator Int	Random.Generator randomValue

Random.generate
    GotSelectedIndex
    randomPhotoPicker
	Cmd Msg	Cmd msg

NOTE Because it takes a function as an argument, Random.generate is another *higher-order function* like List.map or String.filter.

UPGRADING MAIN TO USE BROWSER.ELEMENT

We're almost done, but if we compile our code right now, we'll get an error. This is because Browser.sandbox wants update to return a Model, whereas our update function now returns a (Model, Cmd Msg) tuple. Fortunately, sandbox's older sibling, Browser.element, expects just such a tuple. Let's replace our main declaration with this:

```
main =
    Browser.element
        { init = \flags -> ( initialModel, Cmd.none )
```

```
    , view = view
    , update = update
    , subscriptions = \model -> Sub.none
    }
```

We're passing two things differently from what we passed to `Browser.sandbox`:

1   The `init` record has been replaced by a function that takes `flags` and returns a tuple. We'll revisit `flags` in chapter 5; let's focus on the tuple for now. The first element in that tuple is our initial `Model`, and the second is a command to run when the application loads. (`init` is the only place besides `update` that can specify commands to run.) Because we have nothing to run on startup, we write `Cmd.none`.

2   We've added a `subscriptions` field. Like `flags`, we'll also dive into that in chapter 5; for now, let's disregard it.

ANNOTATING MAIN

Finally, we'll give `main` the following type annotation:

```
main : Program () Model Msg
```

Whoa! What's that funky `()` thing? The `()` value is known as *unit*. It contains no information whatsoever. It's both a value and a type; the `()` type can be satisfied only with the `()` value. We could use it to write a function like this:

```
getUltimateAnswer : () -> Int
getUltimateAnswer unit =
    40 + 2
```

The only way to call `getUltimateAnswer` would be to pass `()` to it; because it accepts `()` as an argument, no other value but `()` will do. A function that takes only `()` as an argument returns the same exact value every time it's called, making it a very boring function.

The reason we see `()` in our `Program` annotation is that `Program`'s three type parameters represent the following pieces of information:

- Our `flags` type. `flags` refers to the argument `init` receives, which we aren't currently using. Using `()` for our `flags` type indicates that we don't accept any flags.
- Our model's type. We can have any type of model we like—it could be a `String`, or an `Int`, or any number of other types. In our case, our model has the type `Model`.
- The type of the message that both `update` and `view` will use. In our case, that type is `Msg`.

Putting these together, we can read `Program () Model Msg` as "an Elm `Program` with no `flags`, whose model type is `Model` and whose message type is `Msg`."

Figure 3.9   Randomly choosing the initially selected photo

THE FINAL BUILD

If you recompile with elm make and open index.html, you should experience a gloriously functional application. Try clicking Surprise Me! to watch it randomly pick a different photo, as shown in figure 3.9.

Ain't it grand? Even after all the changes we made, once it compiled, it just worked—no regressions! Not only that, but our code never came anywhere near causing a runtime exception. This is a normal experience with Elm, yet it never seems to get old.

Compared to where we were at the end of chapter 2, our revised application is not only more feature rich, but also more reliable and better documented. It does more, it does it better, and the code is easier to maintain. Huzzah!

Summary

We've now improved on our application from chapter 2 in several ways:

- We added documentation in the form of type annotations.
- Users can now select from one of three thumbnail sizes.
- It has a Surprise Me! button that selects a thumbnail at random.
- From now on, whenever we add a new Msg value, the compiler will give us a missing-patterns error if we forget to handle it (as when we didn't account for ClickedSize).

Along the way, we covered many new concepts:

- Type variables represent concrete types that have not been specified yet.
- A type alias declaration assigns a name to a type, much as a constant assigns a name to a value.
- A type declaration defines a new custom type, one that did not exist before.

- Custom types can hold more-flexible data than records or tuples can.
- Custom type variants can be either values that are instances of that custom type, or functions that return instances of that custom type.
- You can destructure custom type variants in case-expressions to extract their data.
- If you don't write a fallback _ -> branch in a case-expression, you'll get a compiler error unless your code handles all possible cases.
- `Array.get` prevents runtime crashes by returning a `Maybe` instead of a normal element.
- The () type (known as *unit*) is both a type and a value. The only value of type () is the value ().
- The type `Program () Model Msg` refers to an Elm `Program` with no `flags`, whose model type is `Model` and whose message type is `Msg`.

You also learned some differences between comments and type annotations, as shown in table 3.7.

Table 3.7 Documenting code with comments and type annotations

Comment	Type annotation
Arbitrary string, can describe anything	Can describe only a thing's type
Can be inaccurate or become out of date	Compiler guarantees it's accurate and up to date
Can be written just about anywhere	Always goes on the line above the thing it documents

Finally, you learned about `Maybe`, the container value that `Array.get` returns to represent the potential absence of a value. Table 3.8 compares `Maybe` and `List`.

Table 3.8 Comparing `Maybe` and `List`

Container contents	List	Maybe
Empty	`[] : List a`	`Nothing : Maybe a`
One value	`[ "foo" ] : List String`	`Just "foo" : Maybe String`
Two values	`[ "foo", "bar" ]: List String`	*Not possible!*

In chapter 4, we'll take our application *to the extreme*, by talking to a server to obtain our list of photos to display. Stay tuned!

Listing 3.7 The complete PhotoGroove.elm

```
module PhotoGroove exposing (main)

import Array exposing (Array)
import Browser
import Html exposing (..)
```

```
import Html.Attributes exposing (..)
import Html.Events exposing (onClick)
import Random
```

The type of urlPrefix is String.

```
urlPrefix : String
urlPrefix =
    "http://elm-in-action.com/"
```

Msg is a custom type with four variants.

```
type Msg
    = ClickedPhoto String
    | GotSelectedIndex Int
    | ClickedSize ThumbnailSize
    | ClickedSurpriseMe
```

These variants are containers. Each holds a different type of value.

This variant is not a container. It holds no extra information.

```
view : Model -> Html Msg
view model =
    div [ class "content" ]
        [ h1 [] [ text "Photo Groove" ]
        , button
            [ onClick ClickedSurpriseMe ]
            [ text "Surprise Me!" ]
        , h3 [] [ text "Thumbnail Size:" ]
        , div [ id "choose-size" ]
            (List.map viewSizeChooser [ Small, Medium, Large ])
        , div [ id "thumbnails", class (sizeToString model.chosenSize) ]
            (List.map (viewThumbnail model.selectedUrl) model.photos)
        , img
            [ class "large"
            , src (urlPrefix ++ "large/" ++ model.selectedUrl)
            ]
            []
        ]
```

view is a function that takes a Model and returns an Html Msg value.

The ClickedSurpriseMe variant is not a function.

Arguments are separated by -> because they can be partially applied.

```
viewThumbnail : String -> Photo -> Html Msg
viewThumbnail selectedUrl thumb =
    img
        [ src (urlPrefix ++ thumb.url)
        , classList [ ( "selected", selectedUrl == thumb.url ) ]
        , onClick (ClickedPhoto thumb.url)
        ]
        []
```

The ClickedPhoto variant is a function. Its type is String -> Msg.

```
viewSizeChooser : ThumbnailSize -> Html Msg
viewSizeChooser size =
    label []
        [ input [ type_ "radio", name "size", onClick (ClickedSize size) ] []
        , text (sizeToString size)
        ]
```

```
sizeToString : ThumbnailSize -> String
sizeToString size =
    case size of
        Small ->
            "small"

        Medium ->
            "med"

        Large ->
            "large"
```

This case-expression has no default branch because these three branches already cover all possibilities.

```
type ThumbnailSize
    = Small
    | Medium
    | Large
```

```
type alias Photo =
    { url : String }
```

A type alias gives a name to a type. Anywhere we see the Photo type, we could have written this instead.

```
type alias Model =
    { photos : List Photo
    , selectedUrl : String
    , chosenSize : ThumbnailSize
    }
```

Type aliases can use other type aliases like Photo, as well as custom types like ThumbnailSize.

```
initialModel : Model
initialModel =
    { photos =
        [ { url = "1.jpeg" }
        , { url = "2.jpeg" }
        , { url = "3.jpeg" }
        ]
    , selectedUrl = "1.jpeg"
    , chosenSize = Medium
    }
```

```
photoArray : Array Photo
photoArray =
    Array.fromList initialModel.photos
```

```
getPhotoUrl : Int -> String
getPhotoUrl index =
    case Array.get index photoArray of
        Just photo ->
            photo.url

        Nothing ->
            ""
```

Array.get returns a Maybe because it's possible that there is no value at that index.

```
randomPhotoPicker : Random.Generator Int
randomPhotoPicker =
    Random.int 0 (Array.length photoArray - 1)
```

This Random.Generator Int describes a random number generator that produces integers.

```
update : Msg -> Model -> ( Model, Cmd Msg )
update msg model =
    case msg of
        GotSelectedIndex index ->
            ( { model | selectedUrl = getPhotoUrl index }, Cmd.none )

        ClickedPhoto url ->
            ( { model | selectedUrl = url }, Cmd.none )

        ClickedSize size ->
            ( { model | chosenSize = size }, Cmd.none )

        ClickedSurpriseMe ->
            ( model, Random.generate GotSelectedIndex randomPhotoPicker )
```

Tuples are similar to records. (Model, Cmd Msg) is a tuple with two elements.

Random.generate returns a Cmd that generates a random value, wraps it in GotSelectedIndex, and passes it to update.

```
main : Program () Model Msg
main =
    Browser.element
        { init = \flags -> ( initialModel, Cmd.none )
        , view = view
        , update = update
        , subscriptions = \model -> Sub.none
        }
```

An Elm program with no flags, with Model for its model type and Msg for its message type

Part 2

Production-grade Elm

In the next three chapters, you'll learn techniques that can be found in most Elm applications in the wild: talking to servers, talking to JavaScript, and testing. Strictly speaking, not every Elm application needs these, but in practice, all three are used very widely.

In chapter 4, you'll learn how to communicate with servers. This involves commands, a new concept within The Elm Architecture. Chapter 5 teaches how to communicate with JavaScript, which turns out to be very similar to communicating with servers. Chapter 5 also introduces the last foundational concept of The Elm Architecture: subscriptions.

Just as part 1 of the book ended with a chapter on how to make your code more reliable, so too does part 2, by teaching how to write automated tests for the code you've written in the preceding chapters. You'll learn about Elm's unit tests, fuzz tests, and how to test the user interface itself. By the end, you'll know enough to use Elm professionally.

Talking to servers

This chapter covers

- Using decoders to validate and translate JSON
- Handling descriptive errors with results
- Communicating over HTTP with commands

We've made great progress! Users of our Photo Groove application can now do quite a bit:

- Select a thumbnail to view a larger version
- Choose Small, Medium, or Large thumbnail sizes
- Click the Surprise Me! button to select a random thumbnail

Our manager is impressed with our progress but has even more in mind: "It's time to take Photo Groove to the next level. The highest level. The cloud level. That's right, we're going to have Photo Groove start getting its photo information from our servers!"

As with last time, our manager has one more minor feature request: "There's also going to be some metadata associated with each photo—specifically, download size and an optional caption. We can have it show those on top of the big photo, right?"

Sure, since you asked so nicely.

In this chapter, we'll teach our application how to talk to servers. We'll validate and translate JSON data, communicate over HTTP using The Elm Architecture, and reliably handle errors in client-server communication. Let's get to it!

4.1   Preparing for server-loaded data

Now that we're going to be loading our initial list of photos from the server, our data-modeling needs will change.

4.1.1   Modeling incremental initialization

Right now, our `initialModel` looks like this:

```
initialModel : Model
initialModel =
    { photos = [ { url = "1.jpeg" }, { url = "2.jpeg" }, { url = "3.jpeg" } ]
    , selectedUrl = "1.jpeg"
    , chosenSize = Medium
    }
```

Once we start loading our photos from the server, we'll no longer have any photos when the page loads. Instead, we'll immediately send a request to the server to retrieve them, and once we hear back, we'll either have some photos to display . . . or an error message for the user. Let's translate these new considerations into some changes to our data model.

MODELING LOADED DATA

Our photos can now be in three possible states:

- We're still loading them. This will be our initial state when the program begins.
- There was a server error. In this case, we'll have an error message to display.
- We successfully loaded the data. Now we have photos, and possibly one is selected.

A custom type is the perfect way to represent these distinct possibilities! Let's introduce this custom type right above our `type alias Model` declaration:

```
type Status
    = Loading
    | Loaded (List Photo) String
    | Errored String
```

This neatly represents all three possibilities. We'll begin in the `Loading` state, and then we'll transition to either `Loaded` or `Errored`, depending on whether the server gave us some photos or an error. If we're in the `Errored` state, we have an error message to display, and we have a `List Photo` (and the `String` of which URL is selected) only if the photos `Loaded` successfully.

> **NOTE**   Another way to model this would be using a *list zipper* data structure. We won't dive into list zippers in this book, but they're worth knowing about! A list zipper is like a `List` that has exactly one of its elements marked as

selected. We could replace `Loaded (List Photo) String` with a `Loaded` variant that contains a single value; namely, a list zipper.

Let's replace the `List Photo` in our `Model` and `initialModel` with `Status`:

```
type alias Model =
    { status : Status
    , chosenSize : ThumbnailSize
    }


initialModel : Model
initialModel =
    { status = Loading
    , chosenSize = Medium
    }
```

PROPAGATING CHANGES

Now that we've revised our `Model`, we can lean on the compiler to tell us what parts of our code base were affected by this revision. This will let us reliably propagate these changes throughout our code base!

If we recompile, we'll see three type mismatches: one in `photoArray`, one in `update`, and one in `view`. Let's start with `view`.

FIXING VIEW

`view` has some code that references the obsolete `model.photos`:

```
(List.map (viewThumbnail model.selectedUrl) model.photos)
```

We'll fix this by introducing a case-expression on `model.status`, and moving the code in question to that case-expression's `Loaded` branch—because now our photos are available in only that state. Our new `view` will look like this:

```
view : Model -> Html Msg
view model =
    div [ class "content" ]
        (case model.status of
            Loaded photos selectedUrl ->
                viewLoaded photos selectedUrl model.chosenSize

            Loading ->
                []

            Errored errorMessage ->
                [ text ("Error: " ++ errorMessage) ]
        )

viewLoaded : List Photo -> String -> ThumbnailSize -> List (Html Msg)
viewLoaded photos selectedUrl chosenSize = ...
```

Here we have a case-expression in the middle of our `view`, and we're passing its output to `div [ class "content" ]`. We can totally do that! Using a conditional expression in rendering logic might seem unfamiliar if you're used to HTML (or a restricted templating system), but remember, Elm views are plain old functions. They get to use the language to its fullest!

Each branch in this case-expression evaluates to a List (Html Msg), which will serve as the list of child nodes for the div [class "content"] at the top of view. The Loading branch returns [], which means it won't display anything. (This would also be a reasonable place to display a loading spinner.) The Errored branch only displays the error message, and the Loaded branch calls viewLoaded—which is where most of the action will happen.

RENDERING THE LOADED PHOTOS

The viewLoaded helper function will look almost the same as what we previously had in view. The only difference is that it takes three arguments instead of the one Model, and it returns a List (Html Msg) instead of Html Msg. (After all, view functions can return whatever is most helpful to us!)

Let's move that code over from the old view and replace any obsolete mentions of model with direct references to the arguments instead:

```
viewLoaded : List Photo -> String -> ThumbnailSize -> List (Html Msg)
viewLoaded photos selectedUrl chosenSize =
    [ h1 [] [ text "Photo Groove" ]
    , button
        [ onClick ClickedSurpriseMe ]
        [ text "Surprise Me!" ]
    , h3 [] [ text "Thumbnail Size:" ]
    , div [ id "choose-size" ]
        (List.map viewSizeChooser [ Small, Medium, Large ])
    , div [ id "thumbnails", class (sizeToString chosenSize) ]
        (List.map (viewThumbnail selectedUrl) photos)
    , img
        [ class "large"
        , src (urlPrefix ++ "large/" ++ selectedUrl)
        ]
        []
    ]
```

Spectacular! If we recompile, we'll now see two type mismatches remaining instead of three. Before we fix the next one, though, there's a quick refactor we can make.

USING THE <| OPERATOR

Let's zoom in on our call to div:

```
div [ class "content" ]
    (case model.status of
        ...
    )
```

This code works fine, but it could be shorter if we used the <| operator. "What does that thing do?" I hear you ask, followed immediately by, "Is it a slice of pizza?"

To answer both questions: it is not a slice of pizza, but rather ~~a slice of cake~~ an operator that calls a function. In Elm, these two lines of code do the same thing:

```
String.toUpper   (String.reverse "hello")
String.toUpper <| String.reverse "hello"
```

The `<|` operator takes a function and another value, and passes the value to the function. That might not sound like it does much, but it's handy for situations like the one we have here—where an infix operator would look nicer than parentheses. We can use it to refactor our `div`, as shown in table 4.1.

Table 4.1 Eliminating parentheses by using the `<|` operator

Parentheses	`<|` Operator

`div [ class "content" ]`
`    (case model.status of`
`        ...`
`    )`
	`div [ class "content" ] <|`
	`    case model.status of`
	`        ...`

Lovely! Once we've implemented that refactor, we're ready to resolve our next type mismatch. This one will be a bit more involved.

4.1.2 Resolving data dependencies

The cause of our next type mismatch is that two branches of `update`'s case-expression reference `model.selectedUrl`, which no longer exists:

```
GotSelectedIndex index ->
    ( { model | selectedUrl = getPhotoUrl index }, Cmd.none )

ClickedPhoto url ->
    ( { model | selectedUrl = url }, Cmd.none )
```

Because the selected URL now lives in `model.status`, we'll need to change this logic accordingly.

FIXING UPDATE

Let's add a `selectUrl` helper function below `update` to help us out with this:

```
selectUrl : String -> Status -> Status
selectUrl url status =
    case status of
        Loaded photos _ ->
            Loaded photos url

        Loading ->
            status thought

        Errored errorMessage ->
            status
```

This function doesn't do much. If it's passed a `Status` that is in the `Loaded` state, it returns an updated version of that `Status` that has the thumbnails' `selectedUrl` set to the given URL. Otherwise, it returns the `Status` unchanged.

> **TIP**   This function could be made more robust. Currently, if it gets a photo URL to select before the photos have loaded, it ignores that error and proceeds as if nothing has gone wrong. A more robust implementation might return a `Maybe Status`, so that `update` could fire off a `Cmd` to record the error in a logging service. We won't use a logging service in this book, but although it's good to recover from errors that shouldn't have happened, additionally logging that they happened gives you a way to later investigate what went wrong.

The underscore placeholder

You may have noticed that `Loaded photos _ ->` uses an underscore instead of a descriptive name like `selectedUrl`. The underscore is no ordinary name. It is a special placeholder indicating that there is a value here, but we're choosing not to use it. Attempting to reference _ in our logic would be a compile error.

One handy feature of _ is that you can use it multiple times in the same pattern. For example:

```
Loaded _ _ ->
    status
```

You can use _ in case-expression branches as well as in function arguments:

```
functionThatTakesThreeArguments _ _ _ =
    "I ignore all three of my arguments and return this string!"
```

In contrast to choosing a name like `unusedValue`, the underscore makes it clearer that the value is never used.

Let's use our tasty new `selectUrl` helper function to fix the type mismatch in `update` like so:

```
case msg of
    GotSelectedIndex index ->
        ( { model | status = selectUrl (getPhotoUrl index) model.status }
        , Cmd.none
        )

    ClickedPhoto url ->
        ( { model | status = selectUrl url model.status }, Cmd.none )
```

If we recompile, we can see that we're now down from two type mismatches to one.

REPLACING PHOTOARRAY

The final type mismatch occurs because our top-level `photoArray` is still based on `initialModel.photos`. This was perfectly reasonable back when `initialModel.photos` had a bunch of hardcoded photos in it, but now that we're loading them on the fly, we need a new approach.

Let's start by deleting our existing `photoArray` definition, along with the `get-PhotoUrl` and `randomPhotoPicker` declarations that went with it. This will remove our previous compile error, but will reveal two more once we recompile. This is good! The top-level `photoArray` was only a symptom; now we're getting closer to the actual cause.

DIRECTLY CHOOSING A RANDOM PHOTO

One way we could fix this is by creating `photoArray` on the fly. However, this is a good opportunity to step back and see if we can find a nicer approach.

In chapter 3, we created an `Array Photo` to help us choose a photo at random. We then used a `Random.Generator Int` to get a random index into that array, and `Array.get` with that index to obtain the `Photo` we desired. Is there some way we could randomly choose a `Photo` without the intermediate `Array`? Indeed there is: the `Random.uniform` function!

```
Random.uniform : elem -> List elem -> Random.Generator elem
```

This function produces a `Random.Generator` that randomly picks one of the `elem` values we passed it. It's called `uniform` because it has the same chance of randomly producing any of the elements; their probabilities have a *uniform* distribution.

Why does it take both an `elem` argument as well as a `List elem`? Why not take a `List elem` alone? Because `List elem` could be empty, and it would be impossible for `uniform` to pick one element from a list of zero elements.

> **NOTE** Conceptually, `Random.uniform` "takes a non-empty list." The reason Elm's standard libraries don't include a dedicated `NonEmptyList` type is that it's simple enough for a function that needs one to follow `Random.uniform`'s design: accept a mandatory `elem` as well as a `List elem` of optional additional values. Similarly, a function can "return a non-empty list" by returning an (`elem`, `List elem`) tuple.

We'll use `Random.uniform` to fix the `ClickedSurpriseMe` branch, which depended on the `randomPhotoPicker` value that no longer exists. Let's change the `Clicked-SurpriseMe` branch like so:

```
ClickedSurpriseMe ->
    case model.status of
        Loaded (firstPhoto :: otherPhotos) _ ->
            ( model
            , Random.generate GotRandomPhoto
                (Random.uniform firstPhoto otherPhotos)
            )

        Loading ->
            ( model, Cmd.none )

        Errored errorMessage ->
            ( model, Cmd.none )
```

These two `Loaded` branches use some patterns we haven't seen before.

THE :: PATTERN

Let's zoom in on the first pattern:

```
Loaded (firstPhoto :: otherPhotos) _ ->
```

The `firstPhoto :: otherPhotos` pattern matches `List` values that have at least one element. Their first element is named `firstPhoto` (because it came before the `::` symbol), and the remaining elements are in a list called `otherPhotos`. If we were to annotate their types, we'd write `firstPhoto : Photo` and `otherPhotos : List Photo`.

Now that we have a `Photo` and a `List Photo`, we can pass them as the arguments to `Random.uniform` to get a `Random.Generator Photo` value.

> **TIP** When you encounter a function like `Random.uniform` that takes a "non-empty list," using the `::` pattern in a case-expression is often a good way to obtain the two arguments it needs.

GOTRANDOMPHOTO

Now that we're generating a random photo instead of a random index, our call to `Random.generate` will use a message variant named `GotRandomPhoto` instead of the previous `GotSelectedIndex`. We'll need to change our `Msg` type to reflect this. Let's remove the `GotSelectedIndex Int` variant and add this at the end of our `type Msg` definition:

```
| GotRandomPhoto Photo
```

Then we'll replace the `GotSelectedIndex` branch in `update` with this:

```
GotRandomPhoto photo ->
    ( { model | status = selectUrl photo.url model.status }, Cmd.none )
```

Fantastic! Now our Surprise Me! logic will work with photos loaded from the server, and not only that, we refactored our way out of a dependency. Because we are no longer using `Array`, we can remove `import Array` from the top of our module.

MISSING PATTERNS

If we try to recompile, we'll see one final error:

```
-- MISSING PATTERNS ----------------------------------- src/PhotoGroove.elm
```

Whoops! Our `case model.status` does not handle the possibility that we are in the `Loaded` state with an empty list of photos. The `Loaded (firstPhoto :: other-Photos) _ ->` branch represents only the situation where we got at least one photo, so we'll need to add a second `Loaded` branch for the situation where the server gave us zero photos.

THE [ ] PATTERN

Let's introduce a new branch right below the existing `Loaded` branch:

```
Loaded [] _ ->
    ( model, Cmd.none )
```

This pattern will match `Loaded` variants where the `List Photo` value is empty. It says that if the user clicks Surprise Me! and we loaded zero photos, then the Surprise Me! button does nothing. Thanks to this change, our code compiles again!

USING THE PIPELINE OPERATOR

We have one more change to make: a stylistic one. We're going to express the first `Loaded` branch as a *pipeline* of sequential operations by using `Tuple.pair` and the `|>` operator.

Let's look at `Tuple.pair` first. It's a function that takes two arguments and returns them in a tuple. So writing `Tuple.pair a b` returns `( a, b )`. It works nicely with the `|>` operator, like so:

```
Loaded (firstPhoto :: otherPhotos) _ ->
    Random.uniform firstPhoto otherPhotos
        |> Random.generate GotRandomPhoto
        |> Tuple.pair model
```

The `|>` operator is purely stylistic. This expression is exactly equivalent to writing `Tuple.pair model (Random.generate GotRandomPhoto (Random.uniform firstPhoto otherPhotos))` except it's expressed in a different style. Figure 4.1 compares these two ways to write the same expression.

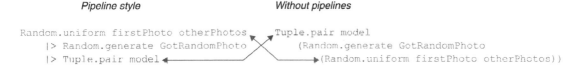

Pipeline style   *Without pipelines*

```
Random.uniform firstPhoto otherPhotos        Tuple.pair model
    |> Random.generate GotRandomPhoto            (Random.generate GotRandomPhoto
    |> Tuple.pair model                          (Random.uniform firstPhoto otherPhotos))
```

Figure 4.1 The same expression, with and without pipelines

The pipelined code is saying the following:

1. Call `Random.uniform firstPhoto otherPhotos`.
2. Pass its return value as the final argument to `Random.generate GotRandom-Photo`.
3. Pass that return value as the final argument to `Tuple.pair model`.

Pipelines can make it easier to read and to modify sequences of transformations like this. We'll be using them later in this chapter and throughout the rest of the book. Go ahead and switch to the pipeline version before we move on.

> **NOTE** Before Elm's compiler generates JavaScript code, it quietly rewrites pipelines into normal function calls. So `"foo" |> String.reverse` compiles to the same thing as `String.reverse "foo"`. Since they compile to the same thing, there's no performance cost to choosing one over the other. Choose whichever makes for nicer code.

THE COMPLETED REFACTOR

Let's review the code changes we've made:

1 Our data model now represents three distinct states: `Loading`, `Loaded`, and `Errored`.

2 We begin in the `Loading` state, but now we access `photos` or `selectedUrl` only when in the `Loaded` state. (Because we now store those values in the `Loaded` variant, we've guaranteed that we can't possibly access them in any other state.)

3 When the user clicks the Surprise Me! button, we randomly select a photo without creating an intermediate `Array`.

Although our code compiles, it no longer does much. We begin in the `Loading` state, but we never transition out of it. Fortunately, our data model is now prepared for us to make that transition using photos we receive from the server. It's time to get some HTTP going!

4.2 Fetching data from a server

One of our helpful coworkers has set up a simple server endpoint that returns a comma-separated list of photo filenames. The list doesn't yet contain the metadata that we'll ultimately need, but it'll give us a good starting point toward that goal. Let's send an `HTTP GET` request to fetch that comma-separated string from a server.

4.2.1 Describing HTTP requests

We'll be using the `Http` module to send HTTP requests to our server. Since `Http` is not one of Elm's core modules, we need to install the `elm/http` package to gain access to it. We'll do that the same way we installed the `elm/browser` package in chapter 2:

```
elm install elm/http
```

Answer y when prompted, and we'll be ready to go!

MANAGED EFFECTS INSTEAD OF SIDE EFFECTS

In chapter 3, we saw how generating random numbers in Elm must be done with a `Cmd` rather than a plain function call. Whereas JavaScript's `Math.random()` can return a different random number each time you call it, Elm functions must be more consistent. When you pass an Elm function the same arguments, it's guaranteed to return the same value.

There's another rule that applies to all Elm functions, and this one affects the HTTP requests we're about to make. The rule is that Elm functions cannot have *side effects*.

> **DEFINITION** An *effect* is an operation that modifies external state. A function that modifies external state when it executes has a *side effect*.

HTTP requests can always modify external state—because even a `GET` request can result in a server changing values in a database—so performing an HTTP request is an effect. This means if we execute a function and it performs an HTTP request, that function has a side effect.

The following listing shows a few JavaScript functions that consistently return the same value, but that have side effects because they modify external state along the way. None of these could be written as plain Elm functions.

> **Listing 4.1 JavaScript functions that have side effects**

```
function storeStuff() {
    localStorage.stuff = "foo";          Modifies the contents
    return 1;                            of localStorage
}

function editField(object) {
    object.foo = "bar";                  Modifies the object
    return object;                       it receives
}

var something = 1;

function editVar() {
    something = 2;                       Modifies an
    return 0;                            external variable
}
```

If you look through all the code we've written for Photo Groove, you won't find a single function that has a side effect. All effects are performed by the Elm Runtime itself; our code only *describes* which effects to perform, by returning values from `update`.

> **NOTE** Calling `update` does not directly alter any state. All `update` does is return a tuple. If you wanted to, you could call `update` a hundred times in a row, and all it would do is give you back a hundred tuples.

This system of *managed effects*, in which the Elm Runtime is in charge of performing all effects, means that Elm programs can be written entirely in terms of data transformations. In chapter 6, you'll see how nice this makes Elm code to test.

To perform an HTTP request, we'll do what we did with random number generation in chapter 3: use `Cmd` to tell the Elm Runtime to perform that effect.

HTTP.GET

The `Http.get` function returns a `Cmd` representing the HTTP request we want to make. It has this type:

```
Http.get : { url : String, expect : Expect msg } -> Cmd msg
```

We pass `Http.get` a URL string, along with an `Expect` value that describes what we expect to get back. Just as in chapter 3 with random number generation, once this `Cmd` completes, it will send a `Msg` to `update` telling us what happened.

Let's see how it works! Suppose we decided to call it like this:

```
Http.get
    { url = "http://manning.com"
    , expect = Http.expectString toMsg
    }
```

Here's what this code is saying:

1 Send an HTTP GET request to http://manning.com.
2 I expect to get back a `String` for the response.
3 When the response comes back, use this `toMsg` function to translate it into a `Msg`.
4 Send that `Msg` to `update`.

Figure 4.2 illustrates this process.

Figure 4.2   The Elm Runtime executing a `Cmd` from `Http.get`

Next, we'll take a look at how to process that response properly.

HTTP.EXPECTSTRING

Let's take a closer look at that `Http.expectString` function. What exactly is it look-ing for in that `toMsg` function?

```
Http.expectString : (Result Http.Error String -> msg) -> Expect msg
```

Unlike the random number generation effect we performed in chapter 3, a lot can go wrong with an HTTP request! What if we send the server an invalid URL? Or an unrecognized one? What if the server has been unplugged by a mischievous weasel?

If the request fails for any reason, we'll want to know what went wrong so we can try to recover—and possibly inform the user. `Http.expectString` uses a value that accounts for this possibility: a `Result`.

RESULT AND MAYBE

To get a feel for how `Result` works, let's compare it to its cousin `Maybe`. In chapter 3, we saw how `Array.get` returned a `Maybe` to account for the possibility of a missing value. The definition of `Maybe` looks like this:

```
type Maybe value
    = Just value
    | Nothing
```

Elm has a similar custom type for representing the *result* of an operation that can fail, such as performing an HTTP request. It's called `Result`, and it looks like this:

```
type Result errValue okValue
    = Err errValue
    | Ok okValue
```

As we can see, `Result` has two type variables:

- `okValue` represents the type of value we'll get if the operation succeeded. For example, if we are trying to obtain a `String` from the server, then `okValue` would be `String`.
- `errValue` represents the type of error we'll get if the operation failed. In our case, `errValue` will refer to a custom type that enumerates various mishaps that can befall HTTP requests. That custom type is called `Http.Error`.

Just as `Maybe` requires that we write logic to handle both the `Just` and `Nothing` cases, so too does `Result` require that we handle both the `Ok` and `Err` cases.

HTTP.GET AND HTTP.EXPECTSTRING

Putting it all together, we can see how `Http.get` and `Http.expectString` work together to provide the ingredients we need to describe a request:

```
expectString : (Result Http.Error String -> msg) -> Expect msg
get          :             { url : String, expect : Expect msg } -> Cmd msg
```

Between the two of them, we have the following:

- A URL string
- The `Msg` that should be sent to `update` if the request fails (meaning we got the `Err` variant of `Result Http.Error String`, which holds an `Http.Error` we can inspect)
- The `Msg` that should be sent to `update` if the request succeeds (meaning we got the `Ok` variant of `Result Http.Error String`, which holds the `String` the server sent back)

Now that you know how to put an HTTP request together, you're ready to send it!

4.2.2   *Sending HTTP requests*

To handle the response from our freshly described HTTP request, we'll start by importing the `Http` module. Let's add this right before `import Random`:

```
import Http
```

Next, let's add a `Msg` variant to handle the `Result` value we'll get from `Http.get`:

```
type Msg
    = ClickedPhoto String
    | ClickedSize ThumbnailSize
    | ClickedSurpriseMe
    | GotRandomPhoto Photo
    | GotPhotos (Result Http.Error String)
```

You'll learn more about the `Http.Error` type in a bit. For now, let's add a branch to our `update` function's case-expression for this new `Msg`. We'll start with something like this:

```
GotPhotos result ->
    case result of
        Ok responseStr ->
            ...translate responseStr into a list of Photos for our Model...

        Err httpError ->
            ( { model | status = Errored "Server error!" }, Cmd.none )
```

With that basic skeleton in place, we can implement these two cases one at a time. We'll start with the `Ok responseStr` case, where the server gave us a valid response and all is well.

READING PHOTO FILENAMES WITH STRING.SPLIT

Remember earlier, when I mentioned how we have a server endpoint that returns a comma-separated list of photo filenames? If not, here it is again:

> *One of our helpful coworkers has set up a simple server endpoint that returns a comma-separated list of photo filenames.*
>
> —This book, earlier

Sure enough, if we visit this endpoint at http://elm-in-action.com/photos/list, we can see the list of filenames. It's a plain old string:

```
"1.jpeg,2.jpeg,3.jpeg,4.jpeg"
```

We wrote `Ok responseStr` a moment ago—that `responseStr` value will refer to exactly this string! Now we can split `responseStr` into a list of individual filenames by using Elm's `String.split` function. It has this type:

```
split : String -> String -> List String
```

We give `String.split` a separator (in this case, a comma) and a string to split, and it gives us back a list of all the strings it found between those separators. Table 4.2 shows what `String.split ","` will do to the string we get from the server.

Table 4.2 Calling `String.split ","` on a string

stringFromServer	String.split "," stringFromServer
"1.jpeg,2.jpeg,3.jpeg,4.jpeg"	["1.jpeg", "2.jpeg", "3.jpeg", "4.jpeg"]

Once we have this list of filename strings, we can use it to set the `photos : List Photo` field in our `Model` as in the following listing.

Listing 4.2 Incorporating `responseStr` into the `Model`

```
Ok responseStr ->
    let
        urls =
            String.split "," responseStr          ⟵  Splits the String
                                                      into a List String

        photos =
            List.map (\url -> { url = url }) urls  ⟵  Translates the List
                                                      String into a List Photo

        firstUrl =
            List.head photos      ⟵  Gets the first
                                      photo in the list
    in
    ( { model | status = Loaded photos firstUrl }, Cmd.none )  ⟵  Sets the photos
                                                                   in the model
```

Now when we successfully receive a `String` response from the server, we'll translate it into a list of `Photo` records, along with a `firstUrl` to use as our `selectedUrl`, and store them both in our `Model`. Now we recompile everything, and . . .

LIST.HEAD

. . . *Whoops!* This code doesn't compile.

The source of the trouble is our call to `List.head`. That function's type looks like this:

```
List.head : List elem -> Maybe elem
```

`List.head someList` and `Array.get 0 someArray` serve essentially the same purpose: returning `Nothing` when passed an empty collection, or `Just whateverElementWasFirst` if the collection had anything in it. Unfortunately for us, this means that our `firstUrl` is not a `String` like the `Loading (List Photo) String` variant expects, but rather a `Maybe String`!

USING THE "AS" KEYWORD

We can use the `::` pattern you learned in section 4.1.2 to remedy this situation. Let's rewrite our `Ok responseStr` branch like so:

```
Ok responseStr ->
    case String.split "," responseStr of
        (firstUrl :: _) as urls ->
            let
                photos =
                    List.map (\url -> { url = url }) urls
```

```
        in
        ( { model | status = Loaded photos firstUrl }, Cmd.none )
    [] ->
        ( { model | status = Errored "0 photos found" }, Cmd.none )
```

This pattern has something you haven't seen before!

```
(firstUrl :: _) as urls ->
```

The `as` `urls` part of this pattern means "give the name `urls` to this entire `List`, while also subdividing it into its first element—which we will name `firstUrl`—and its remaining elements, which we will decline to name by using the _ placeholder."

> **TIP** You can also use as when destructuring function arguments. For example, doSomethingWithTuple ((first, second) as tuple) = ... or perhaps doSomethingWithRecord ({ username, password } as record) = ...

Now everything should compile once again. Notice that we now treat it as an error case if the server returns zero photos. In fact, if this happens, we will set our model's `status` to `Errored`, and it will be as if the server had given us back an invalid response.

When Elm's compiler highlights an edge case like this, we often have a choice to make about how we want to handle it. For example, here we could have set `selectedUrl` to `""` and called it a day. (If we wanted to go that route, though, it would have been better to be more explicit about the possibility of not having a selection; for example, by changing the type of `selectedUrl` to a Maybe String.) We decided not to, but it would have worked fine to take either path.

> **NOTE** Because we now know our List Photo in the Loaded variant will never be empty, we could change the type of Loaded to hold a non-empty list instead of a List Photo. For example, its type could be Loaded Photo (List Photo) String. We won't make that change here, but try it out if you have time.

Before we move on, let's pause for a quick refactor.

USING TYPE ALIASES TO CREATE RECORDS

Declaring `type alias Photo = { url : String }` does more than give us a `Photo` type we can use in type annotations. It also gives us a convenience function whose job is to build `Photo` record instances. This function is also called `Photo`. Here it is in action:

```
Photo "1.jpeg" == { url = "1.jpeg" }
```

This also works with record type aliases involving multiple fields, like the one for `Model`:

```
type alias Model =
    { status : Status
    , chosenSize : ThumbnailSize
    }
```

This declaration gives us a convenience function called `Model` that builds a record and returns it. Because this record has two fields, whereas `Photo` had only one, the `Model` function accepts two arguments instead of one. The type of the `Model` function looks like this:

```
Model : Status -> ThumbnailSize -> Model
```

The order of arguments matches the order of the fields in the `type alias` declaration. So if you were to move the `photos : List Photo` declaration to the end of the `type alias`, then the `Model` function would look like this instead:

```
Model : String -> ThumbnailSize -> List Photo -> Model
```

We can use this knowledge to perform a quick refactor of our `Photo` construction:

```
Old: List.map (\url -> { url = url }) urls
New: List.map Photo urls
```

Lovely!

PATTERN MATCHING

There's one more refactor we can make here. If you zoom out a bit, you'll notice we have a case-expression nested directly inside another case-expression:

```
case msg of

    ...

    GotPhotos result ->
        case result of
            Ok responseStr ->

                ...

            Err _ ->
                ( model, Cmd.none )
```

In situations like this, we can use concise *pattern matching* to express the same logic:

```
case msg of

    ...

    GotPhotos (Ok responseStr) ->
        ...

    GotPhotos (Err _) ->
        ( model, Cmd.none )
```

> **DEFINITION** *Pattern matching* is a way of destructuring values based on how their containers look. In the preceding example, if we have a `GotPhotos` containing an `Ok` containing a value, that value will go into a variable called `responseStr`.

This refactored code is equivalent to what we had before. The difference is that now each of our branches is expressing two conditions at once:

- The `GotPhotos (Ok responseStr)` branch runs if `msg` is a `GotPhotos` variant that contains an `Ok` value.
- The `GotPhotos (Err _)` branch runs if `msg` is a `GotPhotos` variant that contains an `Err` value.

You can nest patterns like these as much as you want, even assembling elaborate creations like `NestAllTheThings (Just (Ok (Listen (This (IsReally "great" _ _)))))` —but try not to overdo it.

RUNNING A COMMAND ON INIT

At this point, we've assembled all the ingredients necessary to launch our HTTP rocket ship in the direction of our server:

- A URL string and `Expect` value that `Http.get` will use to return a `Cmd Msg` that will send the request
- Logic for the `GotPhotos` message that will handle the response

Let's put it all together to create a new value called `initialCmd` by using this call to `Http.get`:

```
initialCmd : Cmd Msg
initialCmd =
    Http.get
        { url = "http://elm-in-action.com/photos/list"
        , expect = Http.expectString (\result -> GotPhotos result)
        }
```

We'll use this `initialCmd` value to run our HTTP request when the program starts up.

The type of initialCmd

Why does `initialCmd` have the type `Cmd Msg`? Let's look at the type of `Http.get` again:

```
Http.get : { url : String, expect : Expect msg } -> Cmd msg
```

Because `msg` is lowercase, it's a type variable like the ones we saw in chapter 3. This means whatever flavor of `Expect` we pass to `Http.get`, we'll get the same flavor of `Cmd` back. Their type parameters will necessarily be the same!

How can we tell what `Expect`'s type parameter will be in this expression? Let's dig one level deeper and look at `Http.expectString` again:

```
Http.expectString : (Result Http.Error String -> msg) -> Expect msg
```

Once again we see a type variable called `msg`. So the `Expect` will be parameterized on whatever type we return from the `(Result Http.Error String -> msg)` function we pass to `Http.expectString`. In our case, that would be this anonymous function:

```
Http.ExpectString (\result -> GotPhotos result)
```

Because that function returns a `Msg`, the call to `Http.expectString` will return an `Expect Msg`, which in turn means `Http.get` will return `Cmd Msg`.

SIMPLIFYING INITIALCMD

This will compile, but we can simplify it. Back in section 2.2.1 of chapter 2, we noted that an anonymous function like `(\foo -> bar baz foo)` can always be rewritten as `(bar baz)` by itself. This means we can replace `(\result -> GotPhotos result)` with `GotPhotos` like so:

```
initialCmd : Cmd Msg
initialCmd =
    Http.get
        { url = "http://elm-in-action.com/photos/list"
        , expect = Http.expectString GotPhotos
        }
```

Now we have a `Cmd` to run, but we want to kick this one off a bit differently than last time. We ran our random number generation command from `update` in response to a user click, but we want to run this command right when the program starts up.

We can do that by updating `main` to use `initialCmd` instead of `Cmd.none` on `init`, like so:

```
main : Program Never Model Msg
main =
    Browser.element
        { init = \_ -> ( initialModel, initialCmd )
        , view = view
        , update = update
        , subscriptions = \_ -> Sub.none
        }
```

We don't use this argument, so name it.

While we're at it, we also updated `init` and `subscriptions` to use `_` for their anonymous functions' arguments, because those arguments never get used.

TIP An anonymous function that ignores its argument (like the `\_ ->` in the preceding code) kinda looks like a hockey stick.

Figure 4.3 illustrates how our revised `init` kicks off the sequence of events leading up to our `update` function receiving a `GotPhotos` message.

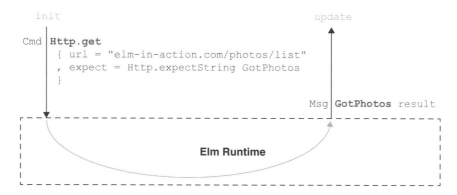

Figure 4.3   Running a `GotPhotos` command on `init`

Now let's recompile and open index.html, so we can bask in the glory of our new server-loaded photos! Figure 4.4 shows how the page should now look.

Figure 4.4   The updated application, with an additional photo loaded

Beautiful! Now that we're loading photos from the server, we're ready to take the final step: obtaining the metadata and complete URLs from the server, rather than filenames alone.

4.3   Decoding JSON

Browsers can talk to servers in many ways: JSON, XML, RPC, BBQ . . . the list goes on. Regardless, when the browser sends off an HTTP request to a server, the response comes back as a bunch of raw bytes. It's up to the program running in the browser to decode those bytes into a useful representation.

The server with the metadata will be sending us that information via JSON. This means we'll need some way to decode a JSON string into something more useful.

4.3.1   Decoding JSON strings into results

To work with JSON, we'll want the elm/json package. Run this at the terminal:

```
elm install elm/json
```

We already had this as an indirect dependency (because the elm/browser package depends on it, and we depend on elm/browser directly), so answer y when prompted to move it into our direct dependencies.

> **NOTE**   We can import modules from only our direct dependencies, not from our indirect dependencies.

THE DECODESTRING FUNCTION

Plenty of things can go wrong during the process of decoding JSON. Suppose the server messes up and sends us XML instead of JSON. Our JSON-decoding logic will certainly fail! Or suppose we get back a response that's valid JSON, but a required field is missing. What then?

The Json.Decode.decodeString function returns a Result. Its complete type is shown here:

```
decodeString : Decoder val -> String -> Result Error val
```

Notice that the Result we get back from decodeString has one concrete type—namely, that errValue is always an Error—and one that matches the type of the given decoder's type variable. (Error is a custom type that the Json.Decode module uses to represent an error that occurred during decoding.) Table 4.3 shows how the decoder passed to decodeString affects its return type.

Table 4.3   How the decoder passed to decodeString affects its return type

Decoder passed in	decodeString returns	Example success value
Decoder Bool	Result Error Bool	Ok True
Decoder String	Result Error String	Ok "Win!"
Decoder (List Int)	Result Error (List Int)	Ok [1, 2, 3]

DECODING PRIMITIVES

The `Json.Decode` module has a `Decoder Bool` called `bool`, which translates a JSON Boolean string (either `"true"` or `"false"`) into an Elm `Bool` (`True` or `False`). Let's try it in `elm repl`!

Listing 4.3 Using `decodeString bool`

```
> import Json.Decode exposing (..)

> decodeString bool "true"
Ok True : Result Error Bool

> decodeString bool "false"
Ok False : Result Error Bool

> decodeString bool "42"
Err … : Result Error Bool

> decodeString bool "@&!*/%?"
Err … : Result Error Bool
```

Besides `bool`, the `Json.Decode` module offers other primitive decoders like `string`, `int`, and `float`. They work similarly to `bool`, as we can see in `elm repl`.

Listing 4.4 Using `decodeString` with `int`, `float`, and `string`

```
> import Json.Decode exposing (..)

> decodeString float "3.33"
Ok 3.33 : Result Error Float

    > decodeString string "\"backslashes escape quotation marks\""
Ok "backslashes escape quotation marks" : Result Error String

> decodeString int "76"
Ok 76 : Result Error Int

> decodeString int "3.33"
Err … : Result Error Int
```

The only primitive decoders are `bool`, `int`, `float`, `string`, and `null`, because JavaScript's `undefined` is not allowed in valid JSON. As you will soon see, there are other ways of handling `null` besides using this primitive decoder.

4.3.2 *Decoding JSON collections*

You've now seen how to decode primitives like Booleans, integers, and strings from JSON into their Elm counterparts. This is a good start, but JSON also supports arrays and objects, and we'll need to decode both of these types in order to receive our list of photos with metadata.

Decoding JSON arrays into lists

Suppose we have the JSON string `"[true, true, false]"`. To decode a list of Booleans from this JSON array, we can write `list bool`. This will give us a `Decoder (List Bool)` value.

Here's how `Json.Decode.bool` and `Json.Decode.list` compare:

```
bool : Decoder Bool
list : Decoder value -> Decoder (List value)
```

Whereas `bool` is a decoder, `list` is a *function* that takes a decoder and returns a new one. We can use it in `elm repl` to make decoders for lists of primitives, or even lists of lists!

Listing 4.5 Using `Json.Decode.list`

```
> import Json.Decode exposing (Decoder, list, bool, string, int)

> list
<function> : Decoder a -> Decoder (List a)          <⊢   elm repl chooses "a" for the
                                                          type variable we called "value".
> list bool
<internals> : Decoder (List Bool)

> list string
<internals> : Decoder (List String)

> list (list int)
<internals> : Decoder (List (List Int))
```

Decoding objects

The simplest way to decode an object is with the `field` function. Suppose we write this:

```
decoder : Decoder String
decoder =
    field "email" string
```

When this decoder runs, it performs three checks:

1 Are we decoding an `Object`?
2 If so, does that `Object` have a field called `email`?
3 If so, is the `Object`'s email field a `String`?

If all three are true, then decoding succeeds with the value of the `Object`'s email field. Table 4.4 shows how this decoder would work on a variety of inputs.

Table 4.4 Decoding objects with field decoders

Decoder	JSON	Result
field "email" string	5	Err … (the number 5 has no fields)
	{"email": 5}	Err … (the email field wasn't a string)
	{"email": "cate@nolf.com"}	Ok "cate@nolf.com"

DECODING MULTIPLE FIELDS

Building a decoder for a single `field` is all well and good, but typically when decoding objects, we care about more than one of their fields. How do we do that? The simplest is with a function like `map2`, which we can see in table 4.5.

Table 4.5 Decoding objects with field decoders

Decoder	JSON	Result

`map2`
    `(\x y -> ( x, y ))`
    `(field "x" int)`
    `(field "y" int)`
	`{"x": 5}`
	
	`{"x": 5, "y": null}`
	
	`{"x": 5, "y": 12}`
		`Err … (y was missing)`
		
		`Err … (y was null, not int)`
		
		`Ok ( 5, 12 )`

DECODING MANY FIELDS

The photo information we'll be getting back from our server will be in the form of JSON that looks like this:

```
{"url": "1.jpeg", "size": 36, "title": "Beachside"}
```

This is an object with three fields: two strings and one `int`. Let's update our `Photo` type alias to reflect this:

```
type alias Photo =
    { url : String
    , size : Int
    , title : String
    }
```

We could decode this by using the technique we just learned, with one slight difference. We'd have to use `map3` instead of `map2`, because we have three fields instead of two:

```
photoDecoder : Decoder Photo
photoDecoder =
    map3
        (\url size title -> { url = url, size = size, title = title })
        (field "url" string)
        (field "size" int)
        (field "title" string)
```

How far can this approach take us? If we added a fourth field, we'd change `map3` to `map4`. The `Json.Decode` module also includes `map5`, `map6`, `map7`, and `map8`, but `map8` is as high as it goes. From there, we can either combine the decoders we've already used . . . or we can introduce a library designed for larger-scale JSON decoding!

PIPELINE DECODING

The `Json.Decode.Pipeline` module is designed to make life easier when decoding large objects. It comes from a popular third-party package called `NoRedInk/elm-json-decode-pipeline`—so let's quickly install it before we proceed:

```
elm install NoRedInk/elm-json-decode-pipeline
```

Let's also add it to our imports. We'll do that by adding all of this to our imports list, right after import Http:

```
import Http
import Json.Decode exposing (Decoder, int, list, string, succeed)
import Json.Decode.Pipeline exposing (optional, required)
```

Now the coast is clear to replace photoDecoder with the code in this listing.

Listing 4.6 photoDecoder

```
photoDecoder : Decoder Photo
photoDecoder =
    succeed buildPhoto
        |> required "url" string
        |> required "size" int
        |> optional "title" string "(untitled)"

buildPhoto : String -> Int -> String -> Photo
buildPhoto url size title =
    { url = url, size = size, title = title }
```

If decoding succeeds, pass these values to the buildPhoto function.

"url" is required and must be a string.

"size" is required and must be an integer.

"title" is optional and defaults to "(untitled)".

Let's break down what's happening here:

1   succeed buildPhoto begins the pipeline. It says that our decoder will decode the arguments to buildPhoto, one by one, and ultimately the whole decoder will succeed unless any of the steps in this pipeline fails. Because buildPhoto accepts three arguments, we'll need three pipeline steps after this. (Otherwise, the compiler will give an error.)

2   required "url" string says that we need what we're decoding to be a JSON object with the string field "url". We're also saying that if decoding succeeds, we should use this first result as the first argument to buildPhoto. Decoding could fail here, either because the "url" field is missing, or because the field is present—but is not a string.

3   required "size" int does the same thing as required "url" string except that it decodes to an integer instead of a string.

4   optional "title" string "(untitled)" is similar to the required steps, but with one important difference: in this example, if the "title" field were either missing or null, this decoder will default on that final argument instead of failing decoding—that is, the title string would default to "(untitled)".

Figure 4.5 shows how the buildPhoto arguments and photoDecoder arguments match up.

```
photoDecoder : Decoder Photo
photoDecoder =
    succeed buildPhoto                                    buildPhoto :
        |> required "url" string                              String
        |> required "size" int                            -> Int
        |> optional "title" string "(untitled)"           -> String
                                                          -> Photo
```

Figure 4.5   The relationship between `photoDecoder` and `buildPhoto`

How "succeed" and "required" interact

To get a deeper understanding of how this works, let's take a closer look at how `succeed` and `required` interact here. Let's start by looking at the type of `Decode.succeed` and `buildPhoto`:

```
succeed : a -> Decoder a
buildPhoto : String -> Int -> String -> Photo
```

Putting the two together, when we call `Decode.succeed buildPhoto`, it returns a decoder of this type:

```
Decoder (String -> Int -> String -> Photo)
```

If we stopped right here, we'd have a pretty unhelpful decoder! It would always succeed, no matter what JSON we gave it, and all it would do is give us that same `buildPhoto` function that we already had to begin with.

We can make this decoder a bit more useful by adding `required`, like so:

```
functionDecoder : Decoder (Int -> String -> Photo)
functionDecoder =
    succeed buildPhoto
        |> required "url" string
```

Whereas the decoder we made with `succeed Photo` would succeed no matter what JSON we gave it, this one will succeed only if we give it a JSON object with a field called `url` that holds a `String`. This decoder also has a slightly different type than the `succeed Photo` one did. It's shrunk by one argument:

Before required: `Decoder (String -> Int -> String -> Photo)`
After required: `Decoder (       Int -> String -> Photo)`

The following table shows how each call to `required` applies one more argument to the `Photo` function we started out with. Doing this a few times shrinks our original `Decoder (String -> Int -> String -> Photo)` down to a `Decoder Photo`.

Step	Type
`succeed buildPhoto`	`Decoder (String -> Int -> String -> Photo)`
`|> required "…" string`	`Decoder       (Int -> String -> Photo)`
`|> required "…" int`	`Decoder              (String -> Photo)`
`|> required "…" string`	`Decoder                        Photo`

By the way, notice anything familiar about what `buildPhoto` does?

All it does is take one argument for each of the fields in `Photo`, and then assign them uncritically without altering them in any way. We already have a function that does this! It's the `Photo` function, which we got for free because we defined the `Photo` type alias.

Let's delete `buildPhoto` and replace `photoDecoder = succeed buildPhoto` with this:

```
photoDecoder =
    succeed Photo
        |> required "url" …
```

Much easier! Finally, let's add this `photoDecoder` definition right below `type alias Photo`.

> **WARNING**   Reordering any function's arguments can lead to unpleasant surprises. Because reordering the fields in the `Model` type alias has the consequence of reordering the `Model` function's arguments, you should be exactly as careful when reordering a type alias as you would be when reordering any function's arguments!

4.3.3   Decoding JSON HTTP responses

You've already seen how we can use `Http.expectString` to obtain a `String` from a server, and how we can use `decodeString` and a `Decoder` to translate a `String` into a list of `Photo` records for our `Model`.

Although we could use `Http.expectString` and `decodeString` to populate our `Model` in this way, another function in the `Http` module will take care of both for us.

HTTP.EXPECTJSON

The `Http.expectJson` function requests data from a server and then decodes it. Here's how the types of `Http.expectString` and `Http.expectJson` match up:

```
expectString : (Result Http.Error String -> msg)                -> Expect msg
expectJson   : (Result Http.Error val    -> msg) -> Decoder val -> Expect msg
```

Comparing types like this suggests how these functions are similar and how they differ. They both accept a function to translate a `Result` into a `msg`. Both `Result` types have `Http.Error` as their `Err` type. However, whereas `expectString` takes no other arguments and always produces a `String` for its `Result`'s `Ok` type, `getJson` additionally accepts a `Decoder val`, and on success produces an `Ok val` result instead of `Ok String`.

As you might expect, if we give `Http.expectJson` a decoder of `(list int)`, and the response it gets back is the JSON payload `"[1, 2, 3]"`, then `Http.get` will successfully decode that into `Ok (List Int)`. If decoding fails, we will instead get `Err BadBody`.

THE BADBODY ERROR

What's BadBody? It's a variant of that `Http.Error` type we said we'd get back to. (Sure enough, here we are getting back to it.) `Http.Error` is a custom type that describes various ways an HTTP request can fail. It looks like this:

```
type Error
    = BadUrl String
    | Timeout
    | NetworkError
    | BadStatus Int
    | BadBody String
```

The `BadBody` variant occurs when the body of the HTTP response failed to decode properly. Because `Error` is a custom type, we can run a case-expression on any `Http.Error` value—with different branches for `Timeout`, `NetworkError`, and so on—to do custom error handling based on what went wrong.

> **TIP** The lower-level `Http.request` function lets you customize requests in greater depth than `Http.get` does.

USING EXPECTJSON IN INITIALCMD

We want to decode the JSON from our server into a `List Photo`, and we have a `Decoder Photo`. This means we can use `Http.expectJson` and `Json.Decode.list` to end up with the information we want.

Let's change `initialCmd` to do just that, while referencing a slightly different URL: instead of /photos/list, from now on we'll use /photos/list.json instead:

```
initialCmd : Cmd Msg
initialCmd =
    Http.get
        { url = "http://elm-in-action.com/photos/list.json"
        , expect = Http.expectJson GotPhotos (list photoDecoder)
        }
```

This means we'll be sending a `List Photo` to `GotPhotos` instead of a `String`, so we'll need to update its definition to match:

```
type Msg
    = SelectByUrl String
    | GotSelectedIndex Int
    | SurpriseMe
    | SetSize ThumbnailSize
    | GotPhotos (Result Http.Error (List Photo))
```

This lets us simplify the `GotPhotos (Ok ...)` branch of update's case-expression quite a bit! Having direct access to photos means we no longer need to build that value up by using a let-expression. We can instead use our new friend *pattern matching* like so:

```
GotPhotos (Ok photos) ->
    case photos of
```

```
first :: rest ->
    ( { model | status = Loaded photos first.url }
    , Cmd.none
    )

[] ->
    ( { model | status = Errored "0 photos found" }, Cmd.none )
```

NOTE The `Http.post` and `Http.jsonBody` functions let you easily send JSON data to servers. In chapter 6, you'll see how the `Json.Encode` module provides a nice way to assemble JSON values—it's much simpler than `Json.Decode`.

RENDERING THE METADATA

Now all that remains is to have our view render the new caption and download size metadata. We can do this by adding one line to `viewThumbnail`:

```
viewThumbnail selectedUrl thumb =
    img
        [ src (urlPrefix ++ thumb.url)
        , title (thumb.title ++ " [" ++ String.fromInt thumb.size ++ " KB]")
        , classList [ ( "selected", selectedUrl == Just thumb.url ) ]
        , onClick (SelectByUrl thumb.url)
        ]
        []
```

Great! At this point, everything should compile, and we can open index.html to see the result, shown in figure 4.6.

Now we're reading our list of photos from the server rather than hardcoding them, and we've given ourselves a nice foundation on which to build an even richer application!

Figure 4.6 The final application

Summary

You learned quite a few things in the course of making Photo Groove talk to servers:

- A `Decoder` can validate and translate JSON into an Elm value.
- The `Json.Decode` module provides primitive decoders like `float`, `int`, and `string`.
- The `Json.Decode.list` function turns a `Decoder Bool` into a `Decoder (List Bool)`.
- Pattern matching lets us trade nested case-expressions for longer branch conditions.
- The `<|` operator can replace parentheses. `foo <| bar 5` is the same as `foo (bar 5)`.
- The `Json.Decode.Pipeline` module offers functions to decode objects in pipeline style.
- A `Result` is either `Ok okValue` in case of success, or `Err errValue` in case of failure.
- `String.split` splits a string around a given separator, resulting in a list of strings.
- `Http.get` takes a URL `String` and an `Expect`, and returns a `Cmd` that sends a request.
- `Http.expectString` requests a plain `String` from the server at the given URL.
- `Http.expectJson` works like `expectString`, except it runs a `Decoder` on the result.
- The `init` field passed to `Browser.element` lets us specify a `Cmd` to run on startup.

You also saw how the pipeline operator (`|>`) lets us write expressions by starting with a value and then running a series of transformations on it. Table 4.6 shows an example of this.

Table 4.6   The same expression with and without pipelines

Pipeline style	Without pipelines

`model.photos`
`    |> Array.fromList`
`    |> Array.get index`
	`Array.get index`
	`    (Array.fromList`
	`        model.photos)`

Now that we've gotten Photo Groove talking to a server, we'll get it talking to Java-Script. This will let us tap into the enormous ecosystem of JavaScript libraries out there. Let's see what that can get us!

Listing 4.7 The complete PhotoGroove.elm

```elm
module PhotoGroove exposing (main)

import Browser
import Html exposing (..)
import Html.Attributes exposing (class, classList, id, name, src, title, type_)
import Html.Events exposing (onClick)
import Http
import Json.Decode exposing (Decoder, bool, int, list, string, succeed)
import Json.Decode.Pipeline exposing (optional, required)
import Random


urlPrefix : String
urlPrefix =
    "http://elm-in-action.com/"


type Msg
    = ClickedPhoto String
    | ClickedSize ThumbnailSize
    | ClickedSurpriseMe
    | GotRandomPhoto Photo
    | GotPhotos (Result Http.Error (List Photo))


view : Model -> Html Msg
view model =
    div [ class "content" ] <|          ⟵  foo (bar baz) == foo <| bar baz
        case model.status of
            Loaded photos selectedUrl ->
                viewLoaded photos selectedUrl model.chosenSize

            Loading ->
                []

            Errored errorMessage ->
                [ text ("Error: " ++ errorMessage) ]


viewLoaded : List Photo -> String -> ThumbnailSize -> List (Html Msg)
viewLoaded photos selectedUrl chosenSize =
    [ h1 [] [ text "Photo Groove" ]
    , button
        [ onClick ClickedSurpriseMe ]
        [ text "Surprise Me!" ]
    , h3 [] [ text "Thumbnail Size:" ]
    , div [ id "choose-size" ]
        (List.map viewSizeChooser [ Small, Medium, Large ])
```

```
        , div [ id "thumbnails", class (sizeToString chosenSize) ]
            (List.map (viewThumbnail selectedUrl) photos)
        , img
            [ class "large"
            , src (urlPrefix ++ "large/" ++ selectedUrl)
            ]
            []
        ]


viewThumbnail : String -> Photo -> Html Msg
viewThumbnail selectedUrl thumb =
    img
        [ src (urlPrefix ++ thumb.url)
        , title (thumb.title ++ " [" ++ String.fromInt thumb.size ++ " KB]")
        , classList [ ( "selected", selectedUrl == thumb.url ) ]
        , onClick (ClickedPhoto thumb.url)
        ]
        []


viewSizeChooser : ThumbnailSize -> Html Msg
viewSizeChooser size =
    label []
        [ input [ type_ "radio", name "size", onClick (ClickedSize size) ] []
        , text (sizeToString size)
        ]


sizeToString : ThumbnailSize -> String
sizeToString size =
    case size of
        Small ->
            "small"

        Medium ->
            "med"

        Large ->
            "large"


type ThumbnailSize
    = Small
    | Medium
    | Large


type alias Photo =
    { url : String
    , size : Int
    , title : String
    }
```

```
photoDecoder : Decoder Photo
photoDecoder =
    succeed Photo
        |> required "url" string
        |> required "size" int
        |> optional "title" string "(untitled)
```

Json.Decode.succeed Photo means we'll call the Photo function to create a Photo record when this pipeline completes.

The first argument to the Photo function will be the "url" string field on the JSON object.

The second argument will be the "size" int field.

The third argument will be the "title" string field if the JSON object has one; otherwise, "(untitled)".

```
type Status
    = Loading
    | Loaded (List Photo) String
    | Errored String


type alias Model =
    { status : Status
    , chosenSize : ThumbnailSize
    }


initialModel : Model
initialModel =
    { status = Loading
    , chosenSize = Medium
    }


update : Msg -> Model -> ( Model, Cmd Msg )
update msg model =
    case msg of
        GotRandomPhoto photo ->
            ( { model | status = selectUrl photo.url model.status }, Cmd.none )

        ClickedPhoto url ->
            ( { model | status = selectUrl url model.status }, Cmd.none )

        ClickedSize size ->
            ( { model | chosenSize = size }, Cmd.none )

        ClickedSurpriseMe ->
            case model.status of
                Loaded (firstPhoto :: otherPhotos) _ ->
                    Random.uniform firstPhoto otherPhotos
                        |> Random.generate GotRandomPhoto
                        |> Tuple.pair model

                Loaded [] _ ->
                    ( model, Cmd.none )

                Loading ->
                    ( model, Cmd.none )

                Errored errorMessage ->
                    ( model, Cmd.none )
```

Matches only nonempty lists. firstPhoto is a Photo, and otherPhotos is a List Photo.

foo (bar baz) == bar baz |> foo.

We would get a Missing Patterns error without this branch. The list might be empty!

```
        GotPhotos (Ok photos) ->
            case photos of
                first :: rest ->
                    ( { model | status = Loaded photos first.url }
                    , Cmd.none
                    )

                [] ->
                    ( { model | status = Errored "0 photos found" }, Cmd.none )

        GotPhotos (Err httpError) ->
            ( { model | status = Errored "Server error!" }, Cmd.none )
```

> **This Msg is a GotPhotos variant, and the Result it holds is an Ok variant.**

```
selectUrl : String -> Status -> Status
selectUrl url status =
    case status of
        Loaded photos _ ->
            Loaded photos url

        Loading ->
            status

        Errored errorMessage ->
            status


initialCmd : Cmd Msg
initialCmd =
    Http.get
        { url = "http://elm-in-action.com/photos/list.json"
        , expect = Http.expectJson GotPhotos (list photoDecoder)
        }
```

> **Json.Decode.list turns photoDecoder : Decoder Photo into a Decoder (List Photo).**

```
main : Program () Model Msg
main =
    Browser.element
        { init = \flags -> ( initialModel, initialCmd )
        , view = view
        , update = update
        , subscriptions = \_ -> Sub.none
        }
```

Talking to JavaScript

5

This chapter covers

- Rendering custom elements
- Sending data to JavaScript
- Receiving data from JavaScript
- Initializing our Elm application by using data from JavaScript

Now we've gotten Photo Groove loading photos from a server. It's looking better and better! However, our manager has a concern: "We have the photos, and they certainly look sharp. But where is the *groove*? This is Photo Groove, not Photo Browse! You know what we need? *Filters*. You know, the kind that make normal photos look all wacky and messed up? Those!"

Sounds groovy.

We collaborate with our team's visual designer to create a mockup of the filtering feature. The final design calls for a display to report on the current activity of the filtering process, and sliders to control the filters' settings. And not just any sliders! Our designer wants these to match the look and feel of some sliders we're using on a different product.

As luck would have it, we won't have to code either the filter effects or the sliders from scratch. They're both available as open source libraries, but there's a catch: these libraries are written in JavaScript, not Elm.

Fortunately, Elm applications are not limited to using only Elm libraries! In this chapter, we'll expand Photo Groove to include a filtering feature. We'll add sliders that let users apply filters in varying degrees to the large photo. We'll create an activity display that shows information from the JavaScript libraries. Along the way, you'll learn two ways to incorporate JavaScript code into an Elm application: *custom elements* and *ports*. Here we go!

5.1   *Using custom elements*

We'll start with the sliders. We want to create three sliders in total: Hue, Ripple, and Noise. Adjusting each value will transform how the large photo appears to the end user. Figure 5.1 shows how the sliders fit into what we'll be building over the course of this chapter.

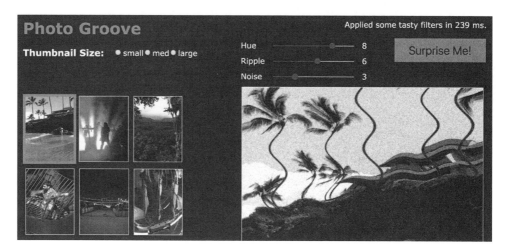

Figure 5.1   Adding sliders that control filtering for the large photo

Each slider controls an integer value that the filtering library will use for the magnitude of the filter effect. Sliding all three to 0 would disable filtering—leaving the photos unaltered, as they look now—whereas setting all three to the maximum value of 11 would apply each filter at full power.

Implementing the sliders by using custom elements will involve three steps:

1   Running some JavaScript code before our Elm code executes, to register custom behavior for all `<range-slider>` elements on the page
2   Writing Elm code to render these `<range-slider>` elements, using plain `Html` values
3   Writing custom event handlers to update our model based on the sliders' states

Along the way, you'll learn a new use for the JSON decoders we saw in chapter 4, and compare two alternative ways of integrating the sliders into our data model.

5.1.1 *Importing custom elements*

To use the third-party JavaScript slider in Elm, we'll first wrap it in a custom element. The slider we'll be importing is written in plain JavaScript with no dependencies, but this Custom Elements Wrapper technique also works with React.js components, jQuery widgets, and just about everything in between!

CUSTOM ELEMENTS

Custom elements arc a part of the Web Components specification. Here's how they work:

- We write some JavaScript to define a new DOM element type. In this case, the new element will be called a `<range-slider>`. (Custom elements must have a dash in their names.)
- We run that JavaScript code when our page loads, to register this custom element with the browser.
- From now on, whenever any code—in JavaScript or in Elm—creates a DOM element whose tag name is `"range-slider"`, that element will behave according to this custom logic.

> **WARNING** Custom elements are implemented in JavaScript, so they may throw runtime exceptions!

REGISTERING CUSTOM ELEMENTS

We'll start by making a custom element that renders a plain old text `<input>` to the page. Then we'll go back and upgrade it to be a proper slider.

Let's start by adding this code right above `</head>` in index.html

---

Listing 5.1 Registering the custom element

```
<script>
    class RangeSlider extends HTMLElement {
        connectedCallback() {
            var input = document.createElement("input");
            this.appendChild(input);
        }
    }

    window.customElements.define("range-slider", RangeSlider);
</script>
</head>
```

You could extract this `<script>` into a slider.js file if you like.

This RangeSlider will be a new Element type in the DOM.

This is called when the slider is about to be added to the DOM.

Creates a new `<input>` element

Adds the `<input>` to the DOM inside the `<range-slider>`

Registers the `<range-slider>` in the browser

Here we're using the `class` keyword that was added to JavaScript in ECMAScript 2015. If you're unfamiliar with `class`, not to worry; in this chapter, all you need to know about it is that `connectedCallback` declares a new method on the class, and we'll be working inside that method declaration to wire up our `RangeSlider`.

> **TIP** Certain older browsers don't support `class`, or for that matter custom elements. Fortunately, the custom elements polyfill offers a solution if you need to support the browsers in question. Visit https://github.com/web components/custom-elements to learn more about it.

Finally, we come to this line:

```
window.customElements.define("range-slider", RangeSlider);
```

This registers the `<range-slider>` on the page. From now on, whenever a DOM element with the tag name `"range-slider"` appears on this page, it will behave according to the implementation we've imported here.

ADDING A <RANGE-SLIDER> TO THE PAGE

Back at the beginning of chapter 2, we saw the `node` function from the `Html` module. It takes three arguments:

- Tag name
- List of attributes
- List of children

Here are two ways to create the same button, one using `node` and the other using `button`:

```
node "button" [ class "large" ] [ text "Send" ]
      button  [ class "large" ] [ text "Send" ]
```

Functions that create elements like `button`, `label`, and `input` have tiny implementations—they do nothing more than call `node`. For example, `label` and `input` can be implemented like so:

```
label attributes children =
    node "label" attributes children

input attributes children =
    node "input" attributes children
```

> **TIP** Because of partial application, we could also have written these as `label = node "label"` and `input = node "input"`. However, it's considered good practice to name all your arguments when defining a named function at the top level like this.

Now that the `<range-slider>` custom element has been registered on the page with our call to `window.customElements.define("range-slider", RangeSlider)`, the only Elm code necessary to use it is to call `node  "range-slider"`. Let's add a function that does this, at the end of PhotoGroove.elm:

```
rangeSlider attributes children =
    node "range-slider" attributes children
```

This `rangeSlider` function will work the same way as functions like `button`, `div`, and so on. It also has the same type as they do:

```
rangeSlider : List (Attribute msg) -> List (Html msg) -> Html msg
```

Add this type annotation right above that `rangeSlider` implementation.

VIEWING THE SLIDERS

Next, let's invoke `rangeSlider` to render the sliders. They won't actually work like sliders yet, but we'll make them work properly afterward. For now, add the following code beneath the `view` function.

Listing 5.2 `viewFilter`

```
viewFilter : String -> Int -> Html Msg
viewFilter name magnitude =
    div [ class "filter-slider" ]
        [ label [] [ text name ]        ← Displays the filter's name
        , rangeSlider                    ← <range-slider> that goes from 0 to 11
            [ max "11"
            , Html.Attributes.property "val" (Json.Encode.int magnitude)  ← Sets the slider's "val" to the current magnitude
            ]
            []
        , label [] [ text (String.fromInt magnitude) ]   ← Displays the current magnitude
        ]
```

That `Json.Encode` module is a new one! Let's add it right above `import Random`, like so:

```
import Json.Encode
import Random
```

HTML.ATTRIBUTES.PROPERTY

Here we're using `Json.Encode.int` not to encode JSON, as the name might suggest, but rather to encode a JavaScript `Value` for the `Html.Attributes.property` function:

```
Html.Attributes.property "val" (Json.Encode.int magnitude)
```

This will set a JavaScript *property* on this `<range-slider>` node, so that our custom element can read it later. The property will be named `val`, and it will be set to our `magnitude` value.

The `Json.Encode.int` function specifies what the property's type will be on the JavaScript side. If we had used `(Json.Encode.string (String.fromInt magnitude))` instead, the property would have been set to a JavaScript string instead of a number.

AMBIGUOUS NAME

If we try to build this code, we'll get a compile error. `max` is ambiguous. It's being exposed by both of these modules:

- `Basics`
- `Html.Attributes`

We're seeing this error because Elm has a built-in math function called `max`. It's in the `Basics` module, and every Elm file has an implicit `import Basics exposing (..)` so that we can use common functions like `negate`, `not`, and `max` without having to qualify them as `Basics.negate`, `Basics.not`, or `Basics.max`.

RESOLVING AMBIGUOUS NAMES

The compiler is reporting an ambiguity in our code: when we wrote `max`, we might have meant either `Basics.max` or `Html.Attributes.max`, since both `max` functions are exposed in this file. Let's clarify which we meant by fully qualifying `max`:

```
Html.Attributes.max "11"
```

This resolves the compiler error, but `Html.Attributes.max` is pretty verbose. We can shorten it by giving `Html.Attributes` an alias of `Attr`, using the `as` keyword:

```
import Html.Attributes as Attr exposing (class, classList, id, name, src,
    title, type_)
```

While we're at it, let's give `Json.Encode` the same treatment:

```
import Json.Encode as Encode
```

Now anywhere we would write `Html.Attributes.foo`, we can write `Attr.foo` instead. Similarly, anywhere we would write `Json.Encode.int`, we can now write `Encode.int` instead.

Let's refactor our `rangeSlider` to look like this:

```
, rangeSlider
    [ Attr.max "11"
    , Attr.property "val" (Encode.int magnitude)
    ]
```

Splendid! This should make everything compile neatly.

RENDERING THREE SLIDERS

Now we can call `viewFilter` in our `viewLoaded` function to get a few sliders rendering. Let's do that right below the code for the Surprise Me! button:

```
viewLoaded photos selectedUrl chosenSize =
    [ h1 [] [ text "Photo Groove" ]
    , button
        [ onClick ClickedSurpriseMe ]
        [ text "Surprise Me!" ]
    , div [ class "filters" ]
        [ viewFilter "Hue" 0
        , viewFilter "Ripple" 0
        , viewFilter "Noise" 0
        ]
```

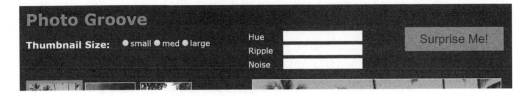

Figure 5.2 **Adding** `rangeSliders` **for Hue, Ripple, and Noise**

Figure 5.2 shows how this looks on the page.

THE CUSTOM ELEMENT RENDERING PROCESS

Notice that although we rendered three `<range-slider>` elements to the DOM, the browser displays an `<input>` for each of them. Let's recap why that is:

1. We defined `class RangeSlider extends HTMLElement` in JavaScript.
2. We gave it a `connectedCallback` method that creates a new `<input>` node and calls `this.appendChild` on it. This method will be called whenever a `<range-slider>` is added to the DOM.
3. We called `window.customElements.define("range-slider", RangeSlider)`, which told the browser to use our `RangeSlider` class as the implementation for all `<range-slider>` nodes on the page.
4. In Elm we called `node "rangeSlider"` to add `<range-slider>` nodes to the page.
5. When the browser added those `<range-slider>` elements to the DOM, it ran their `connectedCallback` methods from the `RangeSlider` class, which appended the `<input>` nodes we requested as their children.

Now we can replace that `createElement("input")` inside `connectedCallback` with some code to instantiate our third-party custom slider instead of an `<input>`, and we'll be all set!

REPLACING <INPUT> WITH THE CUSTOM SLIDER

To use the third-party slider, we'll first need to import the code for it. Let's import its stylesheet and JavaScript code inside the `<head>` of our index.html file, right below our existing `<link rel="stylesheet">` declaration:

```
<link rel="stylesheet" href="http://elm-in-action.com/styles.css">
<link rel="stylesheet" href="http://elm-in-action.com/range-slider.css">
<script src="http://elm-in-action.com/range-slider.js"></script>
```

These tags load both the JavaScript code and CSS styles necessary to render a range slider element. The particular slider library we will be using is the MIT-licensed *JS Range (JSR)*, by Mateusz Koteja. You can find the source code at github.com/mm-jsr/jsr.

The way JS Range creates a slider is by creating a new JSR object and passing it an `<input>` node. We'll use this on the `input` node we conveniently already created in our `connectedCallback` method.

Listing 5.3   Using JSR to turn the `<input>` into a slider

```
connectedCallback() {
    var input = document.createElement("input");
    this.appendChild(input);

    var jsr = new JSR(input, {        ⟵  Creates a new JSR using
        max: this.max,                    the <input> we created
        values: [this.val],
        sliders: 1,
        grid: false
    });
}
```

Uses the Attr.max value we set in Elm → (points to `max: this.max,`)

Uses the Attr.property "val" we set in Elm → (points to `values: [this.val],`)

Tweaks some other JSR knobs—these aren't important (points to `sliders: 1,` / `grid: false`)

Here we've passed JSR the `<input>` it requires as its first argument, as well as a configuration object. We've configured its `max` to be `this.max`, and its `values` to be `this.val`. These correspond to the `Attr.max` and `Attr.property` `"val"` calls we made in Elm:

```
rangeSlider
    [ Attr.max "11"
    , Attr.property "val" (Encode.int magnitude)
    ]
```

TIP Naming this property `val` instead of `value` is no accident. Elm applies special handling to the `value` property, so it's best not to choose that particular name for custom properties.

This is our first example of sending a value from Elm to JavaScript. The `Attr.max` *property* that we set on the Elm side appeared as `this.max` on the JavaScript side, within the custom element's `connectedCallback` method.

NOTE The browser treats DOM element *attributes* and *properties* differently. Both properties and attributes have the type `Attribute` in Elm—so that the node function can accept a `List` of any combination of them—which means the only way to tell them apart is to read their documentation or source code. This distinction is relevant in custom elements because, although DOM element *properties* like `Attr.max` and `Attr.property` are accessible using `this` within any custom element method, DOM element *attributes* are not.

Let's open up our browser to see our custom elements in all their glory! Figure 5.3 shows how the page should look.

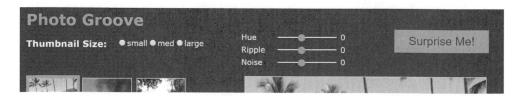

Figure 5.3   Using JSR to instantiate the sliders

> **TIP** Custom elements can wrap pretty much any JavaScript library that uses the DOM. For example, you could replace `this.appendChild(input)` with `ReactDOM.render(this)` inside `connectedCallback`.

Those sliders look slick, but they aren't completely operational yet. We want the numbers next to the sliders to change as the user slides their values around. Let's make that happen!

5.1.2 Handling custom events

If we take a quick glance at JS Range's documentation, we can see that the slider emits a custom event, called `"update"`, from its `range` object as the user slides. This event reports the slider's current value, so we'd like to listen for it and update our `Model` with that value.

Our Elm code can't listen to events emitted by the JSR `range` object itself, but it can listen to events from the `<range slider>` custom element. We can add a quick bit of JavaScript code to listen for the `range` object's `update` event and broadcast its value from the `<range-slider>` so we can hear it over in Elm Land. Let's add this to the end of our `connectedCallback()` method.

Listing 5.4 Broadcasting a `ChangeEvent`

```
connectedCallback() {
    ...

    var rangeSliderNode = this;          // Stores a reference to "this" for later

    jsr.addEventListener("update", function(elem, value) {   // Listens for "update" events from the JSR object
        var event = new CustomEvent("slide", {               // Creates a new "slide" event
            detail: {userSlidTo: value}                      // Stores the value inside that event
        });

        rangeSliderNode.dispatchEvent(event);                // Dispatches the event from the <range-slider>
    });
}
```

Now whenever the user drags the slider around, our `<range-slider>` element will emit a `"slide"` event containing the new value they've chosen.

> **TIP** Internet Explorer has a slightly different API for creating `CustomEvent` values. That API has been deprecated, and modern browsers may drop support for it, but if you need to support IE, here's what to do: `var event = document.createEvent("CustomEvent"); event.initCustomEvent ("slide", true, true, {detail: userSlidTo: value}})`.

LISTENING FOR CUSTOM EVENTS

Now that we're dispatching this `"slide"` event, how might we respond to it on the Elm side? `Html.Events` has a variety of built-in event handler functions such as onClick, but there's no onSlide. The Html.Attributes module has no idea it exists. So how can we specify a handler for it?

HTML.EVENTS.ON

The Html.Events.on function lets us create a custom event handler, just as the Html.node function lets us create a custom element and the Html.Attributes .property function lets us create a custom property. The on function has this type:

```
on : String -> Decoder msg -> Attribute msg
```

The String is the name of the event, which in this case is "slide". The Decoder argument is a Json.Decode.Decoder, the same type of decoder we built in chapter 4 for our HTTP responses. Here we won't be using the Decoder on a JSON string coming back from a server, but rather on a JavaScript event object.

DECODING THE SLIDE EVENT

The CustomEvent object JavaScript will dispatch for "slide" is shaped something like this:

```
{detail: {userSlidTo: 7}}
```

The detail field is what CustomEvent objects use to hold their custom information, which in our case holds a single field we decided to name userSlidTo in listing 5.4. We can use the Json.Decode.field and Json.Decode.int functions to write a decoder for this like so:

```
field "detail" (field "userSlidTo" int)
```

Table 5.1 compares this decoder to the example email decoder we wrote in chapter 4.

Table 5.1   Decoding objects with field decoders

Decoder	JSON	Result
field "email" string	5	Err "Expected object, got 5"
	{"email": 5}	Err "Expected string for 'email', got 5"
	{"email": "cate@nolf.com"}	Ok "cate@nolf.com"

Decoder	JavaScript	Result
field "detail" (field "userSlidTo" int)	9	Err "Expected object, got 9"
	{"detail": 9}	Err "Expected object for detail, got 9"
	{"detail": {"userSlidTo": 9}}	Ok 9

JSON.DECODE.AT

There's a convenience function in `Json.Decode` for the case where we want to call `field` on another `field` like this: `Json.Decode.at`. It takes a list of field strings and traverses them in order. These two decoders do the same thing:

```
field "detail" (field "userSlidTo" int)

at [ "detail", "userSlidTo" ] int
```

DECODING A MSG

This `Decoder Int` will decode an integer from a JavaScript object such as `{detail: {userSlidTo: 7 }}`. But is that what we want? Let's look at the type of on again:

```
on : String -> Decoder msg -> Attribute msg
```

Notice that it wants a `Decoder msg` and then returns an `Attribute msg`. That tells us we want it to decode not an integer, but a message. Ah! We have a message type named `Msg`. So how do we convert between the `Decoder Int` that we have and the `Decoder Msg` that on expects?

USING JSON.DECODE.MAP

The `Json.Decode.map` function is just what the doctor ordered! It converts between decoded values, as shown in table 5.2.

Table 5.2 `Json.Decode.map`

Expression	Description
`Json.Decode.map negate float`	Decodes a float, then negates it.
`Json.Decode.map (\num -> num * 2) int`	Decodes an integer, then doubles it.
`Json.Decode.map (\_ -> "[[redacted]]") string`	Decodes a string, then replaces it with "[[redacted]]" no matter what it was originally. Note that this will still fail if it attempts to decode a nonstring value.

Because `Json.Decode.map` takes a function that converts one decoded value to another, we can use it to convert our decoded `Int` into a `Msg`.

UPDATING IMPORTS

We'll need to expose the on and at functions in our imports in order to reference them:

```
import Html.Events exposing (on, onClick)
import Json.Decode exposing (Decoder, at, string, int, list, succeed)
```

Then we'll be ready to add this `onSlide` function to the end of PhotoGroove.elm.

Listing 5.5 `onSlide`

```
onSlide : (Int -> msg) -> Attribute msg
onSlide toMsg =
    let
        detailUserSlidTo : Decoder Int
        detailUserSlidTo =
            at [ "detail", "userSlidTo" ] int

        msgDecoder : Decoder msg
        msgDecoder =
            Json.Decode.map toMsg detailUserSlidTo
    in
    on "slide" msgDecoder
```

Decodes the integer located at event.detail.userSlidTo

Converts that integer to a message using toMsg

Creates a custom event handler using that decoder

Notice how `onSlide` takes a `toMsg` function? This is because we need it to be flexible. We plan to have multiple sliders on the page, and we'll want each of them to have a unique `Msg` variant so that we can tell their messages apart. The `toMsg` argument lets us pass in the appropriate variant on a case-by-case basis, which will come in handy later.

REFACTORING TO USE PIPELINES

Notice how we assemble this value in three steps (`detailUserSlidTo`, `msgDecoder`, and `on`), and each step's final argument is the previous step's return value? That means we can rewrite this to use the pipeline style you learned in chapter 4! Let's do that refactor:

```
onSlide : (Int -> msg) -> Attribute msg
onSlide toMsg =
    at [ "detail", "userSlidTo" ] int
        |> Json.Decode.map toMsg
        |> on "slide"
```

Try walking through each step in the pipeline and finding the equivalent code in listing 5.5. All the same logic is still there, just reorganized.

ADDING EVENT HANDLING TO VIEWFILTER

Now that we have `onSlide`, we can use it in our `viewFilter` function. Remember how we made `onSlide` accept an `Int -> msg` function, so that we could pass it a different `Msg` variant on a case-by-case basis? We'll want `viewFilter` to have that same flexibility. The only difference will be that because `viewFilter` returns an `Html Msg`, we won't be using a type variable like `msg`; instead, `viewFilter` will accept an `Int -> Msg` function.

Listing 5.6 Using `onImmediateValueChange` in `viewFilter`

```
viewFilter : (Int -> Msg) -> String -> Int -> Html Msg
viewFilter toMsg name magnitude =
    div [ class "filter-slider" ]
```

```
    [ label [] [ text name ]
    , rangeSlider
        [ Attr.max "11"
        , Attr.property "val" (Encode.int magnitude)
        , onSlide toMsg
        ]
        []                                          ◁
    , label [] [ text (String.fromInt magnitude) ]
    ]
```

> **Calling onSlide just
> as we did onClick**

With this shiny new `viewFilter` implementation completed, our display logic is ready to be connected to our model and `update`. Once we've revised those to work with `viewFilter`, our shiny new custom elements will be fully integrated into our application!

5.1.3 Responding to slider changes

We have three filters, each of which has a name and a magnitude. How should we track their current values in our model? Let's walk through two approaches, comparing the pros and cons of each, and then at the end decide which to use.

The first approach would be to add three fields to the model: one for Hue, one for Ripple, and one for Noise. The alternative would prioritize flexibility, and store the filters as a list of { `name : String, amount : Int` } records. Table 5.3 shows these approaches side by side.

Table 5.3 Storing filter data as three `Ints` versus one list of records

Three-integers approach	One-list-of-records approach

``
type alias Model =
    { status : Status
    , chosenSize : ThumbnailSize
    , hue : Int
    , ripple : Int
    , noise : Int
    }
``
	``
	type alias Model =
	    { status : Status
	    , chosenSize : ThumbnailSize
	    , filters : List { name : String,
	      amount : Int }
	    }
	``

``
initialModel : Model
initialModel =
    { status = Loading
    , chosenSize = Medium
    , hue = 5
    , ripple = 5
    , noise = 5
    }
``
	``
	initialModel : Model
	initialModel =
	    { status = Loading
	    , chosenSize = Medium
	    , filters =
	        [{ name = "Hue", amount = 5 }
	        , { name = "Ripple", amount = 5 }
	        , { name = "Noise", amount = 5 }
	        ]
	    }
	``

Each model design has its own strengths and weaknesses, which become clearer when we write code that references this part of the model.

Let's consider how our `update` implementations might compare. In either approach, we'd expand our `Msg` type's variants and then add at least one branch to our `update` function's case-expression. Table 5.4 compares how these revisions would look for each approach.

Table 5.4   Updating the model

Three-integers approach	One-list-of-records approach

<pre>type Msg
    = ClickedPhoto String
    …
    | SlidHue Int
    | SlidRipple Int
    | SlidNoise Int
 	
case msg of
    …
    SlidHue hue ->
        ({ model | hue = hue }
        , Cmd.none
)
 	
    SlidRipple ripple ->
        ({ model | ripple = ripple }
        , Cmd.none
)
 	
    SlidNoise noise ->
        ({ model | noise = noise }
        , Cmd.none
)</pre>
	<pre>type Msg
	    = ClickedPhoto String
	    …
	    | SlidFilter String Int
	
	case msg of
	    …
	    SlidFilter name amount ->
	        let
	            transform filter =
	                if filter.name == name then
	                    { name = name
	                    , amount = amount
	                    }
	                else
	                    filter
	
	            filters =
	                model.filters
	                    |> List.map transform
	        in
	        ({ model | filters = filters }
	        , Cmd.none
	        )</pre>

The list-of-records approach is more flexible. If we decided to add a fourth filter, such as Blur, we could add it to `initialModel`, and boom! It would appear on the page instantly. With the three-integers approach, adding a fourth integer would require not only expanding `initialModel`, but also adding a field to our type alias for `Model`, a variant for our `Msg`, and a branch for `update`'s case-expression. That sure sounds like more work!

Finally, let's compare how rendering would look in table 5.5.

Table 5.5   Viewing filter data from three fields versus one

Three-integers approach	List-of-records approach (assuming `viewFilter` tweaked)

<pre>, div [class "filters"]
    [viewFilter SlidHue "Hue" model.hue
    , viewFilter SlidRipple "Ripple" model.ripple
    , viewFilter SlidNoise "Noise" model.noise
    ]</pre>
	<pre>, div [class "filters"]
	    (List.map viewFilter
	        model.filters)</pre>

In either case, we'd need to change `viewLoaded`'s arguments—either giving it access to `Model` or to a `{ name : String, amount : Int }` record. But after doing that, we could save ourselves a few lines of code with the list-of-records approach, using `List.map` as shown in table 5.5. Once again, a list of records comes out ahead!

CHOOSING AN APPROACH

So far, we've compared these approaches by conciseness, as well as by the amount of effort it would take to add more filters later. However, our analysis is overlooking a crucial consideration, one that tends to make a much bigger difference in Elm than in JavaScript: *which approach rules out more bugs?*

As we've seen, Elm's compiler gives us certain guarantees that can rule out entire categories of bugs. Some code can better leverage these guarantees than others. We can "help the compiler help us" by taking the compiler into consideration when making decisions like these. What potential future headaches would each approach let the compiler rule out?

CONSIDERING POTENTIAL BUGS

Suppose we go with the list-of-records approach, and one of our coworkers makes an innocuous typo—writing `"Rippl"` instead of `"Ripple"`—such that a `SlidFilter "Rippl" 5` message comes through our `update` function. That code will compile, but it won't work properly because our `filter.name == "Rippl"` condition will never pass. We'll have to hope our coworker catches this bug in testing.

What if our coworker makes the same typo in the three-integers approach? Attempting to create a `SlidRippl 5` message will be a compiler error, because we named our `Msg` variant `SlidRipple`, not `SlidRippl`; see table 5.6.

Table 5.6 Making a mistake

	Three-integers approach	**List-of-records approach**
Message	`SlidRippl 5`	`SlidFilter "Rippl" 5`
Outcome	Elm's compiler tells us we have a naming error.	This compiles, but now we have a bug.

CONSIDERING FUTURE CHANGES

What about making changes? Suppose in the future we need to rename `"Ripple"` to `"Swirl"`.

In the three-integers approach, we can rename our `Msg` variant from `SlidRipple` to `SlidSwirl`, and our `Model` field from `ripple` to `swirl`—and then watch Elm's compiler tell us exactly what other parts of our code base need changing as a result. If we miss anything, we'll get a helpful type mismatch error telling us every spot we overlooked.

With the list-of-records approach, we have to hope none of our coworkers ever wrote code using the hardcoded magic string `"Ripple"` instead of a constant. If they did, and something breaks, the only way we'll find out before the bug reaches production is if someone also wrote a test that happens to fail when we change "Ripple" to "Swirl".

CHOOSING RELIABILITY

By using individual fields instead of a list of records, we can rule out the entire category of bugs related to invalid filter names.

Increasing conciseness and saving potential future effort are nice, but preventing bugs in a growing code base tends to be more valuable over time. Verbosity has a predictable impact on a project, whereas the impact of bugs can range from "quick fix" to "apocalyptic progress torpedo." Ruling those out is more valuable than a bit of conciseness!

We'll go with the approach that prevents more bugs. Take a moment to look back at tables 5.3, 5.4, and 5.5, and implement the changes in the first column. Then let's revise our `viewLoaded` function to accept `Model` as its final argument instead of `ChosenSize`, and to use `Model`'s new fields:

```
viewLoaded : List Photo -> String -> Model -> List (Html Msg)
viewLoaded photos selectedUrl model =
…
, div [ class "filters" ]
    [ viewFilter SlidHue "Hue" model.hue
    , viewFilter SlidRipple "Ripple" model.ripple
    , viewFilter SlidNoise "Noise" model.noise
    ]
…
, div [ id "thumbnails", class (sizeToString model.chosenSize) ]
```

Last, but not least, we'll need to change `view` to pass `model` instead of `model.chosenSize` as the final argument to `viewLoaded`:

```
Loaded photos selectedUrl ->
    viewLoaded photos selectedUrl model
```

> **TIP**   It's generally a good idea to keep our types as narrow as possible, so we'd like to avoid passing `viewLoaded` the entire `Model` if we can. However, that's not a refactor we need to do right now.

When the dust settles, you should be able to recompile with `elm make --output=app.js PhotoGroove.elm` and see the number labels change when the user slides, as shown in figure 5.4.

Figure 5.4   Sliding now changes the numbers next to the sliders.

Now that we have our sliders set up, we can move on to introducing the filters themselves!

5.2 Sending data to JavaScript

Now our model has all the data it needs to calibrate the filters. We'll use some Java-Script once again to apply the filters, although this time not custom elements. Instead, we'll write code that passes configuration options and a <canvas> element to a Java-Script function, which will then proceed to draw groovy pictures on it.

First we'll get a basic proof-of-concept working, to confirm that we're successfully communicating across languages, and then we'll smooth out the implementation details until we're satisfied with how things are working.

5.2.1 Creating a command by using a port

You may recall from chapter 4 that an *effect* is an operation that modifies external state. You may also recall that if a function modifies external state when it runs, that function has a *side effect*. Elm functions are not permitted to have side effects, but JavaScript functions are.

TALKING TO JAVASCRIPT IS LIKE TALKING TO SERVERS

Because calling any JavaScript function may result in a side effect, Elm functions cannot call JavaScript functions anytime they please; this would destroy the guarantee that Elm functions have no side effects.

Instead, Elm talks to JavaScript the same way it talks to servers: by sending data out through a command, and receiving data in through a message. Figure 5.5 illustrates this.

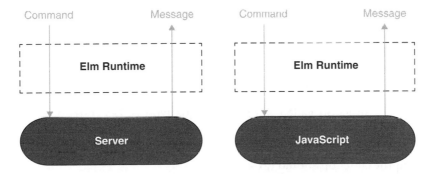

Figure 5.5 Using commands and messages to talk to both servers and JavaScript

This means that talking to JavaScript will have some characteristics in common with what we saw when talking to servers in chapter 4:

- Data can be sent only by using a command.
- Data can be received only by update, and that data must be wrapped in a message.
- We can translate and validate this incoming data by using decoders.

NOTE   In JavaScript, some effects are performed synchronously, with program execution halting until the effect completes. In contrast, an Elm `Cmd` always represents an *asynchronous* effect. This means that when we send data to JavaScript, it's always possible that other JavaScript code might run before data gets sent back to Elm.

CREATING A COMMAND

Let's create a `Cmd` to send some data to JavaScript. First we'll define a `type alias` for the data we're going to send, right above our `type alias` for `Photo`:

```
type alias FilterOptions =
    { url : String
    , filters : List { name : String, amount : Int }
    }
```

This represents all the information our JavaScript library will need in order to apply the filters: the URL of the photo in question, plus the list of filters and their amounts.

PORT MODULES

In chapter 4, we created a `Cmd` using the `Http.send` function, but here we'll instead use a language feature designed specifically for talking to JavaScript: the `port` keyword. Any module that uses the `port` keyword must be declared using the `port module` keyword, which means we'll need to change the first line of PhotoGroove.elm to this:

```
port module PhotoGroove exposing (..)
```

TIP   If you're ever wondering whether a given module talks directly to arbitrary JavaScript code, checking to see if it's a `port` module is generally the quickest way.

USING A PORT TO DEFINE A FUNCTION

Now that we're working with a `port` module, we can use the `port` keyword right above the `type alias` for `FilterOptions` like so:

```
port setFilters : FilterOptions -> Cmd msg
```

This declares a function called `setFilters`. Its type is (`FilterOptions -> Cmd msg`). We don't write an implementation for this function, because the `port` keyword automatically writes one for us. `port` only needs to look at the type we requested to decide what the function should do.

All `port` functions that send data to JavaScript are defined using a very specific pattern:

- The `port` keyword must be followed by a function name and a type annotation.
- The type annotation must be for a function that takes one argument.
- The function must return `Cmd msg`, and nothing else—not even `Cmd Msg`!

PORT COMMANDS NEVER SEND MESSAGES

Our new `setFilters` function returns `Cmd msg`, not `Cmd Msg`—but what's the difference? We know from chapter 3 that the lowercase *m* means msg is a *type variable*, like the `val` type variable we saw in `Array.fromList`:

```
fromList : List val -> Array val
```

This `List String -> Cmd msg` function is the first time you've seen a function annotation with a type variable in its return type, but no type variable in its parameters. As it turns out, though, we've been using a `Cmd msg` for quite some time now! The official documentation for `Cmd.none` shows that it has this type:

```
none : Cmd msg
```

A `Cmd msg` by itself like this is a *command that produces no message after it completes.*

> **NOTE** A command that produces no messages has the type `Cmd msg`, a subscription (for example, `Sub.none`) that produces no messages has the type `Sub msg`, and a list that has no elements—that is, `[]`—has the similar type `List val`. Because their type variables have no restriction, you can use a `Cmd msg` anywhere you need any flavor of `Cmd`, just as you can use an empty list anywhere you need any flavor of `List`. Playing around with empty lists in `elm repl` can be a helpful way to see how types like these interact with other types.

Both `Cmd.none` and `setFilters` produce no message after completing. The difference is that `Cmd.none` has no effect, whereas `setFilters` will perform the effect of sending data to JavaScript. (Specifically, it will send the `FilterOptions` value we pass it.) You can think of `setFilters` as a "fire and forget" command. Table 5.7 compares `Cmd Msg` and `Cmd msg` in different expressions.

Table 5.7 Comparing `Cmd Msg` and `Cmd msg`

Expression	Type	Effect	Message sent back to update

`list photoDecoder`
`  |> Http.get "http://..."`
`  |> Http.send GotPhotos`
	Cmd Msg	Sends HTTP request	GotPhotos

`Cmd.none`	Cmd msg	(None)	(No message sent back)
`setFilters filterOptions`	Cmd msg	Sends `filterOptions` to JavaScript	(No message sent back)

> **NOTE** Although HTTP requests can fail, sending data to JavaScript cannot. We don't miss out on any error-handling opportunities just because `setFilters` sends no message back to update.

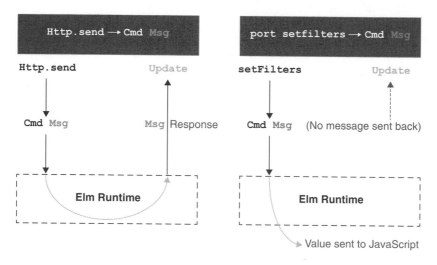

Figure 5.6   Comparing a `Cmd` from `Http.send` to a `Cmd` from a port

Figure 5.6 shows the similarities and differences between a `Cmd` originating from an `Http.send`, and a `Cmd` originating from a `port`.

CALLING SETFILTERS WHEN USERS SELECT PHOTOS

Now that we have our port set up, we need to call `setFilters` in order to send some data to JavaScript. We'll want to apply the filters every time the user selects a photo, so that's when we'll want `update` to return the command we get from `setFilters`. Here's one way we could modify the `ClickedPhoto` branch of `update` to do this.

Listing 5.7   `ClickedPhoto`

```
ClickedPhoto selectedUrl ->
    let
        filters =
            [ { name = "Hue", amount = model.hue }
            , { name = "Ripple", amount = model.ripple }
            , { name = "Noise", amount = model.noise }
            ]

        url =
            urlPrefix ++ "large/" ++ selectedUrl

        cmd =
            setFilters { url = url, filters = filters }
    in
    ( model, cmd )
```

However, the `ClickedPhoto` branch is not the only way a user can select a photo. Users can also click the Surprise Me! button to select a photo at random, and we'll want to apply filters in that situation as well. This means we'll want to reuse the preceding code in two places: both the `ClickedPhoto` branch of our case-expression as well as the `GotRandomPhoto` branch.

SHARING CODE BETWEEN UPDATE BRANCHES

Usually, the simplest way to share code is to extract common logic into a helper function and call it from both places. This is just as true for `update` as it is for any function, so let's do that!

> **NOTE** The structure of `update` permits clever alternatives to this venerable code-sharing technique—for example, having `update` call itself, passing a different `Msg`. This saves us from writing another function, but it's more error-prone. If we do this, and later a teammate innocently changes how that other `Msg` responds to user input, our code breaks. Having `update` call itself also runs a bit slower because we create an unnecessary `Msg` and run an unnecessary case-expression on it. A helper function not only runs faster; it's less error-prone to maintain because it explicitly signals to future maintainers that code is being reused.

We'll name the helper function `applyFilters`, and add it right below `update`.

Listing 5.8 `applyFilters`

```
applyFilters : Model -> ( Model, Cmd Msg )
applyFilters model =
    case model.status of
        Loaded photos selectedUrl ->
            let
                filters =
                    [ { name = "Hue", amount = model.hue }
                    , { name = "Ripple", amount = model.ripple }
                    , { name = "Noise", amount = model.noise }
                    ]

                url =
                    urlPrefix ++ "large/" ++ selectedUrl
            in
            ( model, setFilters { url = url, filters = filters } )

        Loading ->
            ( model, Cmd.none )

        Errored errorMessage ->
            ( model, Cmd.none )
```

Now we can have both `ClickedPhoto` and `GotRandomPhoto` call `applyFilters` directly:

```
GotRandomPhoto photo ->
    applyFilters { model | status = selectUrl photo.url model.status }


ClickedPhoto url->
    applyFilters { model | status = selectUrl url model.status }
```

Lovely! Now whenever a user clicks either a photo or the Surprise Me! button, `set-Filters` will return a `Cmd` that sends the appropriate `FilterOptions` value over to JavaScript. Next, we'll wire up the logic on the JavaScript side, which will receive that `FilterOptions` value and use it to apply some filters.

5.2.2 *Receiving data from Elm*

Now we're going to write a bit more JavaScript code. Whenever we access a JS library from Elm, it's best to write as little JavaScript as possible. This is because if something crashes at runtime, it's a safe bet that the culprit is somewhere in our JavaScript code—so the less of it we have, the less code we'll have to sift through to isolate the problem.

ADDING PASTA

The JavaScript code we need comes from an open source image-filtering library intuitively named Pasta.js. We can import Pasta by adding this `<script>` tag to index.html, right before the `<script>` that imports our compiled app.js file:

```
<div id="app"></div>

<script src="http://elm-in-action.com/pasta.js"></script>
<script src="app.js"></script>
```

This `<script>` adds a global JavaScript function called `Pasta.apply` to the page. It takes two arguments:

- A `<canvas>` element, which is where `apply` will draw the filtered photos
- An `options` object, which—in a remarkable coincidence—has the same structure as the `FilterOptions` record Elm will be sending to JavaScript via our `setFilters` port.

Let's introduce that `<canvas>`. We can do this with a quick change to Photo-Groove.elm, having `viewLoaded` render a canvas instead of an `img` for the `"large"` image. Let's replace our `img [ class "large", ... ] []` in `viewLoaded` with this:

```
canvas [ id "main-canvas", class "large" ] []
```

`Pasta.apply` will take care of drawing the filtered photo onto this `canvas`. (The photo URL to draw will be sent to `Pasta.apply` via the `FilterOptions` we're sending through our `port`.)

RECEIVING DATA FROM THE SETFILTERS PORT

We can set up a callback function that receives data from our `setFilters` function like so:

```
<script src="http://elm-in-action.com/pasta.js"></script>
<script src="app.js"></script>
<script>
  var app = Elm.PhotoGroove.init({node: document.getElementById("app")});

  app.ports.setFilters.subscribe(function(options) {
    Pasta.apply(document.getElementById("main-canvas"), options);
  });
</script>
```

We've never needed the return value of Elm.PhotoGroove.init() before, but now we do. This object, typically named app, lets us subscribe to data that Elm sends to JavaScript via ports like setFilters. When the Elm Runtime executes the Cmd returned by setFilters, the callback function we've passed to app.ports.set-Filters.subscribe will run. The options argument it accepts is the Filter-Options record Elm sent over, but converted from an Elm record to a JavaScript object.

> **WARNING** Like custom elements, ports invoke JavaScript code—which may throw runtime exceptions. If we make a mistake in any of our JavaScript code here, Elm's compiler has no way to help us catch it.

Table 5.8 shows how a port translates immutable Elm values (like the FilterOptions record) into brand-new (potentially mutable) JavaScript values.

Table 5.8 Translating Elm values into JavaScript values via ports

Elm value	Elm type	JavaScript value	JavaScript type
"foo"	String	"foo"	string
4.2	Float	4.2	number
True	Bool	true	boolean
("foo", True, 4.2)	(String, Bool, Float)	["foo", true, 4.2]	Array
["drive", "line"]	List String	["drive", "line"]	Array
{ name = "Shadow" }	{ password : String }	{"name": "Shadow"}	object
Nothing	Maybe val	null	object

> **TIP** Because all Elm values must be immutable, mutable values (such as JavaScript objects and arrays) can't be sent through the port. Instead they automatically get copied into immutable data structures. This process has some overhead. Passing in values like strings and numbers, which are already immutable, has no such overhead.

Because we gave our <canvas> an id of "main-canvas", we can easily pass it to Pasta.apply by calling document.getElementById("main-canvas") to find it on the page by id.

TRYING IT OUT

Let's try it out! If we open the page, we see . . . well, an empty rectangle, as shown in figure 5.7.

That's not what we wanted! We'll figure out that bug later, but first let's see what these sliders do. Crank up that Ripple value, and then . . . hmm, still nothing happens. What's the deal?

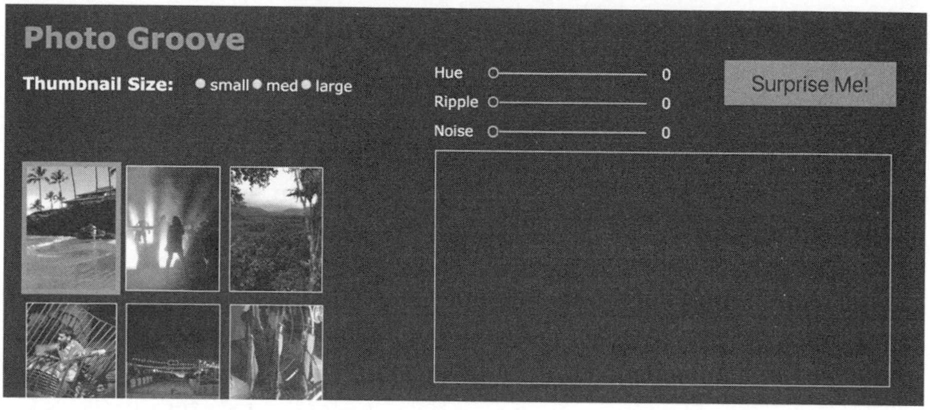

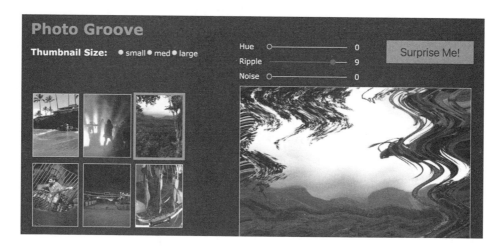

Figure 5.7   An empty rectangle. Yep.

One last idea: maybe try selecting a new photo? Oh hey, look at that! As we can see in figure 5.8, things changed—quite a lot! We are definitely talking to that JavaScript library.

Figure 5.8   Increasing Ripple, then selecting another photo

However, there are some bugs to iron out. Playing around with it some more, we observe the following problems:

- All of the Ripple and Noise values between 1 and 11 have the same effect.
- Changing Hue doesn't seem to do anything.
- When we initially load the page, we see an empty rectangle instead of the first photo.

Clearly, we have some fixing to do!

CONVERTING THE AMOUNT VALUE TO A PERCENTAGE

The reason Hue isn't working is the same reason that the Ripple and Noise values between 1 and 11 do the same thing: we're not quite using the Pasta.js API correctly.

We're sending an `Int` between 1 and 11, but actually Pasta.js is expecting a percentage—a `Float` between 0 and 1. Because JavaScript does not draw a distinction between `Int` and `Float`, this mistake does not result in a type mismatch error—not even at runtime!—and instead, our code simply does not work as expected.

We can fix this by dividing our `Model`'s `hue`, `ripple`, and `noise` fields by 11 before sending them to JavaScript. Let's revise our logic in `applyFilters`:

```
filters =
    [ { name = "Hue", amount = toFloat model.hue / 11 }
    , { name = "Ripple", amount = toFloat model.ripple / 11 }
    , { name = "Noise", amount = toFloat model.noise / 11 }
    ]
```

We need that `toFloat` because Elm's division operator (`/`) works only if you give it two `Float` values. The `Basics.toFloat` function converts an `Int` to a `Float`, so `toFloat model.hue` converts `model.hue` from an `Int` to a `Float`—at which point we can divide it by 11 as normal.

> **NOTE** This is another example of Elm's design emphasizing *being explicit*. If JavaScript required similar explicitness, we'd have caught this bug earlier, when we tried to pass an `Int` to an API expecting a `Float`.

We'll also need to update `FilterOptions` to expect a `Float` for the amount field:

```
type alias FilterOptions =
    { url : String
    , filters : List { name : String, amount : Float }
    }
```

Now if we recompile and try our sliders again, we see a much more interesting range of Hue, Ripple, and Noise values. Lovely! There are still some bugs left, but we're making progress.

CHANGING AS WE SLIDE

This will be way more fun if the photos update every time we slide, right? We know that `applyFilters` calls our `setFilters` port, so to apply the filters every time we slide, all we need to do is to run our `applyFilters` command every time we slide:

```
update : Msg -> Model -> ( Model, Cmd Msg )
update msg model =
    case msg of
        ...
        SlidHue hue ->
            applyFilters { model | hue = hue }

        SlidRipple ripple ->
            applyFilters { model | ripple = ripple }
```

```
SlidNoise noise ->
    applyFilters { model | noise = noise }
```

Recompile, and . . . presto! We're still greeted with an empty rectangle, but now whenever we slide, the photos update in real time to reflect the new filter settings. Whee! Now let's fix that pesky bug where we see an empty rectangle instead of a photo on page load.

5.2.3 *Timing DOM updates*

Showing the initial photo when the page loads takes two steps—a straightforward step and a tricky step. Let's start with the straightforward one: what we do after loading the photos.

APPLYING FILTERS AFTER LOADING PHOTOS

The problem here is that we currently load the photos and then re-render the view, but re-rendering the view is no longer enough to make a photo show up. We now need to call `applyFilters` so that Pasta can render something to the canvas.

To fix this, we need the `GotPhotos` branch of our update function's case-expression to call `applyFilters` after updating `model`:

```
GotPhotos (Ok photos) ->
    case photos of
        first :: rest ->
            applyFilters
                { model
                    | status =
                        case List.head photos of
                            Just photo ->
                                Loaded photos photo.url

                            Nothing ->
                                Loaded [] ""
                }
```

However, if you recompile and reload, you'll see the same behavior. Why wasn't that enough?

TIMING PORTS AND RENDERING

The remaining problem is a matter of timing. Let's break down what is happening:

1. We initialize `model.status` to `Loading`.
2. We request a list of photos from the server.
3. `view` runs, and does not call `viewLoaded` because `model.status` is `Loading`.
4. Because `viewLoaded` is never called, the `<canvas>` is never rendered.
5. The server responds with our photos, meaning `update` gets a `GotPhotos` message.
6. `update` runs its `GotPhotos` branch and returns a new `Model` (with a status that is no longer `Loading`), as well as a `Cmd` that will instruct our JavaScript code to have Pasta render to the `<canvas>`.

See the problem? Step 6 tells Pasta to render to a `<canvas>`, but as we noted in step 4, no such `<canvas>` has been created yet!

This means our JavaScript call to `Pasta.apply(document.getElementById` `("main-canvas"), options)` will silently fail. Shortly after this happens, `view` will run again with the new `model`. This time, `model.status` will not be `Loading`—meaning `viewLoaded` will happily ask for a fresh, blank `<canvas>`. Great.

We were so close, though! If Elm would have rendered the `view` before running the `Cmd` that invoked Pasta, the `<canvas>` would have been on the DOM before the Java-Script executed, and everything would have been fine. So why doesn't Elm do this?

OPTIMIZED DOM UPDATES

One reason the Elm Runtime has good performance is that it skips unnecessary renders. See, browsers repaint the DOM as pixels on users' screens only every so often. If the Elm Runtime changes part of the DOM, and then changes it again before the next repaint, the first change will have been wasted time; only the second change will be painted for users to see.

You might think that if your `update` function gets called a million times in a single second, your `view` would also be called a million times. Not so! Although those million updates will result in a million potential `Model` changes, Elm waits until the browser's next repaint to call `view` even once—with whatever value `Model` has at that moment. Invoking `view` more frequently than that would result in DOM updates that the browser wouldn't bother to paint anyway.

SYNCHRONIZING WITH THE ELM RUNTIME

The JavaScript function `requestAnimationFrame` allows code to run just before the browser's next repaint. Because this is when the Elm Runtime will schedule its next DOM update, we can use `requestAnimationFrame` to delay our call to `document` `.getElementById("main-canvas")` until after our next `view` has added the `<canvas>` we need to the DOM.

Because `requestAnimationFrame` accepts a single callback function, we can finally fix this bug by wrapping our call to `Pasta.apply` in a `requestAnimation-Frame` callback function, like so:

```
app.ports.setFilters.subscribe(function(options) {
  requestAnimationFrame(function() {
    Pasta.apply(document.getElementById("main-canvas"), options);
  });
});
```

> **TIP** Anytime you need to trigger some JavaScript port code to run *after the next time* `view` results in a DOM update, you can synchronize things by wrapping your port code in `requestAnimationFrame` like this.

Let's recompile and bring up the page. Now the initial photo loads right after the page does.

5.3   *Receiving data from JavaScript*

Now we're ready for the final piece of the puzzle: the Pasta activity display, which shows information reported by Pasta. First we'll start subscribing to Pasta's real-time activity updates, which Pasta broadcasts as they occur. Then we'll set an initial activity message that displays the version of Pasta we've loaded. Each change involves a different Elm concept we haven't used before: first *subscriptions* and then *flags*. Let's put them to work!

5.3.1   *Receiving real-time data from JavaScript via ports*

Here we'll be receiving real-time data from JavaScript in the same way we receive user input: through a Msg. Let's start by adding an activity string to our Model, initialModel, and Msg, as shown in table 5.9.

Table 5.9   Adding an activity string to Model, initialModel, and Msg

Model	initialModel	Msg

type alias Model =
    { status : Status
    , activity : String
	initialModel : Model
	initialModel =
	    { status = Loading
	    , activity = ""
		type Msg
		    . . .
		
			GotRandomPhoto Photo
			
				GotActivity String

With these in place, our change to update is straightforward: set the activity field on model when we receive a GotActivity message:

```
update msg model =
    case msg of
        GotActivity activity ->
            ( { model | activity = activity }, Cmd.none )
```

We'll also need viewLoaded to display the activity:

```
, button
    [ onClick ClickedSurpriseMe ]
    [ text "Surprise Me!" ]
, div [ class "activity" ] [ text model.activity ]
, div [ class "filters" ]
```

Nice! We're getting faster at this. Now all that's missing is a source of GotActivity messages. We'll get those from JavaScript.

SENDING DATA FROM JAVASCRIPT TO ELM

Let's modify index.html to add a bit more JavaScript code right below our set-Filters code:

```
var app = Elm.PhotoGroove.init({node: document.getElementById("app")});

app.ports.setFilters.subscribe(function(options) {
    requestAnimationFrame(function() {
        Pasta.apply(document.getElementById("main-canvas"), options);
```

```
    });
});

Pasta.addActivityListener(function(activity) {
    console.log("Got some activity to send to Elm:", activity);
});
```

Pasta calls this function whenever its activity changes.

Logs the new activity value to the developer console

This uses Pasta's `addActivityListener` function to log activity to the browser's JavaScript console. If we reload the page and open the browser's console, we'll see various activity messages flowing through as we play around with the sliders and select photos. Next, we need to send those `activity` strings to Elm instead of to the console.

SUBSCRIPTIONS

Earlier in the chapter, we sent data from Elm to JavaScript by using a command. Now we'll do the reverse: send some data from JavaScript to Elm—using, not a command, but a *subscription*.

> **DEFINITION** A *subscription* represents a way to translate certain events outside our program into messages that get sent to our `update` function.

One use for subscriptions is handling user inputs that aren't tied to a particular DOM element. For example, we've used `onClick` to translate a click event on a specific element into a message that gets sent to `update`. What if we instead want to detect when the user resizes the entire browser window?

We do this by adding a subscription to our program that translates browser window resize events into messages. Those messages get sent to `update` just as the ones for `onClick` do. The difference is that instead of using `Html.Events.onClick` from the `elm/html` package, we'd use `Browser.onResize` from the `elm/browser` package, as shown in figure 5.9.

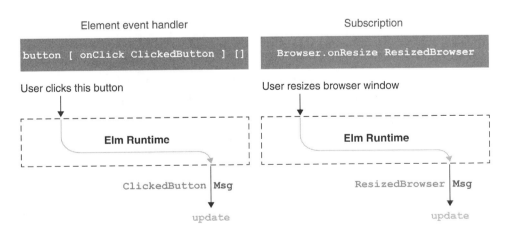

Figure 5.9 A subscription that translates browser window resize events into messages

DEFINING A SUBSCRIPTION PORT

There are also subscriptions that translate data from JavaScript into messages that are sent to `update`. We can get one of these subscriptions by using a slightly different `port` declaration. Let's add another `port` right below the code that defines `setFilters`:

```
port setFilters : FilterOptions -> Cmd msg

port activityChanges : (String -> msg) -> Sub msg
```

We can already see some similarities and differences between our command port and our subscription port. Both define a function that takes one argument, but whereas the first function returns a command (`Cmd msg`), the second returns a subscription (`Sub msg`).

`Cmd` and `Sub` are both parameterized on the type of message they produce. We noted earlier that `setFilters` returns a `Cmd msg` (as opposed to `Cmd Msg`) because it is a command that produces no message after it completes. In contrast, `activity-Changes` returns a `Sub msg`, but here `msg` refers to the type of message returned by the (`String -> msg`) function we pass to `activityChanges`. Table 5.10 shows how various calls to `activityChanges` can yield different return values.

Table 5.10   Calling the `activityChanges` function

Function to pass to `activityChanges`	Expression	Return type
`String.length : String -> Int`	`activityChanges String.length`	`Sub Int`
`String.reverse : String -> String`	`activityChanges String.reverse`	`Sub String`
`GotActivity : String -> Msg`	`activityChanges GotActivity`	`Sub Msg`

> **NOTE**   Whereas it's normal for `setFilters` to return `Cmd msg`, it would be bizarre for `activityChanges` to return `Sub msg`. After all, a `Cmd msg` is a command that has an effect but never sends a message to `update`—but subscriptions do not run effects. Their whole purpose is to send messages to `update`. Subscribing to a `Sub msg` would be like listening to a disconnected phone line: not terribly practical.

If we call `activityChanges GotActivity`, we'll get back a `Sub Msg` subscription. That's all well and good, but what do we do with a `Sub Msg`?

PASSING SUBSCRIPTIONS TO BROWSER.ELEMENT

We use `Sub Msg` with that `subscriptions` field we set up with `Browser.element`:

```
main : Program () Model Msg
main =
    Browser.element
        { init = \_ -> ( initialModel, initialCmd )
        , view = viewOrError
        , update = update
        , subscriptions = subscriptions
        }
```

```
subscriptions : Model -> Sub Msg
subscriptions model =
    activityChanges GotActivity
```

Ever since chapter 3, we've been setting this `subscriptions` field to an anonymous function that always returned `Sub.none`. Now we've made that function return `activityChanges GotActivity` instead, which means that whenever JavaScript sends a string to the `activityChanges` port, it will result in a `GotActivity` message being sent to `update`.

> **NOTE** The argument this anonymous `subscriptions` function accepts is a `Model`. Whenever our model changes, the new model is passed to this function, giving us a chance to return a different `Sub` depending on what's in the new model. This lets us dynamically control which subscriptions our program pays attention to.

Figure 5.10 illustrates how subscriptions fit into Elm programs.

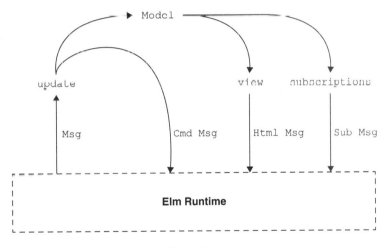

Figure 5.10   How subscriptions fit into Elm programs

Now our `activityChanges` port is fully connected to the rest of our application, meaning we're ready to have our JavaScript code start sending it data!

CALLING APP.PORTS.ACTIVITYCHANGES.SEND

Much as we used `app.ports.setFilters.subscribe` to receive data from Elm, so too, we can use `app.ports.activityChanges.send` to send data to Elm. Let's replace our `console.log` in index.html with a call to `app.ports.activityChanges.send`:

```
Pasta.addActivityListener(function(activity) {
    console.log("Got some activity to send to Elm:", activity);
    app.ports.activityChanges.send(activity);
});
```

Remember, `subscriptions = \_ -> activityChanges GotActivity` specifies that we'll wrap whatever `activity` string we receive from the `activityChanges` port in a `GotActivity` message.

This means that calling `app.ports.activityChanges.send("Reticulating splines")` from JavaScript will ultimately result in a `GotActivity "Reticulating splines"` message being sent to `update` on the Elm side. At that point, our existing activity-rendering logic should kick in, which we can confirm by recompiling and reopening index.html in the browser. Figure 5.11 shows how the page should look.

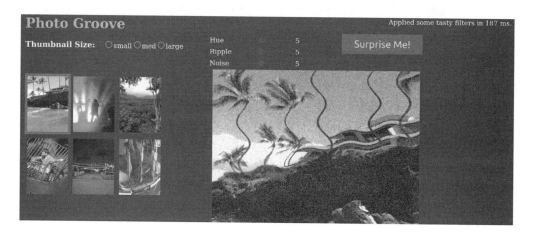

Figure 5.11   Showing the activity when filters change

Fantastic! We have just one more problem to address. Right when we refresh the page, at first there is no activity to show, leading to a brief flicker of nothingness before the first activity update arrives. We'll fix this by showing an initial activity message, using data obtained from Pasta prior to the first activity change it sends us.

5.3.2   *Receiving initialization arguments via flags*

We'd like to display an initial activity report that includes the version of Pasta we're using. It will look something like this:

> *Initializing with Pasta v4.2...*

We can easily obtain the current version from Pasta in JavaScript; all we have to do is reference `Pasta.version`. But how do we get that value into Elm in time for the initial render, to avoid that flicker of missing content?

SENDING INITIALIZATION DATA TO PROGRAM

Calling `app.ports.activityChanges.send(Pasta.version)` won't cut it here. Elm would still render `initialModel` (with `model.activity` being `""`, resulting in

the flicker of missing content) before receiving a message from `activityChanges`
and re-rendering with the new `activity`.

What we want is a way to give Elm a value from JavaScript that's available right away,
early enough to use in our initial render. This means we don't want ports; we want *flags*.

> **DEFINITION** *Flags* are values passed from JavaScript to an Elm program's `init`
> function.

To use flags, we'll revisit the very first piece of configuration we used in our main declaration:

```
main =
    Browser.element
        { init = \flags -> ( initialModel, initialCmd )
```

Remember that `flags` argument the `init` function was receiving? The one we
renamed to `_` because we weren't using it? We're finally about to use it!

Let's give our initialization logic a bit more room to breathe, by moving `init` from
an anonymous function to a named top-level function:

```
main =
    Browser.element
        { init = init
        , view = view
        , update = update
        , subscriptions = \_ -> activityChanges GotActivity
        }

init : Float -> ( Model, Cmd Msg )
init flags =
    let
        activity =
            "Initializing Pasta v" ++ String.fromFloat flags
    in
    ( { initialModel | activity = activity }, initialCmd )
```

> **TIP** `String.fromFloat` is like `String.fromInt`, but for floats. Okay,
> maybe calling this a "tip" is a bit of a stretch, but let's go with it.

Changing the type of `init`'s `flags` argument will affect the type of `main` a bit:

```
main : Program () Model Msg
main : Program Float Model Msg
```

`Program () Model Msg` means "a `Program` with `Model` as its model type, `Msg` as its
message type, and which has no flags." `Program Float Model Msg` means the same
thing, except that its flags are a `Float`. (For a refresher on the `()` type, see chapter 3,
section 3.3.3.)

The type of Browser.element

The complete type of the `Browser.element` function is as follows:

```
{ init : flags -> ( model, Cmd msg )
, view : model -> Html msg
, update : msg -> model -> ( model, Cmd msg )
, subscriptions : model -> Sub msg
}
-> Program flags model msg
```

These three type variables—`flags`, `model`, and `msg`—tie every Elm program together.

Because `view`, `init`, `update`, and `subscriptions` all produce the same `msg` type as the one `update` receives as an argument, you can choose whatever message type you like; `update` will be able to process every message. The Elm Runtime will send messages to `update` only from the sources that you see in this configuration record right here.

Likewise, the `model` that `init` returns has the same type as the one `update` accepts and returns, and the same one `subscriptions` is based on.

Elm has no secret enforcement mechanism behind the scenes making sure all the messages and the model fit together properly. It's all done with plain old type variables right here in this type signature.

SENDING FLAGS TO ELM

Now that our `init` function accepts a `Float` for its flags, we're ready to send that `Float` in from JavaScript. We do this by passing an extra argument to the `Elm.PhotoGroove.init` method we've been using to start the program running:

```
var app = Elm.PhotoGroove.init({
  node: document.getElementById("app"),
  flags: Pasta.version
});
```

Decoding JavaScript values

If we want, we can use the same JSON decoders we used in chapter 4 to translate values from JavaScript into Elm values while gracefully handling errors. In that chapter, we used the `Json.Decode.decodeString` function to decode a `String` of JSON into various Elm values. A similar function, `Json.Decode.decodeValue`, takes a `Json.Decode.Value` instead of a `String`. We can write our `activityChanges` port to expect a `Value` from JavaScript, like so:

```
import Json.Decode exposing (Value)

port activityChanges : (String -> msg) -> Sub msg
port activityChanges : (Value -> msg) -> Sub msg
```

From there, writing a `Decoder Msg` and passing it to `Json.Decode.decodeValue` will give us a `Result String Msg`. We can translate that into a `Msg` by introducing an error-handling `Msg` that ideally displays a helpful message to end users, explaining that something went wrong.

We can use the same technique for flags:

```
main : Program Value Model Msg
```

Using this decoder style is generally a better choice for production applications. For one thing, it lets us give users a better experience by gracefully handling errors. For another, any incoming type other than `Value` is liable to result in a runtime exception if JavaScript passes in something invalid.

Elm will check this immediately upon receiving the value, and will throw the exception early rather than letting it snake its way through our program, but it's better still to do the error handling ourselves. Besides, because Elm performs the automatic check using decoders anyway, there's no performance penalty for doing it explicitly.

That's it! Now when we start up Photo Groove, we'll see the version number proudly displaying for the briefest of moments before the first photo loads. Figure 5.12 shows the initial activity value, captured using an incredibly high-speed screenshotting camera.

Figure 5.12   Showing the activity on page load

Nicely done!

Summary

Photo Groove is now substantially groovier than before. Specifically:

- We added some cool sliders by using custom elements written in JavaScript.
- As users slide their values around, we change the filters on the large photo.
- The filters come from a JavaScript library, which Photo Groove talks to like a server.
- When the JS filtering library sends activity reports, Photo Groove displays them.
- The initial activity report includes the JS filtering library's version number.

In the process, you learned some new concepts and techniques for building Elm applications:

- Asking "Which approach rules out more bugs?" is a good way to decide between different ways to model data.
- Once custom elements have been registered on the page, we can access them by using the `Html.node` function.

- The as keyword lets us alias imported modules; for example, `import Html.Attributes as Attr` and `import Json.Encode as Encode`.
- The `Html.Events.on` function lets us create a custom event handler by using a `Decoder`.
- `requestAnimationFrame` can delay our JavaScript code's execution until the next time Elm calls `view` and renders the result to the DOM.
- A subscription represents a way to translate certain events outside our program into messages that get sent to our `update` function.
- A `port module` can use the `port` keyword to define functions that return commands and subscriptions that talk to JavaScript.
- `init`'s first argument lets us send initialization flags from JavaScript to Elm.

In chapter 6, we'll crank our application's maintainability into overdrive by building it a hearty suite of automated tests. Listings 5.9 and 5.10 show where index.html and PhotoGroove.elm ended up.

Listing 5.9   index.html

```html
<!doctype html>
<html>
    <head>
        <link rel="stylesheet" href="http://elm-in-action.com/styles.css">
        <link rel="stylesheet"
            href="http://elm-in-action.com/range-slider.css">
        <script src="http://elm-in-action.com/range-slider.js"></script>
        <script>
            class RangeSlider extends HTMLElement {
                connectedCallback() {
                    var input = document.createElement("input");
                    this.appendChild(input);

                    var jsr = new JSR(input, {
                        max: this.max,
                        values: [this.val],
                        sliders: 1,
                        grid: false
                    });

                    var rangeSliderNode = this;

                    jsr.addEventListener("update", function(elem, value) {
                        var event = new CustomEvent("slide", {
                            detail: {userSlidTo: value}
                        });

                        rangeSliderNode.dispatchEvent(event);
                    });
                }
            }
```

Defines a RangeSlider class to be the implementation for `<range-slider>` later

The connectedCallback() method gets called whenever a `<range-slider>` is added to the DOM.

Creates an `<input>` and adds it to the DOM

Uses the JSR library to initialize the `<input>`

When the slider updates, dispatches a CustomEvent that Elm can listen for

```
                window.customElements.define("range-slider", RangeSlider);    ◁──┐
        </script>                                                   Defines <range-slider>
    </head>                                                          to use the RangeSlider
                                                                       class for its logic
    <body>
        <div id="app"></div>

        <script src="http://elm-in-action.com/pasta.js"></script>
        <script src="app.js"></script>
        <script>                                                   Passes Pasta.version
            var app = Elm.PhotoGroove.init({node:                  in as a flag to the
    document.getElementById("app"), flags: Pasta.version});  ◁──   Elm program

                                                           ┌───────────────────────
  Run this code  ┌──▷  app.ports.setFilters.subscribe(function(options) {
  when the Elm    │         requestAnimationFrame(function() {               ◁──────┐
  Runtime sends a │             Pasta.apply(
  setFilters Cmd. │                 document.getElementById("main-canvas"),
                  │                 options                       Uses requestAnimationFrame
                  │             );                                to wait for view to be
                  │         });                                   reflected in the real DOM
                  │     });

                        Pasta.addActivityListener(function(activity) {
                            app.ports.activityChanges.send(activity);   │  When Pasta's activity
                        });                                             │  listener fires, sends
                </script>                                               │  activity to the
            </body>                                                     │  activityChanges Sub
        </html>
```

Listing 5.10 PhotoGroove.elm

```elm
port module PhotoGroove exposing (main)

import Array exposing (Array)
import Browser
import Html exposing (..)
import Html.Attributes as Attr exposing (..)
import Html.Events exposing (on, onClick)
import Http
import Json.Decode exposing (Decoder, at, bool, int, list, string, succeed)
import Json.Decode.Pipeline exposing (optional, required)
import Json.Encode as Encode
import Random


urlPrefix : String
urlPrefix =
    "http://elm-in-action.com/"


type Msg
    = ClickedPhoto String
    | SlidHue Int
    | SlidRipple Int
    | SlidNoise Int
```

```
        | ClickedSize ThumbnailSize
        | ClickedSurpriseMe
        | GotRandomPhoto Photo
        | GotActivity String
        | GotPhotos (Result Http.Error (List Photo))


view : Model -> Html Msg
view model =
    div [ class "content" ] <|
        case model.status of
            Loaded photos selectedUrl ->
                viewLoaded photos selectedUrl model

            Loading ->
                []

            Errored errorMessage ->
                [ text ("Error: " ++ errorMessage) ]


viewFilter : (Int -> Msg) -> String -> Int -> Html Msg
viewFilter toMsg name magnitude =
    div [ class "filter-slider" ]
        [ label [] [ text name ]
        , rangeSlider
            [ Attr.max "11"
            , Attr.property "val" (Encode.int magnitude)
            , onSlide toMsg
            ]
            []
        , label [] [ text (String.fromInt magnitude) ]
        ]
```

> Calls our rangeSlider function. It's a plain function like any other, but resembles the usual functions we use to create Html values.

```
viewLoaded : List Photo -> String -> Model -> List (Html Msg)
viewLoaded photos selectedUrl model =
    [ h1 [] [ text "Photo Groove" ]
    , button
        [ onClick ClickedSurpriseMe ]
        [ text "Surprise Me!" ]
    , div [ class "activity" ] [ text model.activity ]
    , div [ class "filters" ]
        [ viewFilter SlidHue "Hue" model.hue
        , viewFilter SlidRipple "Ripple" model.ripple
        , viewFilter SlidNoise "Noise" model.noise
        ]
    , h3 [] [ text "Thumbnail Size:" ]
    , div [ id "choose-size" ]
        (List.map viewSizeChooser [ Small, Medium, Large ])
    , div [ id "thumbnails", class (sizeToString model.chosenSize) ]
        (List.map (viewThumbnail selectedUrl) photos)
    , canvas [ id "main-canvas", class "large" ] []
    ]
```

```
viewThumbnail : String -> Photo -> Html Msg
viewThumbnail selectedUrl thumb =
    img
        [ src (urlPrefix ++ thumb.url)
        , title (thumb.title ++ " [" ++ String.fromInt thumb.size ++ " KB]")
        , classList [ ( "selected", selectedUrl == thumb.url ) ]
        , onClick (ClickedPhoto thumb.url)
        ]
        []


viewSizeChooser : ThumbnailSize -> Html Msg
viewSizeChooser size =
    label []
        [ input [ type_ "radio", name "size", onClick (ClickedSize size) ] []
        , text (sizeToString size)
        ]


sizeToString : ThumbnailSize -> String
sizeToString size =
    case size of
        Small ->
            "small"

        Medium ->
            "med"

        Large ->
            "large"


type ThumbnailSize
    = Small
    | Medium
    | Large


port setFilters : FilterOptions -> Cmd msg


port activityChanges : (String -> msg) -> Sub msg


type alias FilterOptions =
    { url : String
    , filters : List { name : String, amount : Float }
    }


type alias Photo =
    { url : String
    , size : Int
    , title : String
    }
```

Creates app.ports.setFilters and app.ports.activityChanges. The Elm Runtime will create the implementation of setFilters and activityChanges.

```elm
photoDecoder : Decoder Photo
photoDecoder =
    succeed Photo
        |> required "url" string
        |> required "size" int
        |> optional "title" string "(untitled)"


type Status
    = Loading
    | Loaded (List Photo) String
    | Errored String


type alias Model =
    { status : Status
    , activity : String
    , chosenSize : ThumbnailSize
    , hue : Int
    , ripple : Int
    , noise : Int
    }


initialModel : Model
initialModel =
    { status = Loading
    , activity = ""
    , chosenSize = Medium
    , hue = 0
    , ripple = 0
    , noise = 0
    }


update : Msg -> Model -> ( Model, Cmd Msg )
update msg model =
    case msg of
        GotActivity activity ->
            ( { model | activity = activity }, Cmd.none )

        SlidHue hue ->
            applyFilters { model | hue = hue }

        SlidRipple ripple ->
            applyFilters { model | ripple = ripple }

        SlidNoise noise ->
            applyFilters { model | noise = noise }

        GotRandomPhoto photo ->
            applyFilters { model | status = selectUrl photo.url model.status }

        ClickedPhoto url ->
            applyFilters { model | status = selectUrl url model.status }
```

```
            ClickedSize size ->
                ( { model | chosenSize = size }, Cmd.none )

            ClickedSurpriseMe ->
                case model.status of
                    Loaded (firstPhoto :: otherPhotos) _ ->
                        Random.uniform firstPhoto otherPhotos
                            |> Random.generate GotRandomPhoto
                            |> Tuple.pair model

                    Loaded [] _ ->
                        ( model, Cmd.none )

                    Loading ->
                        ( model, Cmd.none )

                    Errored errorMessage ->
                        ( model, Cmd.none )

            GotPhotos (Ok photos) ->
                case photos of
                    first :: rest ->
                        applyFilters { model | status = Loaded photos first.url }

                    [] ->
                        ( { model | status = Errored "0 photos found" }, Cmd.none c

            GotPhotos (Err httpError) ->
                ( { model | status = Errored "Server error!" }, Cmd.none )


applyFilters : Model -> ( Model, Cmd Msg )
applyFilters model =
    case model.status of
        Loaded photos selectedUrl ->
            let
                filters =
                    [ { name = "Hue", amount = toFloat model.hue / 11 }
                    , { name = "Ripple", amount = toFloat model.ripple / 11 }
                    , { name = "Noise", amount = toFloat model.noise / 11 }
                    ]

                url =
                    urlPrefix ++ "large/" ++ selectedUrl
            in
            ( model, setFilters { url = url, filters = filters } )

        Loading ->
            ( model, Cmd.none )

        Errored errorMessage ->
            ( model, Cmd.none )
```

```elm
selectUrl : String -> Status -> Status
selectUrl url status =
    case status of
        Loaded photos _ ->
            Loaded photos url

        Loading ->
            status

        Errored errorMessage ->
            status


initialCmd : Cmd Msg
initialCmd =
    Http.get
        { url = "http://elm-in-action.com/photos/list.json"
        , expect = Http.expectJson GotPhotos (list photoDecoder)
        }


main : Program Float Model Msg
main =
    Browser.element
        { init = init
        , view = view
        , update = update
        , subscriptions = subscriptions
        }


subscriptions : Model -> Sub Msg
subscriptions model =
    activityChanges GotActivity


init : Float -> ( Model, Cmd Msg )
init flags =
    let
        activity =
            "Initializing Pasta v" ++ String.fromFloat flags
    in
    ( { initialModel | activity = activity }, initialCmd )


rangeSlider : List (Attribute msg) -> List (Html msg) -> Html msg
rangeSlider attributes children =
    node "range-slider" attributes children


onSlide : (Int -> msg) -> Attribute msg
onSlide toMsg =
    at [ "detail", "userSlidTo" ] int
        |> Json.Decode.map toMsg
        |> on "slide"
```

Creates a `<range-slider>` element

Handles the custom "userSlidTo" event that `<range-slider>` will emit

6
Testing

Our Photo Groove application has been delighting users in production for a while now, and things have settled down on the development team. Our manager has left for vacation with vague instructions to "keep the lights on," and we find ourselves with time to revisit some of the corners we cut when shipping Photo Groove.

At this point, we know we'll be maintaining this application for the long haul. We'll need to add new features, improve existing ones, and do both without introducing bugs to the existing feature set. That isn't easy! The longer our application is around, the more important it will be that the code we write is not just reliable, but also *maintainable*.

As we saw in chapter 3, Elm's compiler is an invaluable tool for maintainability. It can assist us by finding syntax errors and type mismatches before they can impact our end users, and this is even more helpful after we make a big change to our code.

However, the compiler has no way of knowing how our business logic is supposed to work. We'll need to use a different tool to verify that our business logic is working as expected, and `elm-test` is great for that! In this chapter, you'll learn how to use `elm-test` to write automated tests that verify our business logic, including the following:

- Testing our JSON decoding logic
- Testing our `update` logic
- Testing our `view` logic

By the end, we'll have a more maintainable code base that will be easier to build on as we continue to iterate on Photo Groove's feature set in the chapters to come. Let's rock!

6.1   Writing unit tests

Before you can write your first automated test, we'll need to introduce a new package to our code base: `elm-explorations/test`. Typically, we'd do this using the `elm install` command, but setting up our tests for the first time is a bit more involved. Fortunately, the `elm-test` command-line tool automates this setup for us.

6.1.1   Introducing tests

Let's begin by running this command from the same directory as our elm.json file:

```
elm-test init
```

This will generate three things:

- A new folder called tests
- A file inside that folder called Example.elm
- A new dependency in our elm.json file

NOTE Any package that begins with `elm-explorations/` might begin with `elm/` someday. Depending on when you're reading this, the package name might be `elm/test` instead of `elm-explorations/test`!

Figure 6.1 illustrates how our project's new file structure should look.

Figure 6.1   Our project's file structure after running `elm-test init`

NOTE The elm-stuff folder contains cached files generated by `elm make` to speed up compilation. It should never be checked into source control, and it will be harmlessly regenerated by `elm make` if it gets deleted.

`elm-test init` also installed a package called `elm-explorations/test` as a *test dependency.* A test dependency's modules are available only when running tests—meaning only modules we put in this new tests/ directory will be able to access them.

TIP The application's dependencies and test dependencies are listed in that elm.json file. We'll dive into this file in greater depth in appendix B.

We'll use modules from the `elm-explorations/test` package in the Example.elm file that was created inside the tests/ directory.

RENAMING EXAMPLE.ELM

Let's open up that Example.elm file in the tests/ directory. It should have this line at the top:

```
module Example exposing (..)
```

As vibrant a name as Example.elm might be, it doesn't fit very well with our application. Let's rename the file to PhotoGrooveTests.elm and change the first line to this:

```
module PhotoGrooveTests exposing (..)
```

NOTE Elm module names must match their filenames. If we kept the first line as `module Example` but renamed the file to PhotoGrooveTests.elm, we would get an error when we ran our tests.

This module will contain our *tests,* each of which is an expression that verifies something about our application's logic. Although this chapter focuses on using tests to defend against regressions in our existing application code, this is not the only way to do it. It can be helpful to write tests before finishing the initial version of the business logic itself, to guide implementation and help reveal design shortcomings early.

When we use the `elm-test` command to run our tests, each test will either *pass* or *fail.* Failures might indicate that our application code has a problem, or that our tests have a problem—after all, tests can have bugs too! If every test passes, the *test run* as a whole passes. If any test fails, the test run as a whole fails.

UNIT TESTS

The `suite : Test` value in our `PhotoGrooveTests` module is an example of a unit test in Elm. The term *unit test* means different things depending on who you ask, so let's start by setting a clear definition of what it means in Elm.

DEFINITION In Elm, a *unit test* is a test that runs once, and whose test logic does not perform effects. (In chapter 4, you learned that an *effect* is an operation that modifies external state.)

We'll contrast unit tests with fuzz tests in a bit.

EXPECTATIONS

Every unit test requires a single expression that evaluates to an `Expectation` value.

Here's an `Expectation` that tests whether `1 + 1 == 2`:

```
expectation : Expectation
expectation =
    Expect.equal (1 + 1) 2
```

I have it on good authority that `1 + 1` should be equal to `2`, so it's safe to assume that any test that evaluates to this `Expectation` will pass when we run it.

`Expect.equal` is a function that has the following type:

```
equal : a -> a -> Expectation
```

We pass it two values, and it returns an `Expectation` that claims the two values are equal. If they turn out to be equal, the expectation will pass. If not, it will fail. Failed expectations usually translate to failed tests, as we will see momentarily.

RUNNING OUR FIRST UNIT TEST

Let's replace the implementation of `suite` in PhotoGrooveTests.elm with the following:

```
suite : Test
suite =
    test "one plus one equals two" (\_ -> Expect.equal 2 (1 + 1))
```

Before we get into what this code means, let's run this test and see if it passes.

Run this at the command line:

```
elm-test
```

You should see some output that ends with this:

TEST RUN FAILED

Huzzah! You've written your first passing test!

BREAKING DOWN OUR FIRST UNIT TEST

Figure 6.2 highlights the two arguments we passed to the `test` function.

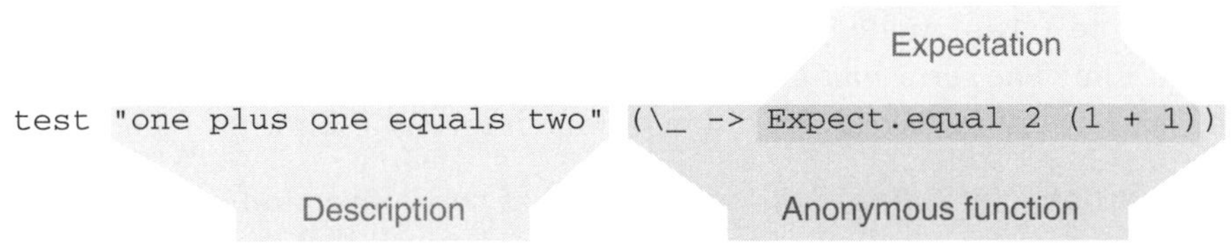

Figure 6.2 Arguments passed to the `test` function

The first argument to `test` is a description of the test. If the test fails, `elm-test` will display this text to let us know which test failed. Because the purpose of these descriptions is to help us identify which test failed, `elm-test` enforces that they must be unique. Now that we've given this test a description of `"one plus one equals two"`, we can't give any other test that same description.

Next, let's look at the argument after the description string:

```
(\_ -> Expect.equal 2 (1 + 1))
```

Oh, hey! It's our friend `Expect.equal` from earlier. When the test ran, `Expect.equal` checked whether the two arguments it received were equal. Because they were, it returned a "pass" `Expectation`. (Otherwise, it would have returned a "fail" `Expectation`.)

Since `2 == (1 + 1)`, it returns a "pass" `Expectation`, which is why the test as a whole passed when we ran it.

Notice that the argument the `test` function receives is not an actual `Expectation` value, but rather an anonymous function that *returns* an `Expectation`. This function wrapper is important, but unit tests never need to reference the argument it receives, so we can always safely disregard that argument by naming it "`_`" the way we did here.

Why the function wrapper?

Although `Expect.equal 2 (1 + 1)` determines whether the test passes, we don't pass that directly to the test function. We wrap it in an anonymous function first; what we actually pass is (`\_ -> Expect.equal 2 (1 + 1)`) instead.

Why does `test` expect us to pass it a function instead of a plain old `Expectation`? This is done in order to postpone evaluation of the test. Compare these two expressions:

```
totalA  = (      10 + 20 + 30)
addNums = (\_ -> 10 + 20 + 30)
```

If we run both of these lines of code, `totalA` will immediately add `10 + 20 + 30` to get a result of `60`. However, `addNums` will not do any addition yet. That line of code only defines a function. The addition won't happen until the function gets called later.

The very first release of `elm-test` did not wrap expectations in functions like this, which led to a problem on large test suites. `elm-test` would print something like "Starting test run . . ." followed by a blank screen, followed by a pile of output only after the last test had finished. There was no opportunity to report progress incrementally, because every test in the module began evaluating, one after the other, as soon as the module loaded!

Delaying evaluation lets `elm-test` control when and how to run each test, giving it the flexibility to do things like report incremental progress on a long-running test suite.

> *(continued)*
>
> At this point, you might be asking yourself, "Self, what exactly is the throwaway value that gets passed to that function?" Clearly the function takes an argument, because every Elm function must take at least one argument. (There is, in fact, no such thing as a zero-argument Elm function.) So what's the value that gets passed in?
>
> To answer that, let's look at the type of the `test` function:
>
> ```
> test : String -> (() -> Expectation) -> Test
> ```
>
> Remember the `()` value that we discussed back in chapter 3? It's called *unit*, and we used it near the end of section 3.3.3 to annotate `main` as `Program () Model Msg`.
>
> Here we can see that the anonymous function we're passing has the type `() -> Expectation`, which means the only possible value it can be passed is `()`. Because a function like that must always return the same value every time it is called, one of the few things it's useful for is to delay evaluation.
>
> Because we define our test case inside an anonymous `() -> Expectation` function, that code does not get evaluated right away when the program starts. Instead, it will be evaluated only when that `() -> Expectation` function is called. This lets `elm-test` control when tests are executed, which in turn lets it perform optimizations such as running tests in parallel.

Great! Next, you'll use what you've learned to write your first real unit test for Photo Groove.

6.1.2   Unit testing a JSON decoder

Take a look back at our `photoDecoder`, which we used to decode `Photo` values from the raw JSON strings our HTTP requests received from the server. `photoDecoder` describes JSON values that have two required fields and one optional field. Here's how we defined it:

```
photoDecoder : Decoder Photo
photoDecoder =
    decode buildPhoto
        |> required "url" string
        |> required "size" int
        |> optional "title" string "(untitled)"
```

We'll write a test for this code that checks whether that optional field is serving the purpose we expect—namely, that if the JSON the server sends us doesn't have a `title` field, the photo ends up with the default title of `"(untitled)"`.

However, our test can't yet access `photoDecoder`. Let's add this to the top of PhotoGrooveTests, right above `import Test exposing (..)`:

```
import PhotoGroove
```

This will import all values exposed by our `PhotoGroove` module. We can check which values a module exposes by looking at its first line. In our case, that line looks like this:

```
port module PhotoGroove exposing (main)
```

Uh-oh! It looks like we're exposing only `main` at the moment. By default, Elm modules hide their values from the outside world—an excellent default, as we will see in chapter 8!—which means that, at the moment, this module is exposing only `main`. If we want to access `photoDecoder` from `PhotoGrooveTests`, we'll have to expose it too.

We can do this by changing the first line of the `PhotoGroove` module like so:

```
port module PhotoGroove exposing (main, photoDecoder)
```

With that change in place, we can move on to writing the test. First we'll write it using only what you know already, and then you'll learn some new Elm techniques to make it nicer to read.

WRITING A FAILING TEST FIRST

Let's start by renaming `suite` to `decoderTest`, and implementing it as a failing test so you can see what failed test output looks like.

Listing 6.1 `decoderTest`

```
module PhotoGrooveTests exposing (..)

import Expect exposing (Expectation)
import Json.Decode exposing (decodeString)
import PhotoGroove
import Test exposing (..)


decoderTest : Test
decoderTest =
    test "title defaults to (untitled)"          ⟵┐ Test
        (\_ ->                                          description        ┌ Anonymous
            "{\"url\": \"fruits.com\", \"size\": 5}"    ⟵┘                 └ function wrapper
                |> decodeString PhotoGroove.photoDecoder          ⟵┐ Decoding
                |> Expect.equal                                     │ the JSON
                    (Ok { url = "fruits.com", size = 5, title = "" })
        )
```

Sample JSON string ⟶ `"{\"url\": \"fruits.com\", \"size\": 5}"`

You may recall the `decodeString` function from chapter 4. It takes a decoder and a string containing some JSON, then returns a `Result`:

```
decodeString : Decoder val -> String -> Result String val
```

Here we've supplied `photoDecoder` as the decoder, and `"{\"url\": \"fruits .com\", \"size\": 5}"` as the JSON string. That JSON string is pretty noisy with all those backslash-escaped quotes, though. Let's clean that up a bit.

TRIPLE-QUOTED STRINGS

Elm has a triple-quote syntax for writing longer quotes. Table 6.1 shows how to use that syntax to rewrite the preceding JSON string.

Table 6.1 Using triple-quote string syntax

Single quote	Triple quote

`jsonSingleQuote =`
 	
 `"{\"url\": \"fruits.com\", \"size\": 5}"`
	`jsonTripleQuote =`
	 `"""`
	 `    {"url": "fruits.com", "size": 5}`
	 `"""`

The triple-quote syntax is more verbose—three quotes is, after all, more than one—but it has two advantages over the more common single-quote syntax:

- Triple-quoted strings can span across multiple lines.
- Triple-quoted strings can contain unescaped quotation marks.

Both of these are particularly useful for JSON strings. For one, they let us dodge a veritable avalanche of backslashes! For another, it's reasonable to have long JSON strings in decoder tests. In those cases, having strings that can span multiple lines really comes in handy.

Because this is a fairly short bit of JSON, we can triple-quote it but keep it on one line. Let's change `"{\"url\": \"fruits.com\", \"size\": 5}"` to `"""{"url": "fruits.com", "size": 5}"""` and keep moving.

RUNNING ALL TESTS

Our test expects that decoding this JSON string with `photoDecoder` will return (`Ok { url = "fruits.com", size = 5, title = "" }`). But in a shocking plot twist, it actually will not!

To see what it returns instead, let's rerun `elm-test` and check out the failure message. The `elm-test` command will search our tests directory for .elm files, and run all the `Test` values they expose. In our case, `elm-test` will find PhotoGrooveTests.elm and an exposed `Test` value called `decoderTest`. If we added a second .elm file to our tests/ directory, its exposed `Test` values would also be included the next time we ran `elm-test`.

> **NOTE** The exposing (`..`) in our module `PhotoGrooveTests` exposing (`..`) declaration means our `PhotoGrooveTests` module exposes all of its top-level values—currently just `decoderTest`—so other modules can `import` them. Later, you'll learn how to reap some major benefits from having our modules intentionally expose less, but for now we'll continue exposing everything.

INSPECTING FAILURE OUTPUT

Let's run our tests by running this at the command line:

```
elm-test
```

We should see the output in figure 6.3.

```
↓ PhotoGrooveTests
✗ title defaults to (untitled)

    Ok { url = "fruits.com", size = 5, title = "(untitled)" }

        │
        │    Expect.equal
        │

    Ok { url = "fruits.com", size = 5, title = "" }
```

TEST RUN FAILED

Figure 6.3   Output from the failed test

See the two `Ok` values with the records inside? Those represent the arguments we passed to `Expect.equal`. They differ in that one has `title = "(untitled)"`, whereas the other has `title = ""`.

It's no coincidence that the record on the bottom is the record at the end of our pipeline:

```
"""{"url": "fruits.com", "size": 5}"""
    |> decodeString PhotoGroove.photoDecoder
    |> Expect.equal
        (Ok { url = "fruits.com", size = 5, title = "" })
```

As long as our test code is written in a pipeline style that ends in `|> Expect.equal`, we should be able to look at our code side by side with the test output and see by visual inspection which value `Expect.equal` received as which argument. The value at the top in our test should line up with the value at the top of the console output, and the value on the bottom in our test should line up with the value on the bottom of the console output.

FIXING THE FAILING TEST

The failing test output also told us why the test failed: we wrote that we expected the `title` field to be `""`, but actually it was `"(untitled)"`. (You'd think the test description we wrote of `"title defaults to (untitled)"` would have tipped us off ahead of time, but here we are.)

This test will pass after we fix the expectation. Let's change the `Expect.equal` call to this:

```
Expect.equal (Ok { url = "fruits.com", size = 5, title = "(untitled)" })
```

Now let's see if that worked, by running `elm-test` once more. The output should look like this:

TEST RUN FAILED

Great success!

> **TIP** It's useful to start with an intentionally failing test and then fix it. This helps avoid the embarrassing situation of accidentally writing a test that always passes! After you've seen the test fail, and then fixed it—or, even better, fixed the implementation it's testing—you can have more confidence that the test is actually verifying something.

REPLACING PARENTHESES WITH THE <| OPERATOR

Our test got easier to read when we switched to the triple-quote syntax, but we still have those clunky parentheses around our anonymous function. We can make things nicer by using the <| operator you learned about in chapter 4.

You may recall that the <| operator takes a function and another value, and passes the value to the function. We can use it to refactor our test as shown in table 6.2.

Table 6.2 Replacing parentheses with the <| operator

Parentheses	Left pipe

`test "title defaults to (untitled)"`
`    (\_ ->`
`        ...`
`    )`
	`test "title defaults to (untitled)" <|`
	`    \_ ->`
	`        ...`

Nice! Things are looking cleaner now, but we can still improve this test.

6.1.3 *Narrowing test scope*

Our test's description says `"title defaults to (untitled)"`, but we're actually testing much more than that. We're testing the structure of the entire `Photo`!

This means if we update the structure of `Photo`—say, to add a new field—this test will break. We'll have to come back and fix it manually, when we wouldn't have needed to if the test did not rely on the entire `Photo` structure. Even worse, if something breaks about `url` or `size`, we'll get failures not only for the tests that are directly responsible for those, but also for this unrelated test of `title`. Those spurious failures will clutter up our test run output!

TESTING ONLY THE TITLE

Here's how our pipeline currently works:

```
"""{"url": "fruits.com", "size": 5}"""
    |> decodeString PhotoGroove.photoDecoder
    |> Expect.equal (Ok { url = "fruits.com", size = 5, title = "(untitled)" })
```

Let's refactor the test to work with `title` only, by introducing a function called `Result.map`:

```
"""{"url": "fruits.com", "size": 5}"""
    |> decodeString PhotoGroove.photoDecoder
```

```
|> Result.map (\photo -> photo.title)
|> Expect.equal (Ok "(untitled)")
```

We've made two changes here:

- We added a step to our pipeline: `Result.map (\photo -> photo.title)`.
- We changed (`Ok { url = "fruits.com", size = 5, title = "(unti-tled)" }`) to the narrower test of (`Ok "(untitled)"`).

RESULT.MAP

You've previously seen two functions—`map`: `List.map` from chapter 2 and `Json.Decode.map` from chapter 5. Now we're adding `Result.map` to your repertoire!

Check out the similarities between the types of `List.map`, `Json.Decode.map`, and `Result.map`:

```
      List.map : (a -> b) -> List      a  -> List      b
Json.Decode.map : (a -> b) -> Decoder  a  -> Decoder  b
    Result.map : (a -> b) -> Result x a  -> Result x b
```

Pretty similar! Each `map` function does the following:

1. Takes a data structure with a type variable we've called a here
2. Also takes an (`a -> b`) function that converts from a to b
3. Returns a version of the original data structure in which the type variable is b instead of a

Here are some examples of `map` functions using `String.fromInt`. Note how `map` consistently transforms the value inside the container from an integer to a string:

```
      List.map     String.fromInt       [ 5 ]  ==        [ "5" ]
Json.Decode.map    String.fromInt   (succeed 5)  == (succeed "5")
    Result.map     String.fromInt      (Ok 5)  ==     (Ok "5")
```

Transforming a container's contents is the main purpose of `map`, but in some cases `map` does not transform anything, and returns the original container unchanged:

```
      List.map     String.fromInt           []  ==            []
Json.Decode.map    String.fromInt  (fail "argh!") == (fail "argh!")
    Result.map     String.fromInt       (Err 1)  ==      (Err 1)
```

As we can see, sometimes `map` functions decline to transform an entire classification of values:

- `List.map` has no effect on `[]`.
- `Json.Decode.map` has no effect on decoders created with `fail`.
- `Result.map` has no effect on `Err` variants.

It's up to each `map` implementation to decide how to handle the values it receives, but in general they should fit this familiar pattern of transforming the contents of a container.

Inferring implementation details from a type

Even without knowing their implementations, we might have been able to guess that `List.map` would not transform empty lists. After all, if a collection is empty, there's nothing to transform!

It's harder to guess that `Result.map` would ignore `Err` values, as there is no equivalent "empty collection" for `Result`. Believe it or not, once you know what to look for, you can find enough information in the type of `Result.map` to be certain that it could not possibly transform `Err` values!

Here's its type again. This time, let's take a closer look at the type variable that refers to `Err`; namely, `x`:

```
Result.map : (a -> b) -> Result x a -> Result x b
```

Suppose the implementation of `Result.map` tried to pass an `x` value to the `(a -> b)` transformation function. That implementation wouldn't compile! `x` and `a` are different types, so passing an `x` value to a function expecting `a` would be a type mismatch. The transformation function can't possibly affect an `Err`, because it can't be passed one.

There is a function that transforms the error, called `Result.mapError`:

```
Result.mapError : (x -> y) -> Result x a -> Result y a
```

Can you spot the difference? `Result.mapError` accepts a transformation function that takes an `x` but not an `a`. It can't transform an `Ok` value because it can't be passed one, and sure enough, `Result.mapError` does nothing when passed an `Ok` value.

Taking this idea even further, have a look at the `identity` function, from the `Basics` module:

```
identity : a -> a
```

This function knows so little about its argument that it can't do anything to it. For example, if it tried to divide whatever it received by 2, it would have to be `identity : Float -> Float` instead. The only way to implement an Elm function with the type `a -> a` is to have it return its argument unchanged:

```
identity : a -> a
identity a = a
```

Inferring implementation details like this can speed up bug hunting. Sometimes you can tell whether a function a coworker wrote might possibly be the culprit behind a bug you're tracking down just by looking at its type. If the function couldn't possibly affect the problematic value, you know you're clear to move on and search elsewhere.

USING THE .TITLE SHORTHAND

We can make one more refactor to our test. Take a closer look at the anonymous function we're passing to `Result.map`:

```
"""{"url": "fruits.com", "size": 5}"""
    |> decodeString PhotoGroove.photoDecoder
    |> Result.map (\photo -> photo.title)
    |> Expect.equal (Ok "(untitled)")
```

Functions like this come up enough that Elm has a shorthand for them. Let's replace this entire anonymous function with `.title`:

```
    |> Result.map .title
```

Writing `.title` by itself gives us a function that takes a record and returns the contents of its `title` field. It's exactly the same as the `(\photo -> photo.title)` function we had there before, except that it's shorter.

THE UNIT TEST WITH NARROWED SCOPE

Here's the original test we began with:

```
decoderTest : Test
decoderTest =
    test "title defaults to (untitled)"
        (\_ ->
            "{\"url\": \"fruits.com\", \"size\": 5}"
                |> decodeString PhotoGroove.photoDecoder
                |> Expect.equal
                    (Ok { url = "fruits.com", size = 5, title = "" })
        )
```

We refactored it to use triple-quoted strings, to test only the decoded title using `Result.map .title`, and to use the `<|` operator instead of parentheses around our anonymous function. The following listing shows our refactored `decoderTest` in all its glory.

Listing 6.2 Refactored `decoderTest`

```
decoderTest : Test
decoderTest =
    test "title defaults to (untitled)" <|
        \_ ->
            """{"url": "fruits.com", "size": 5}"""
                |> decodeString PhotoGroove.photoDecoder
                |> Result.map .title
                |> Expect.equal (Ok "(untitled)")
```

This works great! We can now rerun `elm-test` to confirm that the refactored test still passes.

However, we're testing only this one particular hardcoded JSON string. Next, we'll use fuzz tests to expand the range of values our test covers, without writing additional tests by hand.

6.2   *Writing fuzz tests*

When writing tests for business logic, it can be time-consuming to hunt down *edge cases*—those unusual inputs that trigger bugs that never manifest with more common inputs. In Elm, *fuzz tests* help us detect edge case failures by writing one test that verifies a large number of randomly generated inputs.

> **DEFINITION**   Elm's *fuzz tests* are tests that run several times with randomly generated inputs. Outside Elm, this testing style is sometimes called *fuzzing, generative testing, property-based testing,* or *QuickCheck-style testing.* elm-test went with *fuzz* because it's concise, suggests randomness, and is fun to say.

Figure 6.4 shows what we'll be building toward.

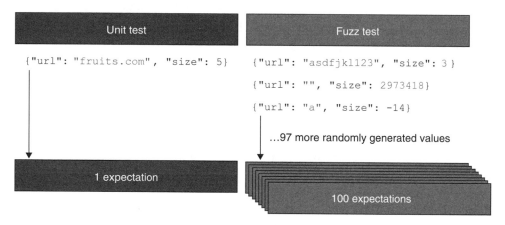

Figure 6.4   Randomly generating inputs with fuzz tests

A common way to write a fuzz test is to start by writing a unit test and then convert it to a fuzz test to help identify edge cases. Let's dip our toes into the world of fuzz testing by converting our existing unit test to a fuzz test. We'll do this by randomly generating our JSON instead of hardcoding it, so we can be sure our default title works properly no matter what the other fields are set to!

6.2.1   *Converting unit tests to fuzz tests*

Before we can switch to using randomly generated JSON, we need to replace our hardcoded JSON string with some code to generate that JSON programmatically.

BUILDING JSON PROGRAMMATICALLY WITH JSON.ENCODE

Just as we use the Json.Decode module to turn JSON into Elm values, we can use the Json.Encode module to turn Elm values into JSON. Let's add this to the top of Photo-GrooveTests.elm, right after import Json.Decode exposing (decodeString):

```
import Json.Encode as Encode
```

Because JSON encoding is the only type of encoding we'll be doing in this file, that `as Encode` alias lets us write `Encode.foo` instead of the more verbose `Json.Encode .foo`. While we're at it, let's give our `Json.Decode` import the same treatment, and change it to this:

```
import Json.Decode as Decode exposing (decodeString)
```

JSON.ENCODE.VALUE

Whereas the `Json.Decode` module centers around the `Decoder` abstraction, the `Json.Encode` module centers around the `Value` abstraction. A `Value` (short for `Json.Encode.Value`) represents a JSON-like structure. In our case, we will use it to represent actual JSON, but it can represent objects from JavaScript (like the JavaScript event objects we decoded in chapter 5) as well.

We'll use three functions to build our `{"url": "fruits.com", "size": 5}` JSON on the fly:

- `Encode.int    : Int                      -> Value`
- `Encode.string : String                   -> Value`
- `Encode.object : List ( String, Value ) -> Value`

`Encode.int` and `Encode.string` translate Elm values into their JSON equivalents. `Encode.object` takes a list of key-value pairs; each key must be a `String`, and each value must be a `Value`. Table 6.3 shows how we can use these functions to create a `Value` representing the same JSON structure as the one our hardcoded string currently represents.

Table 6.3 Switching from `String` to `Json.Encode.Value`

String	Json.Encode.Value

`"""{"url": "fruits.com", "size": 5}"""`	`Encode.object`
	`    [ ( "url", Encode.string "fruits.com" )`
	`    , ( "size", Encode.int 5 )`
	`    ]`

JSON.DECODE.DECODEVALUE

After we have this `Value` we want, we could do two things with it:

- Call `Encode.encode` to convert the `Value` to a `String`, and then use our existing `decodeString photoDecoder` call to run our decoder on that JSON string.
- Don't bother calling `Encode.encode`, and instead swap out our `decodeString photoDecoder` call for a call to `decodeValue photoDecoder` instead.

Like `decodeString`, the `decodeValue` function also resides in the `Json.Decode` module. It decodes a `Value` directly, without having to convert to and from an intermediate string representation. That's simpler and will run faster, so we'll do it that way.

Let's start by editing our `import Json.Decode` line to expose `decodeValue` instead of `decodeString`. It should end up looking like this:

```
import Json.Decode as Decode exposing (decodeValue)
```

Then let's incorporate our new encoding and decoding logic into our test's pipeline.

Listing 6.3   Using programmatically created JSON

```
decoderTest : Test
decoderTest =
    test "title defaults to (untitled)" <|
        \_ ->
            [ ( "url", Encode.string "fruits.com" )
            , ( "size", Encode.int 5 )
            ]
                |> Encode.object
                |> decodeValue PhotoGroove.photoDecoder    <———    We now call
                |> Result.map .title                                decodeValue instead
                |> Expect.equal (Ok "(untitled)")                   of decodeString here.
```

FROM TEST TO FUZZ2

Now we're building our JSON programmatically, but we're still building it out of the hardcoded values `"fruits.com"` and `5`. To help our test cover more edge cases, we'll replace these hardcoded values with randomly generated ones.

The `Fuzz` module will help us do this. Add this after `import Expect exposing (Expectation)`:

```
import Fuzz exposing (Fuzzer, int, list, string)
```

We want a randomly generated string to replace `"fruits.com"`, and a randomly generated integer to replace `5`. To access those, we'll make the substitution shown in table 6.4.

Table 6.4   Replacing a unit test with a fuzz test

Unit test	Fuzz test
`test "title defaults to (untitled)" <|` `    \_ ->`	`fuzz2 string int "title defaults to` `(untitled)" <|` `        \url size ->`

We've done two things here. First we replaced the call to `test` with a call to `fuzz2 string int`. The call to `fuzz2` says that we want a fuzz test that randomly generates two values. `string` and `int` are *fuzzers* specifying that we want the first generated value to be a string, and the second to be an integer. Their types are `string : Fuzzer String` and `int : Fuzzer Int`.

DEFINITION   A *fuzzer* specifies how to randomly generate values for fuzz tests.

The other change we made was to our anonymous function. It now accepts two arguments: `url` and `size`. Because we've passed this anonymous function to `fuzz2 string int`, elm-test will run this function 100 times, each time randomly generating a fresh `String` value and passing it in as `url`, and a fresh `Int` value and passing it in as `size`.

> **NOTE** `Fuzz.string` does not generate strings completely at random. It has a higher probability of generating values that are likely to cause bugs: the empty string, very short strings, and very long strings. Similarly, `Fuzz.int` prioritizes generating 0, a mix of positive and negative numbers, and a mix of very small and very large numbers. Other fuzzers tend to be designed with similar priorities.

USING THE RANDOMLY GENERATED VALUES

Now that we have our randomly generated `url` and `size` values, all we have to do is to use them in place of our hardcoded `"fruits.com"` and 5 values. Here's our final fuzz test.

Listing 6.4   Our final complete fuzz test

```
decoderTest : Test
decoderTest =
    fuzz2 string int "title defaults to (untitled)" <|
        \url size ->
            [ ( "url", Encode.string url )          url and size come from
            , ( "size", Encode.int size )           the string and int fuzzers
            ]                                        we passed to fuzz2.
                |> Encode.object
                |> decodeValue PhotoGroove.photoDecoder
                |> Result.map .title
                |> Expect.equal (Ok "(untitled)")
```

Great! We can now have considerably more confidence that any JSON string containing only properly set `"url"` and `"size"` fields—but no `"title"` field—will result in a photo whose title defaults to `"(untitled)"`.

> **TIP** For even greater confidence, we can run `elm-test --fuzz 5000` to run each fuzz test function 5,000 times instead of the default of 100 times. Specifying a higher `--fuzz` value covers more inputs, but it also makes tests take longer to run. Working as a team can get us more runs without any extra effort. Consider that if each member of a five-person team runs the entire test suite 10 times per day, the default `--fuzz` value of 100 gets us 5,000 runs by the end of the day!

Next, we'll turn our attention to a more frequently invoked function in our code base: `update`.

6.2.2   *Testing update functions*

All Elm programs share some useful properties that make them easier to test:

- The entire application state is represented by a single `Model` value.
- `Model` changes only when `update` receives a `Msg` and returns a new `Model`.
- `update` is a plain old function, so we can call it from tests like any other function.

Let's take a look at the type of `update`:

```
update : Msg -> Model -> ( Model, Cmd Msg )
```

Because this one function serves as the gatekeeper for all state changes in our application, all it takes to test any change in application state is to do the following:

1 Call `update` in a test, passing the `Msg` and `Model` of our choice.
2 Examine the `Model` it returns.

TESTING CLICKEDPHOTO

Let's use this technique to test one of our simplest state changes: when a `SlidHue` message—introduced in chapter 5—comes through the application. For reference, here's the branch of `update`'s case-expression that runs when it receives a `SlidHue` message:

```
SlidHue hue ->
    applyFilters { model | hue = hue }
```

This might seem like a trivial thing to test. It does so little. All it does is update the model's `hue` field, right?

Not quite! Importantly, this logic also calls `applyFilters`. What if `apply-Filters` later returns a different model, introducing a bug? Even writing a quick test for `SlidHue` can give us an early warning against that and potential future regressions in our `update` implementation. The following listing shows a basic implementation, which combines several concepts we've seen elsewhere in the chapter.

Listing 6.5   Testing `SlidHue`

```
slidHueSetsHue : Test
slidHueSetsHue =
    fuzz int "SlidHue sets the hue" <|        Begins with the
        \amount ->                            initial model
            initialModel
                |> update (SlidHue amount)    Discards the Cmd
                |> Tuple.first                returned by update
                |> .hue                       Returns the
                |> Expect.equal amount        model's hue field
```

Calls update directly

The model's hue should match
the amount we gave SlidHue.

You may recall `Tuple.first` from chapter 1. It takes a tuple and returns the first element in it. Because `update` returns a `( Model, Cmd Msg )` tuple, calling `Tuple.first` on that value discards the `Cmd` and returns only the `Model`—which is all we care about in this case.

Let's run the test and . . . whoops! It didn't compile!

EXPOSING VARIANTS

Reading the compiler error message, you might remember that although we previously edited the `PhotoGroove` module to have it expose `photoDecoder`, we haven't done the same for all the values we're using here, like `initialModel` and `update`. Let's change our module declaration to expose these:

```
port module PhotoGroove exposing
    (Model, Msg(..), Photo, initialModel, main, photoDecoder, update)
```

The `(..)` in `Msg(..)` means to expose not only the `Msg` type itself (for use in type annotations such as `Msg -> Model -> Model`), but also its variants. If we'd exposed only `Msg` rather than `Msg(..)`, we still wouldn't be able to use variants like `SlidHue` in our test. In contrast, `Photo` is a type alias, so writing `Photo(..)` would yield an error; `Photo` has no variants to expose.

> **NOTE** We also could have written `port module PhotoGroove exposing (..)` instead of separately listing what we want to expose. However, it's best to avoid declaring modules with `exposing (..)`, except in the case of test modules such as `PhotoGrooveTests`. By explicitly listing only the values and types we want to expose, we avoid unintentionally exposing implementation details that would be better kept hidden within the module.

Because we're using `SlidHue` without qualifying it with its module name—which we could have done by writing `PhotoGroove.SlidHue` instead—we'll need to expose some variants in our `import` declaration to bring them into scope. Let's do that for `Msg`, `Photo`, `Model`, and `initialModel` by changing the `import PhotoGroove` line in `PhotoGrooveTests` like so:

```
import PhotoGroove exposing (Model, Msg(..), Photo, initialModel, update)
```

Making commands testable

As of this writing, `elm-test` does not support testing commands directly. However, you can work around this if you're willing to modify your `update` function. First, make a custom type that represents all the commands your application can run. In our case, that would be the following:

```
type Commands
    = FetchPhotos Decoder String
    | SetFilters FilterOptions
```

(continued)

Then change `update` to have this type:

```
update : Msg -> Model -> ( Model, Commands )
```

Next, write a function that converts from `Commands` to `Cmd Msg`:

```
toCmd : Commands -> Cmd Msg
toCmd commands =
    case commands of
        FetchPhotos decoder url ->
            Http.get { url = url, expect = Http.expectJson GotPhotos
                decoder }

        Setfilters options ->
            setFilters options
```

Finally, we can use these to assemble the type of `update` that `Browser.element` expects:

```
updateForProgram : Msg -> Model -> ( Model, Cmd Msg )
updateForProgram msg model =
    let
        ( newModel, commands ) =
            update msg model
    in
    ( newModel, toCmd commands )
```

Now we can pass `updateForProgram` to `Browser.element`, and everything will work as before. The difference will be that `update` returns a value we can examine in as much depth as we like, meaning we can test it in as much depth as we like.

This technique is useful, but it is rarely used in practice. The more popular approach is to hold off on testing commands until `elm-test` supports them directly.

Excellent! If you rerun `elm-test`, you should see two passing tests instead of one.

6.2.3   *Creating multiple tests with one function*

We've now tested `SlidHue`, but `SlidRipple` and `SlidNoise` are just as prone to mistakes as `SlidHue`. One way to add tests for the other two would be by copying and pasting the `SlidHue` test two more times, and tweaking the other two to use `SlidRipple` and `SlidNoise`. This is a perfectly fine technique! If a test doesn't have another test verifying its behavior, the best verification tool we have is reading the test's code. Sharing code often makes it harder to tell what a test is doing by inspection, which can seriously harm test reliability.

In the case of these sliders, though, we'd like to share code for a different reason than conciseness: they ought to behave the same way. If in the future we changed one test but forgot to change the others, that would almost certainly be a mistake. Sharing code prevents that mistake from happening.

GROUPING TESTS WITH DESCRIBE

The following listing shows how we can use the Test.describe function to make a group of slider tests.

Listing 6.6 Testing SlidHue

```
sliders : Test
sliders =
    describe "Slider sets the desired field in the Model"
        [ testSlider "SlidHue" SlidHue .hue
        , testSlider "SlidRipple" SlidRipple .ripple
        , testSlider "SlidNoise" SlidNoise .noise
        ]
```
> Groups this List of Test values under one description

```
testSlider : String -> (Int -> Msg) -> (Model -> Int) -> Test
testSlider description toMsg amountFromModel =
    fuzz int description <|
        \amount ->
            initialModel
                |> update (toMsg amount)
                |> Tuple.first
                |> amountFromModel
                |> Expect.equal amount
```

> Uses testSlider's description argument as the test's description

(toMsg : Int -> Msg) will be SlidHue, SlidRipple, or SlidNoise.

> (amountFromModel : Model -> Int) will be .hue, .ripple, or .noise.

The Test.describe function has this type:

```
describe : String -> List Test -> Test
```

When one of the tests in the given list fails, elm-test will print out not only that test's description, but also the string passed to describe as the first argument here. For

```
↓ PhotoGroveTests
↓ Slider sets the desired field in Model
✗ SlidHue
```

Figure 6.5 Failure output after using describe

example, if a test with a description of "SlidHue" were listed as one of the tests inside a describe "Slider sets the desired field in the Model", its failure output would look like figure 6.5.

RETURNING TESTS FROM A CUSTOM FUNCTION

The testSlider function is a generalized version of our slidHueSetsHue test from earlier. Table 6.5 shows them side by side.

Table 6.5 Comparing slidHueSetsHue and testSlider

slidHueSetsHue	testSlider
```fuzz int "SlidHue sets the hue" <| \amount -> initialModel |> update (SlidHue amount) |> Tuple.first |> .hue |> Expect.equal amount```	```fuzz int description <| \amount -> initialModel |> update (toMsg amount) |> Tuple.first |> amountFromModel |> Expect.equal amount```

Have a look at the type of `testSlider`:

```
testSlider : String -> (Int -> Msg) -> (Model -> Int) -> Test
testSlider description toMsg amountFromModel =
```

Its three arguments correspond to what we want to customize about the `SlidHue` test:

- `description : String` lets us use descriptions other than `"SlidHue sets the hue"`.
- `toMsg : Int -> Msg` lets us use messages other than `SlidHue`.
- `amountFromModel : Model -> Int` lets us use `model` fields other than `.hue`.

Because the `testSlider` function returns a `Test`, and `describe` takes a `List Test`, we were able to put these together to obtain our customized hue, ripple, and noise tests like so:

```
describe "Slider sets the desired field in the Model"
    [ testSlider "SlidHue" SlidHue .hue
    , testSlider "SlidRipple" SlidRipple .ripple
    , testSlider "SlidNoise" SlidNoise .noise
    ]
```

This compiles because the `SlidHue` variant is a function whose type is `SlidHue : Int -> Msg`, which is what the `toMsg` argument expects, and because the `.hue` shorthand is a function whose type is `.hue : Model -> Int`, which is what the `amount-FromModel` argument expects.

RUNNING THE COMPLETE TESTS

Let's take them out for a spin! If you rerun `elm-test`, you should still see four happily passing tests.

> **TIP** Notice how `elm-test` always prints `"to reproduce these results, run elm-test --fuzz 100 --seed"` and then a big number? That big number is the random number seed used to generate all the fuzz values. If you encounter a fuzz test that is hard to reproduce, you can copy this command and send it to a collaborator. If they run it on the same set of tests, they will see the same output you do; fuzz tests are deterministic given the same seed.

We've now tested some decoder business logic, confirmed that running a `SlidHue` message through `update` sets `model.hue` appropriately, and expanded that test to test the same logic for `SlidRipple` and `SlidNoise` by using one function that created multiple tests. Next, we'll take the concepts you've learned so far and apply them to testing our rendering logic as well!

6.3   *Testing views*

Our application has several rules concerning how we render thumbnail photos. For example:

- Initially, we don't render any thumbnails.

- Once the photos load, we render a thumbnail for each of them.
- When you click a thumbnail, that photo becomes selected.

It's important that these features keep working as we expand our application. By writing tests for each of them, we can guard against not only future business logic regressions in `update`, but also visual regressions in `view`. In the remainder of the chapter, we will write tests to verify all three of these rules.

6.3.1 *Testing DOM structure*

The functions to test DOM structure come from different modules. Let's import the ones we'll be using by adding the following to PhotoGrooveTests.elm:

```
import Html.Attributes as Attr exposing (src)
import Test.Html.Query as Query
import Test.Html.Selector exposing (text, tag, attribute)
```

> **NOTE** It's common to alias `Test.Html.Query` as `Query` like this for brevity's sake. We'll refer to this as "the `Query` module" in this chapter, even though the fully qualified name would be "the `Test.Html.Query` module."

We'll also need to have our `PhotoGroove` module declaration expose `view` so we can import it. While we're at it, let's also expose `Status(..)` and `urlPrefix`, which we'll use in the next section:

```
exposing (Model, Msg(..), Photo, Status(..),
    initialModel, main, photoDecoder, update, urlPrefix, view)
```

We'll also expose them when we import them in `PhotoGrooveTests`:

```
import PhotoGroove exposing (Model, Msg(..), Photo, Status(..),
    initialModel, update, urlPrefix, view)
```

With these changes in place, we're ready to write our first `view` test!

NO PHOTOS? NO THUMBNAILS.

The first rule we'll test is this one:

- Initially, we don't render any thumbnails.

Here's the test we'll write for that:

```
noPhotosNoThumbnails : Test
noPhotosNoThumbnails =
    test "No thumbnails render when there are no photos to render." <|
        \_ ->
            initialModel
                |> PhotoGroove.view
                |> Query.fromHtml
                |> Query.findAll [ tag "img" ]
                |> Query.count (Expect.equal 0)
```

This pipeline has several steps, so let's break them into two parts.

BUILDING A QUERY.SINGLE

The first part of the pipeline is this:

```
initialModel
    |> PhotoGroove.view
    |> Query.fromHtml
```

This code kicks things off by building a representation of the DOM that our test can examine. Table 6.6 breaks down the types involved in this expression.

Table 6.6   Types involved in `initialModel |> view |> Query.fromHtml`

Expression	Type
`initialModel`	`Model`
`PhotoGroove.view`	`Model -> Html Msg`
`Query.fromHtml`	`Html msg -> Query.Single msg`

`initialModel`
`    |> PhotoGroove.view`
`    |> Query.fromHtml`
	`Query.Single msg`

Passing `initialModel` to `view` gives us the `Html` that will display on Photo Groove's initial render. The functions in the `Query` module descend into this `Html`, starting from its root node and proceeding down the tree of DOM nodes it describes. Once we've narrowed it down to the nodes we care about, we call one final function to verify something about them, and produce an `Expectation`.

Figure 6.6 shows the `img` tags `Query.findHtml` will find.

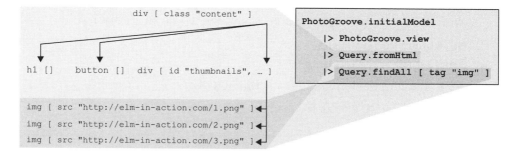

Figure 6.6   Finding all the `img` tags in the DOM

QUERYING HTML

Query functions make use of two types as they descend into `Html`:

- `Query.Single`, which represents a single DOM node
- `Query.Multiple`, which represents multiple DOM nodes

Some functions work in terms of `Single` nodes, whereas others work in terms of `Multiple` nodes. Representing these as distinct types makes it easier to tell when we expect a query to have one result versus several. For example, the `Query.count` function takes `Multiple`, whereas the `Query.children` function takes `Single` and returns `Multiple`.

CONVERTING FROM HTML TO QUERY

The `Query.fromHtml` function begins the process of descending into an `Html` value, by returning a `Single` representing the `Html`'s root node. What is that root node in our case? We can tell by looking at the `view` function that returned that `Html`; namely, `PhotoGroove.view`:

```
view : Model -> Html Msg
view model =
    div [ class "content" ]
```

Because `view` returns a `div` with a `class` of `"content"`, when our `Query.fromHtml` function returns a `Query.Single` value, that `Single` value will refer to this `div`.

> **NOTE** The complete type of `Query.fromHtml` is `fromHtml : Html msg -> Query.Single msg`. Notice the type variable `msg` in there? Because `view` returns an `Html Msg`, calling `Query.fromHtml` will return a `Query.Single Msg` value.

CONVERTING FROM QUERY TO EXPECTATION

Now that we have our `Single` value representing the `div [ class "content" ]` at the root of our `Html`, let's look at the rest of the pipeline—where we transform that `Single` into an `Expectation`. Table 6.7 breaks down the types involved in this process.

Table 6.7 Transforming a `Query.Single` into an `Expectation`

Expression	Type

`initialModel`
`    |> PhotoGroove.view`
`    |> Query.fromHtml`
	`Query.Single msg`

`Query.findAll [ tag "img" ]`	`Query.Single msg -> Query.Multiple msg`
`Query.count (Expect.equal 0)`	`Query.Multiple msg -> Expectation`

We've used two functions to get from `Single` to `Expectation`: `Query.findAll` and `Query.count`. Here's the type of `Query.findAll`:

```
findAll : List Selector -> Single msg -> Multiple msg
```

We give it a list of selectors—ways to identify a particular DOM node—and a `Single`, and it returns a `Multiple` representing all the descendant nodes that match the given selectors. We gave it only one selector—`tag "img"`—which means `findAll` will return all the `img` tags in the DOM tree beneath the `div [ "content" ]` at the root of our `Single` query.

Finally, once we have our `Multiple` nodes, we're ready to make a claim about them. In this case, our test is that we expect no thumbnails to be rendered, so we want to make the claim that the `Multiple` query contains zero nodes. This is where `Query.count` comes in:

```
count : (Int -> Expectation) -> Multiple msg -> Expectation
```

PARTIALLY APPLYING EXPECT.EQUAL

Notice that `Query.count` takes an `(Int -> Expectation)` function, which we satisfied by passing it a partially applied `Expect.equal`:

```
Query.count (Expect.equal 0)
```

As you may recall, `Expect.equal` takes two arguments and compares them to verify that they're equal. That means these two expressions are equivalent:

```
Query.count (Expect.equal 0)
Query.count (\count -> Expect.equal 0 count)
```

One way to read `Query.count (Expect.equal 0)` is, "Count the results in the query, and expect that count to equal 0."

COMPLETE VIEW TEST

Here's the complete implementation of our `noPhotosNoThumbnails` test once again, from `Model` to `Expectation` by way of `Html` and some `Query` operations.

> ### Listing 6.7 `noPhotosNoThumbnails`

```
noPhotosNoThumbnails : Test
noPhotosNoThumbnails =
    test "No thumbnails render when there are no photos to render." <|
        \_ ->
            initialModel
                |> PhotoGroove.view          ◁── Generates Html by
                |> Query.fromHtml                 rendering initialModel
                |> Query.findAll [ tag "img" ]
                |> Query.count (Expect.equal 0)   ◁── Finds the img nodes
                                                      inside that Query.Single
```

Returns Query.Single for that Html's root div ──▷

Finds the img nodes inside that Query.Single ◁──

Counts the img nodes, expects it to be 0

Sure enough, when we run the test, it should pass!

> **TIP** As our test suites get larger, it can be handy to run only a few tests at a time. Take a look at the `Test.skip` and `Test.only` functions in the documentation for the elm-explorations/test package on the https://package.elm-lang.org website. We can also run only a few test files at a time by passing them as arguments to elm-test; for example, `elm-test tests/DecoderTests.elm` or `elm-test tests/User/*.elm`.

Next, we'll expand this test to verify views resulting not only from the initial model, but also from models that have photos loaded.

6.3.2 *Fuzzing view tests*

The second business rule we want to test is this one:

- Once the photos load, we render a thumbnail for each of them.

CHECKING IF A GIVEN THUMBNAIL WAS RENDERED

Let's start by writing a function to check whether a given URL has been rendered as a thumbnail. Add this at the end of PhotoGrooveTests.elm:

```
thumbnailRendered : String -> Query.Single msg -> Expectation
thumbnailRendered url query =
    query
        |> Query.findAll [ tag "img", attribute (Attr.src (urlPrefix ++ url)) ]
        |> Query.count (Expect.atLeast 1)
```

This function starts with a `Query.Single`—which will represent the root of our page's DOM—and finds all the `img` elements within it that have the expected `src` attribute. Then it runs a `Query.count`, which expects that our query found at least one `img` element like that.

> **NOTE** It's better to use `Expect.atLeast 1` than `Expect.equal 1` because our business logic permits duplicate thumbnail URLs, and we wouldn't want our test to incorrectly reject repeats as invalid.

We use `(urlPrefix ++ url)` for our `src` check instead of `url` because that's what our `viewThumbnail` implementation does. The `urlPrefix` is `"http://elm-in-action.com/"`, so without prepending that, we would be searching for a `src` of `"foo.jpeg"` when in actuality a `src` of `"http://elm-in-action.com/foo.jpeg"` was rendered—meaning this test would never pass.

CHECKING IF ALL THUMBNAILS WERE RENDERED

Now that we have a function to test whether a single thumbnail was rendered, let's use it to build a function that tests whether *all* thumbnails were rendered. We could test this by hardcoding some example photos, but why bother? We can get better test coverage by using fuzz tests to randomly generate URLs, and build photos from those!

We'll start by adding a function to build a photo from a single URL, and then randomly generate a list of URLs. Add this to the end of PhotoGroove.elm:

```
photoFromUrl : String -> Photo
photoFromUrl url =
    { url = url, size = 0, title = "" }
```

Next, we'll want to generate some random strings to use as URLs.

FUZZING COLLECTIONS

We can call the `Fuzz.list` function, passing `Fuzz.string` to randomly generate a list of strings. This is the type of `Fuzz.list`:

```
list : Fuzzer a -> List (Fuzzer a)
```

If we call `fuzz (list string)`, it will give us a `Fuzzer (List String)` that we could use as our list of URLs:

```
fuzz (list string) "URLs render as thumbnails" <|
    \urls ->
```

However, there's a subtle problem here: the list fuzzer can potentially generate hundreds of elements. That might not sound like a big deal, but let's recap what we want this test to do:

1   Generate a list of URLs
2   Render a page that creates a thumbnail `Html` element for each of these URLs
3   Convert that entire `Html` structure to a `Query.Single`
4   Traverse every element inside the `Query.Single`, looking for an `img` with the right `src`
5   Repeat the previous step for every single one of the URLs

If the list fuzzer generates 300 URLs on average, that means for each of those 300 URLs, `Query.findAll` has to traverse 300 nodes searching for the one that matches. That's a total of 90,000 nodes to traverse, and we're not even done yet! Remember that fuzz tests run 100 times by default. If those tests generate 300 URLs on average, the total traversal count would be $300 \times 300 \times 100$—so we'd be looking at *nine million traversals* in a single test run. That test would take, uh . . . a bit of time to run. So let's not do that!

When test suites start taking a long time to run, it slows down the whole team. Tests accumulate, and it's important to be mindful of their performance characteristics to avoid letting slowdowns accumulate as well.

CUSTOMIZING LIST SIZES

We can prevent this combinatorial explosion by restricting the sizes of the lists we generate. Let's start our test like this:

```
thumbnailsWork : Test
thumbnailsWork =
    fuzz (Fuzz.intRange 1 5) "URLs render as thumbnails" <|
        \urlCount ->
```

`Fuzz.intRange` will randomly generate an integer from 1 to 5. We'll use it to build a list of one to five elements. (We already have a test covering the zero-elements case: our `noPhotosNoThumbnails` test from earlier.)

Here's how we can convert from `urlCount` to a list of URLs:

```
urls : List String
urls =
    List.range 1 urlCount
        |> List.map (\num -> String.fromInt num ++ ".png")
```

The `List.range` function takes two integers and makes a list containing all the numbers in between. We can see it in action in `elm repl`:

```
> List.range 1 5
[1,2,3,4,5] : List Int
```

Now that we have a reasonably sized list of URLs, we can build photos from them by using the `photoFromUrl` function we wrote earlier. Then we can build a query using a pipeline similar to the one created for our last `view` test. This time, instead of leaving `initialModel` unchanged, we'll override its `photos` field to be the list of photos we just created using `photoFromUrl` on the fly:

```
{ initialModel | status = Loaded (List.map photoFromUrl urls) "" }
    |> view
    |> Query.fromHtml
```

This gives us a `Query.Single`, which we can use to create an `Expectation` to complete our test.

COMBINING EXPECTATIONS WITH EXPECT.ALL

Let's pause and take a look at what we've put together so far:

- A `Query.Single` representing the root DOM node of our page
- A function that checks whether a `Query.Single` renders the given URL as a thumbnail: `thumbnailRendered : String -> Query.Single msg -> Expectation`
- A list of URLs: `urls : List String`

We can distill these down to a single `Expectation` by using the `Expect.all` function:

```
Expect.all : List (subject -> Expectation) -> subject -> Expectation
```

The purpose of `Expect.all` is to run a series of checks on a single subject value, and return a passing `Expectation` only if they all pass. In our case, the `subject` will be the `Query.Single` value we've built up, meaning we need to pass `Expect.all` a list with this type:

```
List (Query.Single msg -> Expectation)
```

We can use `thumbnailRendered` to get just such a list! Let's take a look at its type again:

```
thumbnailRendered : String -> Query.Single msg -> Expectation
```

We can get our list of checks by partially applying `thumbnailRendered` like so:

```
thumbnailChecks : List (Query.Single msg -> Expectation)
thumbnailChecks =
    List.map thumbnailRendered urls
```

Because we've passed a `List String` to `List.map`, it will pass each `String` in that list as the first argument to `thumbnailRendered`. The result of this `List.map` is the `List (Query.Single msg -> Expectation)` we needed for `Expect.all`.

THE FINAL TEST

Putting it all together, here's what we get.

Listing 6.8   The complete thumbnail test

```
thumbnailsWork : Test
thumbnailsWork =
    fuzz (Fuzz.intRange 1 5) "URLs render as thumbnails" <|
        \urlCount ->
            let
                urls : List String
                urls =
                    List.range 1 urlCount
                        |> List.map (\num -> String.fromInt num ++ ".png")

                thumbnailChecks : List (Query.Single msg -> Expectation)
                thumbnailChecks =
                    List.map thumbnailRendered urls
            in
            { initialModel | status = Loaded (List.map photoFromUrl urls) ""
            }
                |> view
                |> Query.fromHtml
                |> Expect.all thumbnailChecks
```

Now that we've verified that the thumbnails display as expected, we can move on to testing that they work properly when a user clicks one.

6.3.3   *Testing user interactions*

The final piece of business logic we'll be testing is this:

- When you click a thumbnail, that photo becomes selected.

Here we can benefit from the test coverage we've obtained through tests we wrote earlier in the chapter. We already have tests that verify the following:

- When the photos load, the first one gets selected.
- Whenever `update` receives a `ClickedPhoto` message, that photo becomes selected.

Having that logic independently verified simplifies what it takes to test this requirement: all we need to do is test that when the user clicks a thumbnail, the Elm Runtime will send an appropriate `ClickedPhoto` message to `update`.

FUZZ.MAP

Once again, we'll want a list of URLs, and once again we'll want to avoid a combinatorial explosion by limiting the number of photos we generate to only a handful. Now that we have multiple tests that want a short list of URL strings, we can avoid code duplication by creating a custom `Fuzzer (List String)` value that has these characteristics, using `Fuzz.map`.

Earlier in the chapter, you learned about `Result.map`, and saw how it compared to `List.map` and `Json.Decode.map`. Buckle up, because `Fuzz.map` is going to be *super duper different* from those other map functions:

```
       Fuzz.map : (a -> b) -> Fuzzer   a -> Fuzzer   b
Json.Decode.map : (a -> b) -> Decoder  a -> Decoder  b
       List.map : (a -> b) -> List     a -> List     b
     Result.map : (a -> b) -> Result x a -> Result x b
```

Okay, not really. `Fuzz.map` works the same way as these other map functions do: it takes a function that converts from one contained value to another. The following listing shows how we can use `Fuzz.map` to implement our custom fuzzer.

Listing 6.9   Custom fuzzer with `Fuzz.map`

```
urlFuzzer : Fuzzer (List String)
urlFuzzer =
    Fuzz.intRange 1 5
        |> Fuzz.map urlsFromCount


urlsFromCount : Int -> List String
urlsFromCount urlCount =
    List.range 1 urlCount
        |> List.map (\num -> String.fromInt num ++ ".png")
```

Now that we have this fuzzer, we can refactor our `thumbnailsWork` test to use it. First we'll remove the `urls` definition from inside its let-expression, and then we'll replace the test definition with this:

```
thumbnailsWork =
    fuzz urlFuzzer "URLs render as thumbnails" <|
        \urls ->
```

SIMULATING CLICK EVENTS

Next, we'll write a fuzz test that renders a list of photos and simulates clicking one of them. Let's think about the structure of that test. It needs two ingredients:

- A list of one or more photos
- Knowing which photo in that list to click

One way we could set this test up is the same way we did with `thumbnailsWork` previously:

```
fuzz urlFuzzer "clicking a thumbnail selects it" <|
    \urls->
```

There's a problem with this approach. What if `urlFuzzer` happens to generate an empty list? We'd have no photo to click!

GENERATING A NON-EMPTY LIST

We can fix this by generating a single URL, plus a list of other URLs to go after it. It's okay if that second list happens to be empty, because we'll still have the single URL to work with:

```
fuzz2 string urlFuzzer "clicking a thumbnail selects it" <|
    \urlToSelect otherUrls ->
        let
            photos =
                [ urlToSelect ] ++ otherUrls
```

THE :: OPERATOR

Incidentally, when we have a single element to add to the front of a list like this, the `::` operator is both more concise and more efficient than what we've done here. The following two expressions produce the same list, but the version that uses `::` is more efficient because it does not create an extra list in the process:

```
[ urlToSelect ] ++ otherUrls
    urlToSelect :: otherUrls
```

CHOOSING WHICH PHOTO TO CLICK

This test is looking better, but there's another problem. How do we decide which photo to click? We could decide to choose the first one every time, but then our test wouldn't be very complete. We'd be testing only that clicking the *first* thumbnail works, not that clicking *any* thumbnail works.

Could we select which photo to click at random? Well, as we saw in chapter 3, generating random numbers is an effect (represented in Elm as a `Cmd`), and `elm-test` tests are not permitted to run effects.

What we can do instead is to generate two lists at random: one list to go before the URL we'll click, and another to go after it:

```
fuzz3 urlFuzzer string urlFuzzer "clicking a thumbnail selects it" <|
    \urlsBefore urlToSelect urlsAfter ->
        let
            photos =
                urlsBefore ++ urlToSelect :: urlsAfter
```

We almost have the list we want, but not quite. Because we want to make sure we click the right one, its URL needs to be unique within the list of photos. We can do this by giving it a different extension from the others; we used `".png"` in our `urlFuzzer` definition, so we'll use `".jpeg"` here:

```
url =
    urlToSelect ++ ".jpeg"

photos =
    urlsBefore ++ url :: urlsAfter
```

HTML.TEST.EVENT

It's time to simulate the click event! We'll use the `Html.Test.Event` module to do this, so let's add it at the top of PhotoGrooveTests and alias it to `Event` for brevity:

```
import Test.Html.Event as Event
```

This gives us access to a function called `Event.simulate` that simulates user events, such as clicks, and checks whether they result in the expected message being sent to update. Here's how we'll use it.

> **Listing 6.10** `Event.simulate`

```
clickThumbnail : Test
clickThumbnail =
    fuzz3 urlFuzzer string urlFuzzer "clicking a thumbnail selects it" <|
        \urlsBefore urlToSelect urlsAfter ->
            let
                url =
                    urlToSelect ++ ".jpeg"

                photos =
                    (urlsBefore ++ url :: urlsAfter)
                        |> List.map photoFromUrl

                srcToClick =
                    urlPrefix ++ url
            in
            { initialModel | status = Loaded photos "" }
                |> view
                |> Query.fromHtml
                |> Query.find [ tag "img", attribute (Attr.src srcToClick) ]
                |> Event.simulate Event.click
                |> Event.expect (ClickedPhoto url)
```

Simulates that a user clicked this img ⟵ (points to `Query.find` line)

Expects that this message was sent to update ⟵ (points to `Event.expect` line)

Those last three lines are new! Here's what's different about them:

- We used `Query.find` instead of `Query.findAll`. This is different in that `Query.find` expects to find exactly one node, and returns a `Single` instead of a `Multiple`. If it finds zero nodes, or multiple nodes, it immediately fails the entire test.
- `Event.simulate Event.click` simulates a click event on the node returned by `Query.find`. It returns an `Event` value, representing what the Elm Runtime will produce in response to that click event.
- `Event.expect (ClickedPhoto url)` converts the `Event` into an `Expectation`, by checking that the event resulted in a `(ClickedPhoto url)` message being sent to update.

If we run all this, sure enough, it works!

FINAL TESTS

With this test in place, we have now covered all three cases of our rendering logic that we set out to cover:

- Initially, we don't render any thumbnails.
- Once the photos load, we render a thumbnail for each of them.
- When you click a thumbnail, that photo becomes selected.

Marvelous!

Summary

You've learned plenty in this chapter, including the following:

- How to introduce tests to an existing Elm application
- The similarities between `Result.map`, `Fuzz.map`, `List.map`, and `Json.Decode.map`
- Building JSON values using `Json.Encode`
- How to use `Json.Decode.decodeValue` instead of `decodeString`
- Describing expectations using `Expect.equal`, `Expect.atLeast`, and `Expect.all`
- Writing unit tests using the `test` function
- Writing fuzz tests by passing fuzzers to `fuzz`, `fuzz2`, and `fuzz3`
- Testing the `update` function by passing handcrafted messages to it in tests
- Assembling `Html` values and querying them with `Test.Html.Query`
- Descending through the DOM by using `Query.findAll`
- Simulating sending events to rendered `Html` by using `Event.simulate`

Here's the final PhotoGrooveTests.elm file.

Listing 6.11   PhotoGrooveTests.elm

```
module PhotoGrooveTests exposing
    (clickThumbnail, decoderTest, photoFromUrl, sliders, testSlider,
    thumbnailRendered, thumbnailsWork, urlFuzzer, urlsFromCount)

import Expect exposing (Expectation)
import Fuzz exposing (Fuzzer, int, list, string)
import Html.Attributes as Attr exposing (src)
import Json.Decode as Decode exposing (decodeValue)
import Json.Encode as Encode
import PhotoGroove
    exposing
        ( Model
        , Msg(..)
        , Photo
        , Status(..)
        , initialModel
        , update
```

> The (..) means to expose not only the type—so we can use it in type annotations—but also the variants, so we can use them in expressions.

```
                    , urlPrefix
                    , view
                    )
        import Test exposing (..)
        import Test.Html.Event as Event
        import Test.Html.Query as Query
        import Test.Html.Selector exposing (attribute, tag, text)


        decoderTest : Test
        decoderTest =
            fuzz2 string int "title defaults to (untitled)" <|
                \url size ->
                    [ ( "url", Encode.string url )
                    , ( "size", Encode.int size )
                    ]
                        |> Encode.object
                        |> decodeValue PhotoGroove.photoDecoder
                        |> Result.map .title
                        |> Expect.equal (Ok "(untitled)")


        sliders : Test
        sliders =
            describe "Slider sets the desired field in the Model"
                [ testSlider "SlidHue" SlidHue .hue
                , testSlider "SlidRipple" SlidRipple .ripple
                , testSlider "SlidNoise" SlidNoise .noise
                ]


        testSlider : String -> (Int -> Msg) -> (Model -> Int) -> Test
        testSlider description toMsg amountFromModel =
            fuzz int description <|
                \amount ->
                    initialModel
                        |> update (toMsg amount)
                        |> Tuple.first
                        |> amountFromModel
                        |> Expect.equal amount


        thumbnailsWork : Test
        thumbnailsWork =
            fuzz (Fuzz.intRange 1 5) "URLs render as thumbnails" <|
                \urlCount ->
                    let
                        urls : List String
                        urls =
                            List.range 1 urlCount
                                |> List.map (\num -> String.fromInt num ++ ".png")

                        thumbnailChecks : List (Query.Single msg -> Expectation)
                        thumbnailChecks =
                            List.map thumbnailRendered urls
```

url will be a string, and size will be an int, because of fuzz2 string int.

Result.map is similar to List.map and Json.Decode.map.

Encode.object returns a Value, so we use decodeValue instead of decodeString.

.hue, .ripple, and .noise are (Model -> Int) functions that take a Model and return the specified field.

toMsg will be SlidHue, SlidRipple, or SlidNoise, each of which is a function with the type (Int -> Msg).

amountFromModel will be .hue, .ripple, or .noise.

intRange prevents us from getting huge URL lists that would slow our test way down.

Expect.all runs each of the given expectations on the given subject.

```
            in
            { initialModel | status = Loaded (List.map photoFromUrl urls) "" }
                |> view
                |> Query.fromHtml
                |> Expect.all thumbnailChecks
```

view converts a Model to Html Msg, and Query.fromHtml converts Html to a Query.Single, which we can run checks on.

```
thumbnailRendered : String -> Query.Single msg -> Expectation
thumbnailRendered url query =
    query
        |> Query.findAll [ tag "img", attribute (Attr.src (urlPrefix ++ url))
      ]
        |> Query.count (Expect.atLeast 1)


photoFromUrl : String -> Photo
photoFromUrl url =
    { url = url, size = 0, title = "" }


urlFuzzer : Fuzzer (List String)
urlFuzzer =
    Fuzz.intRange 1 5
        |> Fuzz.map urlsFromCount


urlsFromCount : Int -> List String
urlsFromCount urlCount =
    List.range 1 urlCount
        |> List.map (\num -> String.fromInt num ++ ".png")


clickThumbnail : Test
clickThumbnail =
    fuzz3 urlFuzzer string urlFuzzer "clicking a thumbnail selects it" <|
        \urlsBefore urlToSelect urlsAfter ->
            let
                url =
                    urlToSelect ++ ".jpeg"
```

url :: urlsAfter operator adds the url String to the beginning of the urlsAfter List of Strings.

```
                photos =
                    (urlsBefore ++ url :: urlsAfter)
                        |> List.map photoFromUrl

                srcToClick =
                    urlPrefix ++ url
            in
            { initialModel | status = Loaded photos "" }
                |> view
                |> Query.fromHtml
                |> Query.find [ tag "img", attribute (Attr.src srcToClick) ]
                |> Event.simulate Event.click
                |> Event.expect (ClickedPhoto url)
```

Simulates a click on the img, and checks that the appropriate ClickedPhoto message was sent to update

Part 3

Building bigger

The final two chapters deal with more advanced topics: data modeling and single-page applications. These chapters build on everything you've learned so far, and introduce new concepts such as routing, working with recursive data, and a powerful performance optimization technique.

In chapter 7, you'll learn how to model an interactive folder tree, involving two important data structures: dictionaries and recursive custom types. It also introduces a second page to the application. Chapter 8 then connects this page with the page you built in chapters 1 through 6, creating a single-page application with routing and navigation. It also introduces the most common performance optimization technique in Elm.

By the end of these two chapters, you'll know enough to dive into just about any Elm project and be able to make changes to it. There might be some unfamiliar terms or techniques here and there, but everything else in Elm involves variations on what you've learned in this book. You'll know everything you need to build your next fully featured user interface in Elm

Data modeling

This chapter covers

- Storing values with associated keys by using dictionaries
- Building interactive trees by using recursive custom types
- Using intermediate representations to decode JSON incrementally
- Decoding recursive data structures with recursive JSON decoders

Our manager is back from vacation and eager to tell the team about a poolside revelation for a new Photo Groove feature: Photo Folders. (The original name was "Photo Pholders" but Marketing said *no*.) As our users' photo collections grow, they've been asking for ways to organize them. Folders are a tried-and-true way to offer exactly that!

To build this feature, we'll introduce a second page to Photo Groove. It will let users navigate through a folder hierarchy, with each folder potentially holding several photos as well as several other folders.

This Photo Folders page will also showcase a new feature one of our coworkers built: Related Photos. This feature automatically analyzes a user's photos, detects which ones are related to which others, and tags those photos as related on the server. The Photo Folders page will be the first to display these new Related Photos relationships. When the user selects a photo in a particular folder, we'll show them a larger version of the photo, as well as thumbnails of its related photos.

As we implement all this, I'll introduce new concepts you haven't seen before. To implement the Selected Photo display, we'll try out a new data structure: a *dictionary*. Once we're done with that, we'll see how to build our Folders display by using a *recursive custom type*, and how to model its expanding and collapsing by using *recursive messages*. Finally, we'll write some JSON decoders to load all this from the server, using *intermediate representations* and *recursive decoders* to handle the nested JSON format our server will send us for this page.

Let's get started!

7.1   *Storing values by keys in dictionaries*

The new Photo Folders page we'll be building will have two main sections: the folders themselves, followed by a large display of the selected photo and its related photos. When the user clicks a photo in either the Folders display or in the Related display, that photo will become the selected photo that we show in the Selected Photo display, along with its related photos. Figure 7.1 shows the page we'll be building in this chapter.

Because we can't implement a "click to select a photo" functionality for the Folders display until the Selected Photo display exists, we'll implement the Selected Photo display first and build the Folders display afterward.

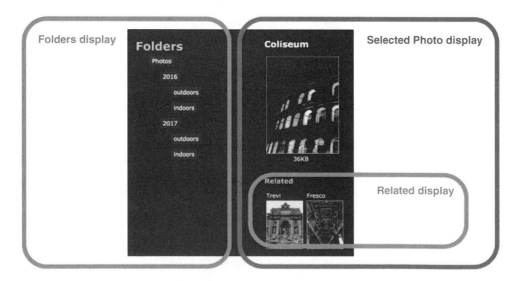

Figure 7.1   The Photo Folders page we'll be building in this chapter

7.1.1   *Setting up the page*

It's normal to put the code for each page in an Elm application in its own .elm file. This means we'll be giving the PhotoGroove.elm file we've been working on in the previous chapters a sibling .elm file.

Our new file will have its own Model, view, update, and main. Like PhotoGroove.elm, the first thing it will do when the page loads is to fetch Model data from the server by using the Http module, similarly to the way we did it in chapter 4. The new file will be completely independent of PhotoGroove.elm—at least until we start linking the two pages together in chapter 8.

Over the last several chapters, we've built up PhotoGroove.elm gradually. First we used a record for our Msg, and then later a custom type. We also moved from Browser.sandbox to Browser.element.

This time, we can use the knowledge acquired over the previous chapters to cut right to the chase, by using Browser.element with a custom type for our Msg from the get-go. Let's create a file named PhotoFolders.elm in the src/ directory, with the following contents.

Listing 7.1   PhotoFolders.elm

```
module PhotoFolders exposing (main)                        ◁──┐ We'll define
                                                                │ main later.
import Http
import Json.Decode as Decode exposing (Decoder, int, list, string)   ◁─
import Json.Decode.Pipeline exposing (required)
                                                    "as Decode" lets us call (for
                                                      example) Decode.succeed
                                                    instead of Json.Decode.succeed.
type alias Model =
    { selectedPhotoUrl : Maybe String         ◁──┐ The selected photo, if the
    }                                             │ user has selected one


initialModel : Model
initialModel =
    { selectedPhotoUrl = Nothing }


init : () -> ( Model, Cmd Msg )
init _ =                                  Uses initialModel as the        Begins an HTTP
    ( initialModel           ◁──────┘      model when the page loads       request to load
    , Http.get                                                             data from the
        { url = "http://elm-in-action.com/folders/list"                    server when
        , expect = Http.expectJson GotInitialModel modelDecoder            the page loads
        }
    )


modelDecoder : Decoder Model
modelDecoder =                             For now, ignore the server's response
    Decode.succeed initialModel      ◁──┘  and succeed with initialModel.
```

```
type Msg
    = ClickedPhoto String
    | GotInitialModel (Result Http.Error Model)
```

> **We'll use this when the user clicks a photo to select it.**

```
update : Msg -> Model -> ( Model, Cmd Msg )
update msg model =
    case msg of
        ClickedPhoto url ->
            ( { model | selectedPhotoUrl = Just url }, Cmd.none )

        GotInitialModel (Ok newModel) ->
            ( newModel, Cmd.none )

        GotInitialModel (Err _) ->
            ( model, Cmd.none )
```

> **The SelectPhotoUrl message sets selectedPhotoUrl in the model.**

> **Accepts the new model we received from the server**

> **We'll ignore page load errors for now.**

This gets our new page's Model started with a single field: selectedPhotoUrl, a
Maybe String that is initially Nothing—indicating the user has not selected a photo
yet—and that will be set to a particular photo's URL string if the user selects that photo.

We've also defined two Msg values:

- The ClickedPhoto message sets the selectedPhotoUrl field in the model
  to be the URL contained in the message. We'll use this later, in the page's view
  function, when the user clicks a photo.

- The GotInitialModel message contains data coming back from the server.
  Just as in chapter 4, our update function will receive that data after the HTTP
  request we specified in init either fails or successfully completes. If it completes, update will replace our Model with the contents of this message.

We can use what we have here to describe a page that loads photos from the server
and then lets users click them to select them. To complete this, we'll need to define a
view function to render it all, as well as a main function to tie everything together.

RENDERING THE NEW PAGE

We'll begin by adding a few imports to support our view. These go at the top of our
imports:

```
import Browser
import Html exposing (...)
import Html.Attributes exposing (class, src)
import Html.Events exposing (onClick)
```

Next, let's add these view and main definitions to the end of PhotoFolders.elm:

```
view : Model -> Html Msg
view model =
    h1 [] [ text "The Grooviest Folders the world has ever seen" ]


main : Program () Model Msg
main =
    Browser.element
```

```
{ init = init
, view = view
, update = update
, subscriptions = \_ -> Sub.none
}
```

This won't display any actual photos yet, but it will at least get us to a point where we can bring up the page in a browser. We'll make this `view` function more featureful later.

VIEWING THE PAGE

Let's compile this new file by using a command similar to the one we've been running in the previous chapters, but this time with PhotoFolders.elm instead of Photo-Groove.elm:

```
elm make --output=app.js src/PhotoFolders.elm
```

Now we can bring up the page in our browser to see how it looks so far. Before we can do this, we'll need to make one small tweak so that our new `PhotoFolders` code gets used instead of the `PhotoGroove` code as before. To do that, we'll need to replace the final `<script>` tag in index.html (the one that starts off `var app = ...`) with this much smaller one:

```
<script>
    var app = Elm.PhotoFolders.init({node: document.getElementById("app")});
</script>
```

> **NOTE** Not only does the word `PhotoGroove` in this `var app =` declaration change to `PhotoFolders`, but we also stop passing `Pasta.version` and delete all the code in the `<script>` related to `ports`.

Great! Save it and open the page in your browser. You should see something like figure 7.2.

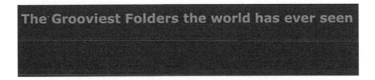

The Grooviest Folders the world has ever seen

Figure 7.2   Viewing the majestic new Photo Folders page

Now that we have a basic page up and running, we're ready to start making it useful.

7.1.2   Storing photos by URL in a dictionary

As impressive as this page already is, it'll be even better when it does something! When the user selects a photo, we want to show a large version of it, along with some smaller thumbnails of its related photos. Figure 7.3 shows how we want it to look.

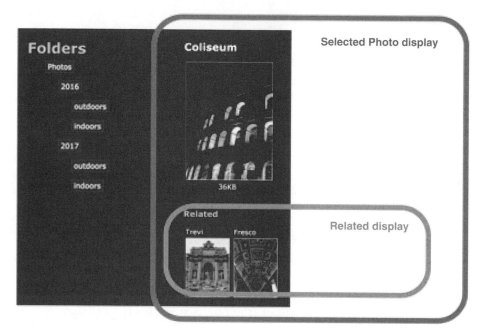

Figure 7.3   The Selected Photo and Related displays we'll be rendering

To implement this, we'll begin by creating two new functions, `viewSelectedPhoto` and `viewRelatedPhoto`, which we'll call from `view` to render the selected photo and its related thumbnails. Let's add the contents of the following listing to the end of PhotoFolders.elm.

Listing 7.2   PhotoFolders.elm

```
type alias Photo =
    { title : String
    , size : Int
    , relatedUrls : List String      ⟵─┐ We didn't have this field
    , url : String                          in PhotoGroove.elm.
    }


viewSelectedPhoto : Photo -> Html Msg         Calling this function will require getting
viewSelectedPhoto photo =                      a Photo from our Model somehow.
    div
        [ class "selected-photo" ]
        [ h2 [] [ text photo.title ]
        , img [ src (urlPrefix ++ "photos/" ++ photo.url ++ "/full") ] []
        , span [] [ text (String.fromInt photo.size ++ "KB") ]
        , h3 [] [ text "Related" ]
        , div [ class "related-photos" ]
            (List.map viewRelatedPhoto photo.relatedUrls)
        ]
```

Calls
viewRelatedPhoto
on each URL in
photo.relatedUrls

```
viewRelatedPhoto : String -> Html Msg
viewRelatedPhoto url =
    img
        [ class "related-photo"
        , onClick (ClickedPhoto url)          Uses the ClickedPhoto
        , src (urlPrefix ++ "photos/" ++ url ++ "/thumb")   message we defined earlier
        ]
        []


urlPrefix : String
urlPrefix =
    "http://elm-in-action.com/"
```

We started by defining a `type alias` `Photo` much like the one we used in Photo-Groove.elm, except the one we defined before didn't have a `relatedUrls` field. (After all, the Related Photos feature didn't exist back then!) We then used `Photo` to annotate `viewSelectedPhoto`.

STORING AND RETRIEVING PHOTOS

Our new `viewSelectedPhoto` function takes a `Photo` as an argument, but our `Model` currently holds only a `Maybe String`. We'll need to begin storing some full-blown `Photo` records in our `Model` if we want to call that function.

Fortunately, our server will provide our `Model` with every `Photo` value we need when the page loads. This begs the question: once we obtain these `Photo` records from the server, how should we store them?

USING A LIST OF PHOTOS

One way to store the photos would be to add a `photos : List Photo` field to our `Model`. Is a `List` the best choice we could make for this use case? Let's think through how `view` would use that `List Photo` to call `viewSelectedPhoto : Photo -> Html Msg`.

To call `viewSelectedPhoto`, we'd take the selected URL from `model.selectedPhotoUrl` (assuming it's a `Just` rather than a `Nothing`) and look through every single record in our `List` in search of a `Photo` whose `url` field matches that selected URL. If we found a matching `Photo` record, we'd pass it to `viewSelectedPhoto`. Otherwise, we'd have nothing to render and would do nothing.

Although this approach works, it has two issues:

- It's not terribly efficient for the task at hand. If the selected photo happens to be the final one in a list of a thousand photos, we have to examine every single one of those photos, one at a time, to find it. It would be more efficient to use a data structure that didn't have to look through every single `Photo` in that situation.
- In the event that multiple `Photo` records happen to have the given URL, it's not immediately clear how we will handle that.

USING A DICTIONARY OF PHOTOS

We can avoid both of these problems by storing the photos, not in a list, but in a *dictionary*.

DEFINITION   A *dictionary* is a collection in which each *value* is associated with a unique *key*.

Back in chapter 1, we talked about how *lists* in Elm must have elements of the same type: we can have [1, 2], or ["a", "b"], but not ["a", 1]. This is because lists can be iterated over—using functions like `List.map`—and reliable iteration depends on elements having consistent types. We also covered how *records* in Elm can store content with mixed types, which comes at the cost of making it impossible to iterate over their fields or values.

Dictionaries have some of the characteristics of lists and some of the characteristics of records. As with lists, we can iterate over them. As with records, the values in a dictionary have no notion of a position—but we can efficiently look up any value by providing the associated key. Each key is guaranteed to be unique within the dictionary, so it is impossible to encounter multiple matches. This makes a dictionary a great choice for our use case. Table 7.1 summarizes these trade-offs among the three data structures.

Table 7.1   Comparing records, lists, and dictionaries

Structure	Iteration	Mixed type elements	Lookup by position	Lookup by key
Record	Unsupported	Supported	Unsupported	Efficient
List	Supported	Unsupported	Supported	Inefficient
Dictionary	Supported	Unsupported	Unsupported	Efficient

Let's get a better feel for dictionaries by playing around in `elm repl`. The following listing shows how to create a dictionary and retrieve values from it by using `Dict.fromList` and `Dict.get`.

Listing 7.3   Creating dictionaries and accessing their values

```
> import Dict
> dict = Dict.fromList [ ( "pi, give or take", 3.14 ), ( "answer", 42 ) ]
Dict.fromList [ … ] : Dict String Float          ◁── Dict String Float
                                                       means "strings
                                                       for keys, floats
                                                       for values."
> Dict.get "a key we never added!" dict     │ Dict.get returns Nothing
Nothing : Maybe Float                        │ if the key is not found.

> Dict.get "pi, give or take" dict     │ Dict.get returns Just
Just 3.14 : Maybe Float                │ and the value if found.

> Dict.get "answer" dict          │ Dict.get on a Dict String Float
Just 42 : Maybe Float             │ always returns a Maybe Float.
```

The `Dict.fromList` function takes a list of tuples and returns a `Dict`. Each tuple represents a key-value pair that will be stored in the dictionary.

If we call `Dict.get` on the resulting dictionary, passing a particular key, it will return the associated value—but only if it finds one. Remember that in chapter 3 we saw that `Array.get` returns a Maybe value to represent the possibility that the requested element was not found? `Dict.get` does the same thing here: it returns `Nothing` if the given key was not present in the dictionary, and if the key was present, it returns the corresponding value wrapped in a `Just`.

> **TIP** It's common for functions that look up values within Elm data structures to return a Maybe if the desired element might not be found. This approach is used in `Array.get`, `Dict.get`, `List.head`, and more.

DICT'S TYPE PARAMETERS

You may recall that `List` and `Array` are parameterized on one type—for example, `List String` or `Array Int`. In contrast, `Dict` has two type parameters: one for the key, and one for the value—for example, `Dict Char Int` or `Dict String Photo`. In listing 7.2, we had a `Dict String Float` because we passed a `List ( String, Float )` to `Dict.fromList`, which meant this dictionary would have a `String` for each of its keys, and a `Float` for each of its values.

Constrained type variables: comparable, number, appendable

The type annotation for `Dict.get` is (`comparable -> Dict comparable value -> Maybe value`). That `comparable` is no ordinary type variable! In chapter 3, we noted that type variables can have *almost* any name you like. The exceptions responsible for that "almost" are the type variable names reserved for Elm's *constrained* type variables, which behave differently from other type variables:

- `number`, which can resolve to `Int` or `Float`
- `appendable`, which can resolve to `String` or `List`
- `comparable`, which can resolve to `Int`, `Float`, `Char`, `String`, `List` or a tuple of these

As an example of what these do, let's look at the multiplication operator, (`*`). If the type of (`*`) were `a -> a -> a`, you could use it to multiply anything—numbers, strings, you name it. However, its actual type is `number -> number -> number`. Because `number` is one of Elm's constrained type variables, `number -> number -> number` can resolve to only one of the following:

```
Int -> Int -> Int
Float -> Float -> Float
```

The `number -> number -> number` function will resolve to one of these after it gets passed either an `Int` or a `Float` as one of its arguments. This means that multiplying two `Int` values will return an `Int`, multiplying two `Float` values will return a `Float`, and attempting to multiply an `Int` by a `Float` will result in a type mismatch. (The most common way to resolve this type mismatch is by calling `toFloat` on the `Int`.)

If you need to annotate a function that takes two independent `number` types, you can add more characters after the word `number` to create distinct type variable names that are still constrained by `number`. For example, `number`, `numberB`, `number2`, and `numberOfCats` all have different names but the same `number` constraint.

> **(continued)**
>
> The number constraint typically appears in core functions having to do with mathematics. appendable is used by the (++) operator. comparable appears in the definitions of Dict and Set, as well as in List.sort and mathematical inequality operators like (<) and (>=). Data structures like Dict and Set use the comparable constraint to store their contents efficiently, which involves sorting them—and only the comparable types have implicit sorting functions built in.
>
> In the case of Dict, its keys must be comparable, but its values can be any type. We can have a Dict String Photo because Photo is the value type, which can be anything, and String is comparable, making it an acceptable key type. We could not have a Dict Photo String, though, because Photo is a type alias for a record, and neither records nor custom types are comparable.
>
> To create a dictionary-like collection with non-comparable keys, you can use a third-party package like pzp1997/assoc-list. Its API differs from Dict only in that its keys do not have the comparable restriction, and as a consequence, its runtime performance is worse than Dict's.

ADDING A DICTIONARY TO MODEL

Let's introduce a dictionary of photos to our model. First we'll import the Dict module:

```
import Dict exposing (Dict)
```

Then we'll update Model to include a Dict String Photo field—with the String being the photo URL we'll use as the key, and the Photo being the corresponding value:

```
type alias Model =
    { selectedPhotoUrl : Maybe String
    , photos : Dict String Photo
    }
```

If we recompile, we'll get an error. initialModel now needs to include a photos field. We'll have it initialize that field to an empty dictionary by using Dict.empty like so:

```
initialModel : Model
initialModel =
    { selectedPhotoUrl = Nothing
    , photos = Dict.empty
    }
```

Later in the chapter, we'll override this empty dictionary with some Photo records loaded from the server, but for now, having it start off empty will be enough to get our code compiling again.

CALLING VIEWSELECTEDPHOTO FROM VIEW

Now we have a `viewSelectedPhoto` that does what we want, but only if `view` passes it a single `Photo` argument. How can `view` do that? The only argument `view` receives is `Model`, which has a `Dict String Photo` field and a `Maybe String` field, but no other sources of `Photo` values. How can we get a single `Photo` from this combination of values?

In situations like this, it's useful to take stock of the types we have to work with and the type we want to get to. It often turns out only a few functions or language features do anything useful with those types.

Here's a summary of where we are:

- We *want* a `Photo` for the selected photo, so `view` can pass it to `viewSelected-Photo`.
- We *have* a `Maybe String` indicating which photo is selected, if any.
- We *have* a `Dict String Photo` of all the photos.

How can we use what we *have* to get what we *want*?

USING DICT.GET WITH A MAYBE STRING

To get from a `Maybe String` of our selected photo's URL (assuming we actually have one) to a `Photo` record for that selected photo, we'll need to do three things:

1 Handle the possibility that `selectedPhotoUrl` is `Nothing`.
2 If it isn't `Nothing`, pass the selected photo URL to `Dict.get` on `model.photos`.
3 Handle the possibility that `Dict.get` returns `Nothing`.

We can do this with `Dict.get` and a nested case-expression, as shown in the following listing.

Listing 7.4 Implementing `view` as a nested case-expression

```
selectedPhoto : Html Msg
selectedPhoto =
    case model.selectedPhotoUrl of           Confirms selectedPhotoUrl
        Just url ->                            is not nothing
            case Dict.get url model.photos of      Confirms that url is present
                Just photo ->                       in the dictionary
                    viewSelectedPhoto photo

                Nothing ->
                    text ""
                                          Empty text nodes
        Nothing ->                        render invisibly.
            text ""
```

REFACTORING TO USE MAYBE.ANDTHEN

We can express this same logic more concisely using the `Maybe.andThen` function:

```
Maybe.andThen : (original -> Maybe final) -> Maybe original -> Maybe final
```

Whenever we have two nested case-expressions like this, with both of them handling `Nothing` the same way, `Maybe.andThen` does exactly the same thing as the code we had before.

We'll use `Maybe.andThen` when we define `selectedPhoto` in our actual `view` function. Let's replace our existing `view` function with the following definition.

Listing 7.5   Implementing `view` using `Maybe.andThen`

```
view : Model -> Html Msg
view model =
    let
        photoByUrl : String -> Maybe Photo      ┐ Returns the photo with the
        photoByUrl url =                        │ given URL in model.photos
            Dict.get url model.photos           ┘

        selectedPhoto : Html Msg
        selectedPhoto =
            case Maybe.andThen photoByUrl model.selectedPhotoUrl of
                Just photo ->                       ┐ photo is the selected photo,
                    viewSelectedPhoto photo         ┘ if found in model.photos.

                Nothing ->                      ┐ Finishes view by wrapping
                    text ""                     │ selectedPhoto in the
    in                                          ┘ structure the page needs
    div [ class "content" ]
        [ div [ class "selected-photo" ] [ selectedPhoto ] ]
```

Comparing andThen and map

In chapter 6, you learned about `Result.map`, and compared it to `Json.Decode.map` and `List.map` in section 6.1.3. There is also a `Result.andThen` function, which works a bit like the `map` function we discussed in chapter 6. Here's how their types compare:

```
Result.andThen : (a -> Result x b) -> Result x a -> Result x b
Result.map     : (a ->          b) -> Result x a -> Result x b
```

Both functions accept a callback and a `Result`; both return the given value unchanged when given an `Err` variant; and when given an `Ok`, both pass the value inside that `Ok` to their callbacks.

They differ in that if `Result.map` receives an `Ok` variant, it always returns an `Ok` variant. The content of that `Ok` variant might be different, but it will definitely be an `Ok` and not an `Err`. In contrast, `Result.andThen` returns whatever its callback returns—which means it can potentially receive an `Ok` and turn it into an `Err`.

The `Maybe.map` function has a very similar relationship to `Maybe.andThen`:

```
Maybe.andThen : (a -> Maybe b) -> Maybe a -> Maybe b
Maybe.map     : (a ->       b) -> Maybe a -> Maybe b
```

Similarly to the behavior of `Result.map`, if `Maybe.map` receives a `Just`, it always returns a `Just`. If it receives `Nothing`, it returns `Nothing`.

Similarly to the behavior of `Result.andThen`, `Maybe.andThen` returns whatever its callback returns—meaning it can potentially receive a `Just` and turn it into a `Nothing`. As we will see later in the chapter, a similar `Json.Decode.andThen` function can likewise turn successes into failures.

This additional capability makes `andThen` strictly more powerful than `map`. Anything we can implement with `map`, we could implement with `andThen` instead. However, `map` is often preferred in practice because it's more concise, and more often than not, the extra power of `andThen` is not needed.

RENDERING THE SELECTED PHOTO

Now everything compiles, but we can't see if it's working properly because we initialize our photo dictionary to `Dict.empty` and never change it. If we pretend we're already able to decode some useful `Photo` data from the server, we'll be able to try out our new page.

Let's change `modelDecoder` to this:

```
modelDecoder : Decoder Model
modelDecoder =
    Decode.succeed
        { selectedPhotoUrl = Just "trevi"
        , photos = Dict.fromList
            [ ( "trevi"
                , { title = "Trevi"
                  , relatedUrls = [ "coli", "fresco" ]
                  , size = 34
                  , url ="trevi"
                  }
                )
            , ( "fresco"
                , { title = "Fresco"
                  , relatedUrls = [ "trevi" ]
                  , size = 46
                  , url ="fresco"
                  }
                )
            , ( "coli"
                , { title = "Coliseum"
                  , relatedUrls - [ "trevi", "fresco" ]
                  , size = 36
                  , url ="coli"
                  }
                )
            ]
        }
```

If we rerun `elm make --output=app.js PhotoFolders.elm` and open the result in the browser, we can now see a lovely large photo with some related photos below it, as shown in figure 7.4.

Figure 7.4   Viewing the selected photo with related photos below it

Fantastic! Not only does this page display the related photos below the selected one, but we can click them to change which one is selected. Next, we'll introduce the pholders—er, *folders!*

7.2   *Modeling trees by using recursive custom types*

Because another of our coworkers is taking care of the page where users can edit their folders, we are free to focus on the page that lets users browse through them. Later in the chapter, we'll load the folders and their contents from the server, but we'll start by hardcoding them just as we did with the Related Photos feature. This way, we can get the interaction working to our satisfaction before we have to deal with whatever data format the server happens to give us.

Each folder could contain one or more photos, as well as one or more subfolders—each of which can also contain more photos and more subfolders, and so on. This relationship forms a *tree*, which is a data structure we never used in the previous chapters.

7.2.1   *Defining trees by using custom types*

Let's say we tried to represent our folder tree structure with a type alias, like so:

```
type alias Folder = { name : String, subfolders : List Folder }
```

This won't work! If we try to compile it, we'll get an error. What's the problem with it?

The purpose of `type alias` is to name a type annotation. When the compiler encounters this name, it substitutes in the type annotation we associated with that name and proceeds as normal.

Now let's suppose the compiler encounters a `Folder` annotation and begins to expand it into the complete type. What happens? The expansion would go something like this:

```
{ name: String, photoUrls : List String, subfolders : List
    { name : String, photoUrls : List String, subfolders : List
        { name : String, photoUrls : List String, subfolders : List …
```

Uh-oh. Trying to expand that type annotation would never end! This is why defining a `type alias` in terms of itself doesn't work, and why we'll need to use something else to define this `Folder` type.

RECURSIVE CUSTOM TYPES

Fortunately, whereas type aliases give a name to an existing type, custom types actually define a brand-new type—and they can refer to themselves in their own definitions. Custom types that do this are known as a *recursive* custom types.

One of the many data structures we can define using a recursive custom type is a linked list—such as the `List` type we all know and love. Under the hood, an Elm `List` is structured like this custom type:

```
type MyList elem
    = Empty
    | Prepend elem (MyList elem)
```

> **NOTE** When we write `[ 1, 2, 3 ]`, it's essentially syntax sugar for `Prepend 1 (Prepend 2 (Prepend 3 Empty))`. No other language support is necessary; every `List` function we've been using in this book—map, head, and so on—can be built using nothing more than case-expressions on this custom type.

DEFINING FOLDER AS A RECURSIVE CUSTOM TYPE

We can use a similar approach to define `Folder` as a recursive custom type:

```
type Folder =
    Folder
        { name : String
        , photoUrls : List String
        , subfolders : List Folder
        }
```

Let's add this `type Folder` declaration right above our `type alias Model` declaration in PhotoFolders.elm.

Notice that whereas other custom types we've seen have had multiple variants—for example, `type Msg = ClickedPhoto String | ClickedSize ThumbnailSize`—this custom type has only one variant. It holds plenty of information, though, because that one variant contains a record: `type Folder = Folder { name : String, ... }`.

This is a common technique in Elm: when a `type alias` is the wrong fit, you can upgrade it to a custom type with a single variant. It's typical when doing this to give the single variant the same name as the type itself—in this case, `type Folder = Folder { ... }`—but we just as easily could have called it something like `type Folder = SingleFolder { ... }` instead.

> **TIP** This upgrade has no runtime cost when you run `elm make` with the `--optimize` flag. When Elm's compiler sees a custom type with a single variant, it "unboxes" it, such that `type Foo = Foo String` compiles down to a plain `String` at runtime.

ADDING HARDCODED DATA TO MODEL AND INIT

Now that we've defined `Folder`, let's make these changes to `Model` and `init`:

1 Add a `root : Folder` field to the end of our type alias `Model` declaration. This will represent our root folder, which will contain all the subfolders inside it.

2 Add `root = Folder { name = "Loading...", photoUrls = [], subfolders = [] }` to the end of the `initialModel` record. This defines a placeholder root folder that says `"Loading..."` while we wait for the server to respond with the actual folders.

> **NOTE** It would be nicer to represent this by using something like a `Maybe Folder` to model that the data has not loaded yet. In chapter 8, we'll switch to an approach more like that.

Let's also give ourselves some example folders to work with, by adding a hardcoded root folder to our `modelDecoder` like so:

```
modelDecoder : Decoder Model
modelDecoder =
    Decode.succeed
        { selectedPhotoUrl = …
        , photos = …
        , root =
            Folder
                { name = "Photos", photoUrls = []
                , subfolders =
                    [ Folder
                        { name = "2016", photoUrls = [ "trevi", "coli" ]
                        , subfolders =
                            [ Folder
                                { name = "outdoors"
                                , photoUrls = [], subfolders = []
                                }
                            , Folder
                                { name = "indoors"
                                , photoUrls = [ "fresco" ], subfolders = []
                                }
                            ]
                        }
                    , Folder
                        { name = "2017", photoUrls = []
                        , subfolders =
```

```
                              [ Folder
                                  { name = "outdoors"
                                  , photoUrls = [], subfolders = []
                                  }
                              , Folder
                                  { name = "indoors"
                                  , photoUrls = [], subfolders = []
                                  }
                              ]
                          }
                      ]
                  }
          }
```

Now we can access model.root from our view function, and use it to render some folders.

RENDERING FOLDERS

To render the folders, we'll start by writing a viewFolder function that renders a single folder. Let's add the contents of the following listing right after viewRelated-Photo.

Listing 7.6 viewFolder

```
viewFolder : Folder -> Html Msg
viewFolder (Folder folder) =                    ◁——  Inline pattern
    let                                               match
        subfolders =
            List.map viewFolder folder.subfolders   ◁——  viewFolder
    in                                                     calls itself.
    div [ class "folder" ]
        [ label [] [ text folder.name ]
        , div [ class "subfolders" ] subfolders
        ]
```

This viewFolder implementation demonstrates a couple of new tricks.

DESTRUCTURING SINGLE-VARIANT CUSTOM TYPES

First up is that viewFolder (Folder folder) syntax. This is a syntax shorthand that makes our code more concise. Our Folder type is a custom type that holds a single variant, and inside that variant is a record we want to access (with { name : String } and so on).

One way to access that record is to use a case-expression to destructure our custom type's one and only variant (the variant named Folder, just like the type itself), the way we did in chapter 3:

```
viewFolder : Folder -> Html Msg
viewFolder wrappedFolder =
    case wrappedFolder of
        Folder folder ->
            ..."folder" now refers to the record we want...
```

Inside that one branch of the case-expression, `folder` would refer to the record we want, and we could then use it however we pleased. There's nothing wrong with this code, except that it could be shorter without losing any clarity.

Because the `Folder` custom type has exactly one variant, Elm lets us avoid writing a full case-expression by using the shorthand `viewFolder (Folder folder)` = to destructure it inline instead. That shorter version is equivalent to the preceding longer case-expression version.

RECURSIVE FUNCTIONS

Next, we have this expression: `List.map  viewFolder  folder.subfolders`. Notice that `viewFolder` is calling itself, making it a *recursive* function.

> **DEFINITION**   A function that calls itself is known as a *recursive* function.

INCORPORATING VIEWFOLDER INTO VIEW

Let's use our hardcoded `Model` data to try out this `viewFolder` function. Add `div [ class "folders" ]` right before `div [ class "selected-photo" ]`, with the following inside it:

```
div [ class "content" ]
    [ div [ class "folders" ]
        [ h1 [] [ text "Folders" ]
        , viewFolder model.root
        ]
    , div [ class "selected-photo" ] [ selectedPhoto ]
    ]
```

Let's recompile and check out the results of our efforts in the browser; see figure 7.5.

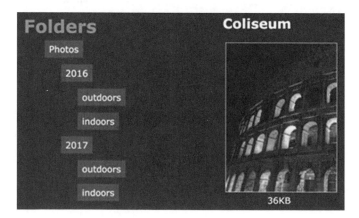

Figure 7.5   Viewing folders

Looking good! We can see our hardcoded folders rendered to the screen, but clicking them still does nothing at this point. Next, we'll introduce the ability to expand and collapse them.

7.2.2 Recursive messages

Whenever the user clicks a folder, we want it to toggle between being expanded and collapsed. This means we'll need to introduce a new piece of state to our `Folder`: a `Bool` indicating whether the folder is expanded. Let's start by making these changes:

1 Add an `expanded : Bool` field to the end of the record in our type `Folder` definition.
2 Add `expanded = True` to each of the `Folder` records in our hardcoded `modelDecoder`. (A quick way to do this is to find/replace all instances of `photo-Urls =` with `expanded = True, photoUrls =` in our PhotoFolders.elm file.)

DESCRIBING DESCENT

To implement this feature, we'll need to add an `onClick` handler to each folder, to toggle its expanded state. Here's how we'll do this:

1 Pass `onClick` a new `Msg` that tells `update` which folder the user clicked.
2 When `update` receives one of these messages, descend from the root folder into the folder tree and toggle the appropriate folder's expanded field in the `Model`.

The following listing shows the code we'll add to the end of PhotoFolders.elm to accomplish this.

Listing 7.7 `toggleExpanded` and `FolderPath`

```
type FolderPath                                          ◁──┐ A path from a folder to
    = End                                                    │ a particular subfolder
    | Subfolder Int FolderPath      ◁──┐ Like Folder, FolderPath is
                                        │ also a recursive custom type.

toggleExpanded : FolderPath -> Folder -> Folder
toggleExpanded path (Folder folder) =               ◁──┐ Destructuring the Folder
    case path of                                        │ custom type inline
        End ->
            Folder { folder | expanded = not folder.expanded }

        Subfolder targetIndex remainingPath ->      ◁──┐ targetIndex is an Int.
            let                                          │ remainingPath is a FolderPath.
                subfolders : List Folder
                subfolders =
                    List.indexedMap transform folder.subfolders

                transform : Int -> Folder -> Folder
                transform currentIndex currentSubfolder =
                    if currentIndex == targetIndex then
                        toggleExpanded remainingPath currentSubfolder      ◁──┐

                    else                                        toggleExpanded is
                        currentSubfolder                        recursive; it calls itself.
            in
            Folder { folder | subfolders = subfolders }
```

"not" swaps True for False, and vice versa. (annotation pointing to `Folder { folder | expanded = not folder.expanded }`) `toggleExpanded` takes a `FolderPath` and a `Folder`, and does one of the following:

- If `FolderPath` is `End`, there are no subfolders to traverse into, so toggle the expanded value on the given folder.
- If `FolderPath` is `Subfolder targetIndex`, look through the given root's subfolders until we find the one at position `targetIndex`. Then call `toggleExpanded` again, this time passing that subfolder as the new root folder, and passing the remaining `FolderPath` after discarding the `Subfolder` value we just handled.

Technically, the function always toggles only the "root folder," but its notion of which folder is the root changes as it processes `Subfolder` values.

Once it has resolved all the subfolders, the final call to `toggleExpanded` will receive the originally desired subfolder as its "root" argument, along with `Root` as its `FolderPath`, meaning it will toggle the expanded value as we want. Figure 7.6 shows how `FolderPath` can model a path to whichever folder the user clicks, and how `toggleExpanded` recurses along that path.

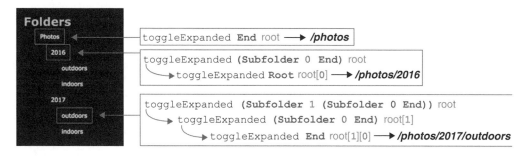

Figure 7.6 Using `toggleExpanded` to represent user interaction with folders

LIST.INDEXEDMAP

To update only the subfolder at the desired index, `toggleExpanded` uses `List.indexedMap`, a function we haven't used before. It works similarly to `List.map`, but with one difference. Here are their types side by side:

```
List.map        :         (oldVal -> newVal) -> List oldVal -> List newVal
List.indexedMap : (Int -> oldVal -> newVal) -> List oldVal -> List newVal
```

The only thing `List.indexedMap` does differently from `List.map` is that it passes an additional value to the transformation function: an `Int` representing the element's index within the list.

If you call `List.indexedMap` on the list `[ "foo", "bar", "baz" ]`, the transformation function will receive 0 and `"foo"`, then 1 and `"bar"`, and finally 2 and `"baz"`.

TRANSFORMING SUBFOLDERS BASED ON INDEX

Here's how `toggleExpanded` uses `List.indexedMap` to alter subfolders:

```
subfolders : List Folder
subfolders =
    List.indexedMap transform root.subfolders
```

When `transform` gets called by `indexedMap`, it receives not only the particular subfolder it's about to transform, but also that subfolder's index within the `subfolders` list. It makes use of that index like so:

```
transform : Int -> Folder -> Folder
transform currentIndex currentSubfolder =
    if currentIndex == targetIndex then
        toggleExpanded remainingPath currentSubfolder
    else
        currentSubfolder
```

Because the `else` branch returns the original `subfolder` unchanged, this `transform` function actually transforms `subfolder` only if `currentIndex == targetIndex`. It transforms the subfolder at the requested `targetIndex` and leaves the others alone.

INCORPORATING FOLDERPATH INTO MSG

Next, we'll connect `toggleExpand` to `update` by expanding our `Msg` type, introducing a `ClickedFolder` variant to go with our existing `ClickedPhoto` and `GotInitialModel` variants. This new variant will fire whenever the user clicks a folder, and it will use a `FolderPath` to describe where in the folder hierarchy the user clicked. The following listing shows the changes we'll make to `Msg` and `update`.

> **Listing 7.8 Adding `ClickedFolder` to `Msg` and `update`**

```
type Msg
    = ClickedPhoto String
    | GotInitialModel (Result Http.Error Model)      We'll make this fire when
    | ClickedFolder FolderPath                  ◁─── a user clicks a folder.


update : Msg -> Model -> ( Model, Cmd Msg )
update msg model =
    case msg of                            Adds a branch to cover
        ClickedFolder path ->         ◁─── our new Msg variant
            ( { model | root = toggleExpanded path model.root }, Cmd.none )

        ClickedPhoto url -> …
```

Next, we'll make things interactive by connecting this `update` logic to `view`.

7.2.3   *Event handlers with recursive messages*

Now that `update` supports a `Msg` called `ClickedFolder` that toggles the expanded state of a particular folder, we can modify our `viewFolder` function to make the folders toggle between being expanded and collapsed on the user's click. While we're at it, we can also start rendering the folders differently depending on whether they are expanded. The following listing shows how we'll make both of these changes.

Listing 7.9   `viewFolder` **with toggling expanded**

```
viewFolder : FolderPath -> Folder -> Html Msg
viewFolder path (Folder folder) =
    let
        viewSubfolder : Int -> Folder -> Html Msg          ⎫ Each subfolder's
        viewSubfolder index subfolder =                    ⎬ FolderPath is
            viewFolder (appendIndex index path) subfolder  ⎭ nested one deeper.

        folderLabel =                                                    ← Click the folder's name
            label [ onClick (ClickedFolder path) ] [ text folder.name ]    to toggle expanded.
    in
    if folder.expanded then
        let                                                ⎫ Renders each
            contents =                                     ⎬ subfolder by
                List.indexedMap viewSubfolder folder.subfolders  ⎭ using its index
        in
        div [ class "folder expanded" ]
            [ folderLabel                     ← Renders the folder's label
            , div [ class "contents" ] contents   before its contents
            ]
    else
        div [ class "folder collapsed" ] [ folderLabel ]  ← Don't render contents
                                                             of collapsed folders.

appendIndex : Int -> FolderPath -> FolderPath
appendIndex index path =
    case path of
        End ->
            Subfolder index End                ← Replaces the original End
                                                 with (Subfolder index End)
        Subfolder subfolderIndex remainingPath ->      ← Recurses until
            Subfolder subfolderIndex (appendIndex index remainingPath)  we reach the End
```

APPENDINDEX

The `appendIndex` function is another recursive function. (As it turns out, they come up a lot when working with tree structures.) This one adds a new subfolder index onto the end of a `FolderPath`, so that `viewFolder` can build up a `FolderPath` as it works its way from the root folder through the subfolders.

> **NOTE**   If we wrote (`Subfolder index path`) instead of (`appendIndex index path`) inside `viewFolder`, the folder paths would get reversed. This wouldn't make a noticeable difference for the root folder and its first subdirectories, but it would result in some funky behavior when toggling other subfolders.

MODIFYING VIEW

We'll also need to modify our top-level `view` function to change how it renders the root folder:

```
viewFolder End model.root
```

Thanks to our new `view` function, a `ClickedFolder` message will be sent to `update` whenever the user clicks a folder. Figure 7.7 shows the exact `Msg` that will be sent to `update` when each folder is clicked.

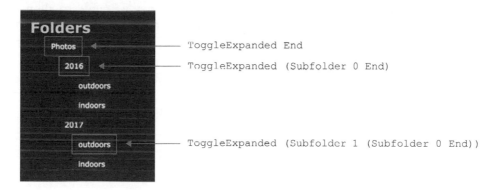

Figure 7.7   User clicks a subfolder, and `ClickedFolder` gets sent to `update`

Great! We have only one step remaining: make it so when the user clicks a photo, it becomes the selected one.

SELECTING A PHOTO ON CLICK

First we'll introduce a `viewPhoto` function above `viewSelectedPhoto`, which will render an individual photo within a folder. We'll have this function reuse our existing `ClickedPhoto` message from section 7.1.1 like so:

```
viewPhoto : String -> Html Msg
viewPhoto url =
    div [ class "photo" , onClick (ClickedPhoto url) ]
        [ text url ]
```

Next, we'll use `viewPhoto` to render the photos right below where we're rendering the subfolders. Let's change the definition of `contents` in the let-expression at the end of `viewFolder` to look like this:

```
let
    contents =
        List.append
            (List.indexedMap viewSubfolder folder.subfolders)
            (List.map viewPhoto folder.photoUrls)
in
```

> **NOTE**   If you want an extra challenge, at the end of this chapter try introducing a feature whereby clicking the Related Photo causes the tree to expand to that photo.

Now the user can click a photo either within its folder or in the Related display, and have it become the selected photo. We've made things nicely interactive!

7.3   *Decoding graphs and trees*

We've now built an interface that renders a tree of folders, each of which can contain photos and subfolders, as well as a Selected Photo display that includes related photos. We defined hardcoded data for these displays so that we could try them out, but now it's time to load that data on the fly—by decoding JSON from our server.

7.3.1   *Decoding dictionaries*

The `Model` we defined in section 7.1 stores its photos in a field called `photos : Dict String Photo`. We'll start by defining a `Decoder (Dict String Photo)` that can decode one of those dictionaries from JSON.

SAMPLE JSON

Here's an example of the JSON format our server will send us to represent the photos:

```
{
    "2turtles": {
        "title": "Two Turtles ",
        "related_photos": ["beach"],
        "size": 27
    },
    "beach": {
        "title": "At Chang's Beach!",
        "related_photos": ["wake", "2turtles"],
        "size": 36
    },
    "wake ": {
        "title": "Boat wake",
        "related_photos": ["beach"],
        "size": 21
    }
}
```

In this structure, each photo's URL is a field in a JSON object, and the value associated with that URL holds the rest of the information about that photo. Translating this JSON into a `Photo` record will require decoding techniques that go beyond the basics we learned in chapter 4.

COMPARING PHOTO REPRESENTATIONS

First, let's compare how a `Photo` will be represented in our Elm code with the corresponding JSON representation coming from the server; see table 7.2.

Table 7.2 Comparing type alias `Photo` and the JSON object we get from the server

Elm record	JSON object

`type alias Photo =`
`    { title : String`
`    , size : Int`
`    , relatedUrls : List String`
`    , url : String`
`    }`
	`{`
	`    "title": "Chang's Beach",`
	`    "size": 24,`
	`    "related_photos": ["maui.jpg"]`
	`}`

INTERMEDIATE REPRESENTATIONS

The JSON object has three fields: `title`, `size`, and `related_photos`. That's not enough data for us to build a complete `Photo` record, but we can at least write a decoder that handles three of the four fields. We can figure out how to obtain the `url` field afterward. Let's begin by adding the code in the following listing to the end of PhotoFolders.elm.

Listing 7.10 Creating a `jsonPhotoDecoder`

```
type alias JsonPhoto =
    { title : String
    , size : Int
    , relatedUrls : List String     A type alias to represent the
    }                               Photo info we get from JSON


jsonPhotoDecoder : Decoder JsonPhoto     Decodes these fields from the JSON
jsonPhotoDecoder =                       object into a JsonPhoto record
    Decode.succeed JsonPhoto  ◁─┘
        |> required "title" string
        |> required "size" int                       As we saw in chapter 4, section
        |> required "related_photos" (list string) ◁─┘  4.3.2, this decodes a List String into
                                                       JsonPhoto's third field: relatedUrls.
```

The `JsonPhoto` type we've introduced here is an *intermediate representation*—a value we'll use only to help us translate from one value to another. In particular, a `Json-Photo` value will help us get from JSON to a `Photo` record.

DECODING URL STRINGS FROM ENCLOSING OBJECTS

We can now decode a `JsonPhoto` record, which holds all the information necessary to make a `Photo` record except a URL string. If we can find some way to decode a URL string, we could combine that with our `JsonPhoto` to end up with the `Decoder Photo` we want.

With that in mind, let's take another look at our sample JSON:

`{ "2turtles.jpg": { ... }, "beachday.jpg": { ... }, "day1maui.jpg": { ... } }`

Hey, there are the URLs we need, right in the object's keys!

DECODE.KEYVALUEPAIRS

We can decode those keys by using the `Decode.keyValuePairs` function. It has this type:

```
keyValuePairs : Decoder val -> Decoder (List ( String, val ))
```

This gives us a decoder that translates JSON objects into key-value tuples. The key's type is always `String`, because JSON object keys are strings by definition. The value's type depends on the `Decoder` we pass to the `keyValuePairs` function.

As an example, suppose we called `keyValuePairs jsonPhotoDecoder` and ran the resulting decoder on our JSON sample from earlier:

```
{ "turtles.jpg": { … }, "beach.jpg": { … }, "maui.jpg": { … } }
```

The output would be a list of (`String`, `JsonPhoto`) tuples like so:

```
output : List ( String, JsonPhoto )
output =
    [ ( "2turtles.jpg", { title = "Turtles & sandals", … } )
    , ( "beachday.jpg", { title = "At Chang's Beach!", … } )
    , ( "day1maui.jpg", { title = "First day on Maui", … } )
    ]
```

TRANSLATING THE LIST OF TUPLES INTO A DICTIONARY

Now we can decode a list of (`String`, `JsonPhoto`) tuples, where the `String` is a photo's URL and `JsonPhoto` is everything else but the URL. We're getting closer!

Let's write a function that translates that list into the dictionary we want, by converting each (`String`, `JsonPhoto`) tuple into a (`String`, `Photo`) tuple and then passing a list of those to `Dict.fromList`. Here's the code we'll add to the end of PhotoFolders.elm to do this:

```
finishPhoto : ( String, JsonPhoto ) -> ( String, Photo )
finishPhoto ( url, json ) =
    ( url
    , { url = url
      , size = json.size
      , title = json.title
      , relatedUrls = json.relatedUrls
      }
    )


fromPairs : List ( String, JsonPhoto ) -> Dict String Photo
fromPairs pairs =
    pairs
        |> List.map finishPhoto
        |> Dict.fromList
```

Just as we did back in section 7.1.2 with `viewSelectedPhoto`, let's once again take stock of the values we *have*, and see if we can combine them to get the value we *want*:

- We *want* a `Decoder (Dict String Photo)` for which each key is the `Photo`'s url.

- We *have* a Decoder (List (String, JsonPhoto)) for which each String is the URL that goes with that JsonPhoto.

How can we use what we *have* to get what we *want*?

COMBINING THE INGREDIENTS WITH DECODE.MAP

Just as before, often only a few functions or language features do anything useful with these types. In this case, we can reach our goal by using the Decode.map function, whose type may look familiar to fans of related artists List.map, Maybe.map, and Result.map:

```
Decode.map : (original -> goal) -> Decoder original -> Decoder goal
```

Here, our original type is List (String, JsonPhoto), and our goal type is Dict String Photo. Do we have a function that takes the one and returns the other?

We sure do! The fromPairs function we just wrote does exactly that. (What are the odds?) Let's add this to the end of PhotoFolders.elm, so that modelDecoder can use it later:

```
photosDecoder : Decoder (Dict String Photo)
photosDecoder =
    Decode.keyValuePairs jsonPhotoDecoder
        |> Decode.map fromPairs
```

TIP This "How can we use what we have to get what we want?" technique works out quite often. It's a useful approach beyond just the two examples in this chapter, with views and with JSON decoding.

Our quest for a Decoder (Dict String Photo) is at an end. Huzzah!

7.3.2 Decoding recursive JSON

Now that we've added a JSON decoder for our Photo record, all we need is to do the same for Folder, and we should be able to load a complete Model from our server. Let's see what JSON the server gives us for folders.

RECURSIVE JSON

Figure 7.8 shows a sample of the JSON we'll receive from the server to describe our folders.

```
{                       our Decoder (Dict String Photo) decodes this
  "name": "All Photos",
  "photos": {"2turtles": {title: "Turtles & sandals", … }},
  "subfolders": [
      {"name": "2016", "photos": {…}, "subfolders": […]},
      {"name": "2017", "photos": {…}, "subfolders": […]}
  ]
}            Each subfolder has the same structure as this outer Folder
```

Figure 7.8 Sample of the JSON we will get back from the server to describe a Folder

Let's focus on the outermost JSON object, which has this structure:

```
{"name": <folder name>, "photos": <photos>, "subfolders": <subfolders> }
```

Each of the `<subfolders>` also has this structure, and so do the subfolders' subfolders, and so on all the way down. It's a *recursive* JSON structure! Thankfully, our `Folder` type is already recursive, so it'll be able to store the data this JSON describes.

There's a catch: this is the one and only JSON structure the server will ever give us. That means we'll need to assemble our entire `Model` by using only JSON in this format.

DECODING THE COMPLETE MODEL

Can this possibly be enough data to decode a complete `Model`? For that, we need values for the `Model`'s `root : Folder` field as well as its `photos : Dict String Photo` field. Also, the `Dict String Photo` needs to be a single source of truth for all photos across all subfolders; otherwise, we won't be able to click any photo in any folder to select it.

But where is our single source of truth in this JSON? Sure, each subfolder has its own `photos` field containing some `Photo` values, but that's not a single source of truth. Technically, this JSON contains all the information we need, but it's not organized in our ideal format; the photo data is intermixed with the folder data, whereas we want them to be neatly separated.

GATHERING NESTED PHOTOS

We ask the team members who maintain this server endpoint if they'd be willing to make changes to their code to provide the JSON in our preferred format. But they're swamped lately—something about a "primary key overflow," whatever that means—and can't accommodate us.

Instead of contorting the lovely data model we've built up over the course of the chapter to fit this JSON we happened to get from the server, we'll write a decoder that translates it into the format we want. After all, the whole point of decoders is to decouple our application's data model from whatever curveball external data formats the world decides to throw at us. In a different situation, we could be accessing a third-party service that gives us no say whatsoever in how the data gets formatted.

DECODING A FOLDER

Let's write a decoder for our root `Folder` first. Here's the sample JSON we'll be working with:

```
{"name": "pics from 2016", "photos": { … }, "subfolders": [ … ]}
```

We want to translate this into a `Folder` value:

- The folder's name is `"pics from 2016"`.
- The folder's `photoUrls` value corresponds to the keys in that `"photos"` object.
- Each of the folder's subfolders is represented the same way this one is.

To do this, we'll add the contents of the following listing to the end of PhotoFolders.elm.

Listing 7.11 Decoding both folders and photos in a single decoder

```
folderDecoder : Decoder Folder
folderDecoder =
    Decode.succeed folderFromJson
        |> required "name" string
        |> required "photos" photosDecoder
        |> required "subfolders" (list folderDecoder)

folderFromJson : String -> Dict String Photo -> List Folder -> Folder
folderFromJson name photos subfolders =
    Folder
        { name = name
        , expanded = True
        , subfolders = subfolders
        , photoUrls = Dict.keys photos
        }
```

We defined photosDecoder in section 7.3.1.

On success, passes decoded name, photos, and subfolders to folderFromJson

Yikes! This decoder is defined in terms of itself!

These argument types match the preceding "require" calls.

We'll expand each folder by default.

photos is a Dict String Photo; its keys are photo URLs.

Let's compare the way we built our `Decoder Photo` to the way we've built a `Decoder Folder` here.

Here are the steps we used to create our `Photo` decoder:

1. We used type alias `JsonPhoto` as an intermediate representation, which gave us a `JsonPhoto : String -> Int -> List String -> JsonPhoto` function.

2. We called `Decode.succeed JsonPhoto`, meaning this `JsonPhoto` function would be called if all the decoding steps succeed.

3. We used `required` several times, to build up a `Decoder JsonPhoto` by specifying the fields and types we wanted to decode and then pass to the `JsonPhoto` function, which then returns a decoded `JsonPhoto` value.

4. We used `Decode.map` to translate a `Decoder JsonPhoto` into the `Decoder Photo` we ultimately wanted.

Here we're using a different approach to get a similar outcome:

1. Instead of using an intermediate representation like `JsonPhoto`, we handcraft a `folderFromJson : String -> Dict String Photo -> List Folder -> Folder` function.

2. We call `Decode.succeed folderFromJson`, meaning this `folderFromJson` function will be called if all the decoding steps succeed.

3. We use `required` several times, to build up a `Decoder Folder` by specifying the fields and types we want to decode and then pass to the `folderFromJson` function, which returns a decoded `Folder` value.

NOTE   With this approach, we do not use an intermediate representation like JsonPhoto, so we do not need to use Decode.map to translate between that representation and the final decoder type we want.

This decoder ends up doing a bit more "postprocessing" than other decoders we've written—namely, calling Dict.keys on photos to get a List String of its keys, and adding expanded = True—but not much!

IDENTIFYING A CYCLIC DEFINITION

Our folderDecoder implementation from listing 7.5 almost works . . . but not quite! If we try to compile it, we'll get a cyclic-definition error.

The trouble is that we've defined a value in terms of itself. Imagine if we'd written this:

```
myString : String
myString =
    List.reverse myString
```

This has a problem similar to the one we saw in section 7.2.1, when we tried to make a type alias Folder that referenced Folder in one of its fields. Because a type alias is shorthand for a type we could have written by hand, when the compiler went to expand that alias out to the full type, it discovered that the resulting type would never end.

Just as a type alias declaration names a *type*, this myString = declaration names an *expression*. Anytime the compiler encounters myString, it will substitute the expression after the equals sign. This is where things go wrong.

Let's look at how the compiler would expand myString:

```
List.reverse (List.reverse (List.reverse (List.reverse …
```

The expansion never ends, because the compiler substitutes in List.reverse str as soon as it sees myString, then sees a myString in that List.reverse myString expression, and therefore substitutes List.reverse myString into *that* expression . . . and so on forever.

THE CYCLIC DEFINITION IN FOLDERDECODER

Our current folderDecoder definition has this same problem. Here it is again:

```
folderDecoder : Decoder Folder
folderDecoder =
    Decode.succeed folderFromJson
        |> required "name" string
        |> required "photos" photosDecoder
        |> required "subfolders" folderDecoder
```

Just as in the case of str = List.reverse str, we're trying to define a value in terms of a value we haven't finished defining yet. This definition will also expand forever.

FIXING THE CYCLIC DEFINITION BY USING DECODE.LAZY

We can solve this problem by using Decode.lazy. It has this type:

```
Decode.lazy : (() -> Decoder val) -> Decoder val
```

NOTE We first saw the () type in chapter 3. It's called *unit,* and it holds no information.

We can use Decode.lazy to remove the cyclic definition from folderDecoder like so:

```
folderDecoder =
    Decode.succeed folderFromJson
        |> required "name" string
        |> required "photos" photosDecoder
        |> required "subfolders" (Decode.lazy (\_ -> list folderDecoder))
```

NOTE The list here can go on either side of Decode.lazy; we could also have written this as (list (Decode.lazy (_ -> folderDecoder))). Although that way also works, it adds more visual separation between list and folderDecoder, making it harder to see which decoder we'll use for "subfolders".

Here we no longer have the never-ending expansion problem, because after the compiler reaches (_ -> list folderDecoder), it stops expanding. That expression is already a fully formed anonymous function, which needs no further expansion.

Sure, later on, when this decoder actually gets run on some real JSON, Decode.lazy will call this anonymous function to obtain folderDecoder—but that will work just fine. By that time, folderDecoder will already have been successfully defined. This is the situation Decode.lazy was created to solve, and it will do the trick nicely here.

TIP If you see this cyclic-definition error on a decoder, it's likely that Decode.lazy can resolve it.

Now that we have a working decoder for root : Folder, we'll turn to the last decoder our model requires: a decoder for its photos : Dict String Photo field, the single source of truth for our detailed photo data.

7.3.3 *Accumulating while decoding*

We already have a Decoder Folder that works on this JSON structure, but it's perfectly reasonable for us to create a second decoder that also works on the same JSON. We'll do that when we create the final Photo dictionary we'll use in our Model. Add this to the end of your PhotoFolders.elm file:

```
modelPhotosDecoder : Decoder (Dict String Photo)
modelPhotosDecoder =
    Decode.succeed modelPhotosFromJson
        |> required "photos" photosDecoder
        |> required "subfolders" (Decode.lazy (\_ -> list
    modelPhotosDecoder))


modelPhotosFromJson :
    Dict String Photo
    -> List (Dict String Photo)
```

```
        -> Dict String Photo
modelPhotosFromJson folderPhotos subfolderPhotos =
    List.foldl Dict.union folderPhotos subfolderPhotos
```

> **NOTE** `modelPhotosDecoder` doesn't bother to decode the `"name"` field because it never uses the folders' names, only their photos.

This new `modelPhotosDecoder` will traverse the same JSON structure as `folderDecoder`, which is why they have so many similarities:

- Both use `required "photos" photosDecoder`.
- Both use `Decode.lazy` with `list` to recursively decode the `"subfolders"` field.
- Both give `Decode.succeed` a handwritten function instead of a record variant.

We see some new functions in `photosFromJson`; namely, `Dict.union` and `List.foldl`. What do they do?

DICT.UNION

Let's start with `Dict.union`. Here is its type:

```
union : Dict comparable val -> Dict comparable val -> Dict comparable val
```

It iterates over the first dictionary and calls `Dict.insert` on each of its keys and values, inserting them into the second dictionary. The returned dictionary has the combined contents of both dictionaries.

> **NOTE** Because the calls to `Dict.insert` use keys and values from the first dictionary, anytime the second dictionary already happens to have an entry for a particular key, it will get overridden.

We can use this to combine our various `Photo` dictionaries into the single dictionary that `Model` needs. However, because `Dict.union` combines only two individual dictionaries—and we need to combine many dictionaries—`Dict.union` will need some help. That's where `List.foldl` comes in.

LIST.FOLDL AND LIST.FOLDR

The `List` module offers two *fold* functions: `List.foldl` and `List.foldr`.

> **NOTE** `foldl` is short for "fold from the left," and `foldr` is short for "fold from the right." JavaScript calls these functions `reduce` and `reduceRight` because they can *reduce* collections down to a single value. Any naming similarity between the `foldr` function and our `Folder` type is purely coincidental.

We can compare what `foldl` and `foldr` do by calling both functions in `elm repl`, passing the same arguments in each case:

```
> List.foldl
    (\letter str -> str ++ "-" ++ String.fromChar letter)
    "start"
    [ 'a', 'b', 'c', 'd' ]
"start-a-b-c-d" : String
> List.foldr
```

```
    (\letter str -> str ++ "-" ++ String.fromChar letter)
    "start"
    [ 'a', 'b', 'c', 'd' ]
"start-d-c-b-a" : String
```

Let's walk through what's happening here.

NAMING THE INGREDIENTS

First, note that both `List.foldl` and `List.foldr` have the same type:

```
(element -> state -> state) -> state -> List element -> state
```

We'll give those arguments some names:

- `(element -> state -> state)` is our update function.
- `state` is our initial state.
- `List element` is our list.

We've named the first argument the *update function* because it works similarly to The Elm Architecture's `update` function, specifically the version we used in chapter 2:

```
Elm Architecture update:       Msg -> Model -> Model
Fold function update:          element -> state -> state
```

Whenever the Elm Runtime calls `update`, it passes a `Msg` and the current `Model`, and gets back the updated `Model` it will use the next time it calls `update`. Similarly, each time a fold calls its update function, it passes an `element` and the previous `state`, and gets back the updated `state` to use the next time it calls the update function.

The first time the fold function calls its update function, it passes the *initial state* as the `state` argument and the first element in the *list* as the other argument. After repeating this process with the remaining elements in the list, it returns the final `state` value. (If the list is empty, it returns the initial state immediately.)

DIFFERENCES BETWEEN FOLDL AND FOLDR

Although `foldl` and `foldr` both call their update functions on each element in the list, they differ in the order in which they pass those elements to their update functions. Table 7.3 compares the calls `foldl` and `foldr` make for the same arguments.

Table 7.3 Calling `foldl` and `foldr` on the same arguments

List.foldl update ['a', 'b', 'c', 'd'] "start"	List.foldr update ['a', 'b', 'c', 'd'] "start"

"start"
    |> update 'a'
    |> update 'b'
    |> update 'c'
    |> update 'd'
	"start"
	    |> update 'd'
	    |> update 'c'
	    |> update 'b'
	    |> update 'a'

Both `foldl` and `foldr` begin with the initial state and then call the `update` function on it four times. But whereas `foldl` passes each element in its list to the `update` function in the same order as they appear in that list, `foldr` passes them in the reverse order.

USING LIST.FOLDL WITH DICT.UNION

Now that we know how `foldl` works, let's break down the types involved in the expression where we've called it; see table 7.4.

Table 7.4   **Types involved in (`List.foldl Dict.union`) plus two more arguments from `Decoder` outputs**

Value	Type
`List.foldl`	`(element -> state -> state) -> state -> List element -> state`
`Dict.union`	`Dict comparable val -> Dict comparable val -> Dict comparable val`
`folderPhotos`	`Dict String Photo`
`subfolderPhotos`	`List (Dict String Photo)`

In this expression, `folderPhotos` is our start value, so `List.foldl` will perform these steps:

1 Pass `Dict.union` the first dictionary in the `subfolderPhotos` list, with `folderPhotos` as the second argument. The result is our first state value.

2 Call `Dict.union`, passing the next dictionary in the `subfolderPhotos` list, with the previous outcome as the second argument. The result is our new state value.

3 Repeat the previous steps until we've iterated through the entire `subfolder-Photos` list. `List.foldl` returns the final state value.

In this way, we end up with a `Dict String Photo` value that combines all the photo information from the current folder as well as its subfolders.

> **NOTE** The only time `List.foldl Dict.union` and `List.foldr Dict.union` will produce different values is when duplicate keys exist in the dictionaries involved. If that happens, the choice of `foldl` or `foldr` will change which values get overridden. We don't expect any duplicate keys (and even if we did, we wouldn't care how they got overridden), so we're choosing `foldl` only because it runs faster than `foldr`.

JOINING TWO DECODERS

Finally, it's time for our `folderDecoder` and `modelPhotosDecoder` to team up and form a working `modelDecoder`. Let's replace the definition of `modelDecoder` with this:

```
modelDecoder : Decoder Model
modelDecoder =
    Decode.map2
```

```
(\photos root ->
    { photos = photos, root = root, selectedPhotoUrl = Nothing }
)
modelPhotosDecoder
folderDecoder
```

Like its smaller cousin map, the `Decode.map2` function transforms the *contents* of a value—in this case, a `Decoder` value—rather than the entire value. The difference is that map2 takes an extra argument. Here are their types side by side:

```
map   : (val          -> final) ->                Decoder val -> Decoder final
map2  : (one -> two -> final) -> Decoder one -> Decoder two  -> Decoder final
```

We used map2 instead of map because building our `Model` requires the outputs of both decoders. We also could have used `Decode.andThen` for this purpose, which works similarly to the `Maybe.andThen` function we saw in section 7.1.2, but it's generally better to use the simpler function (in this case, map2) when either of two functions would do the job. (In practice, `Decode.andThen` tends to be used to perform validation on freshly decoded values.)

> **TIP** Many other modules, like `Result` and `Random`, offer similar map2 and andThen functions.

With these two decoders' powers combined, our `modelDecoder` is now fully operational!

> **NOTE** If you're looking for extra challenges, you can try combining model-PhotosDecoder and folderDecoder into a single Decoder (Folder, Dict String Photo) that decodes both the folders and the photos in one pass. That version would use Decode.map instead of Decode.map2 here.

VIEWING THE FINISHED PAGE

After we recompile, the page should now load both photos and folders from the server. The result should be more folders and more photos than we previously had hardcoded. The final page should look something like figure 7.9, depending on which photo you select.

Now the Photo Folders page is loading its model data from the server. It gathers all the photos it finds in the folder JSON into a single `Dict String Photo`, which the rest of our page uses to make the folders and photos interactive. We did it!

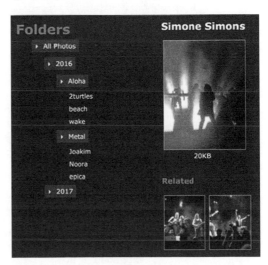

Figure 7.9   The final Photo Folders page

Summary

In this chapter, we built a whole new page from scratch! The Photo Folders feature is sure to be a hit, thanks to our efforts. Along the way, you learned several new techniques:

- Using `Dict String Photo` to store photos by their URL.
- Using a recursive custom type of `type Folder = Folder { subfolders : List Folder, ... }` to represent a tree of folders with subfolders nested inside.
- Using a recursive `Msg` variant to implement expanding and collapsing on that tree.
- Using `Decode.keyValuePairs` to decode an object into key-value pairs for further processing with functions like `Decode.map`.
- Creating intermediate representations like `Decoder JsonPhoto` to decode what we can from a particular JSON object, then using `Decode.map` to use additional information to translate from `Decoder JsonPhoto` into a `Decoder Photo`. We used this technique to decode a photo's URL from its key in the enclosing JSON object.
- Using recursive decoders to decode tree structures, and seeing how `Decode.lazy` can fix cyclic-definition errors in recursive decoders.
- Using `Dict.union` to combine the contents of two dictionaries into one.
- Using `List.foldl` to reduce a list of values down to one value.
- Using the `map2` function to combine and transform two values—in this case, JSON decoders—into one value.

Here is the final PhotoFolders.elm file.

Listing 7.12   PhotoFolders.elm

```
module PhotoFolders exposing (main)

import Dict exposing (Dict)
import Html exposing (...)
import Html.Attributes exposing (class, src)
import Html.Events exposing (onClick)
import Http
import Json.Decode as Decode exposing (Decoder, int, list, string)
import Json.Decode.Pipeline exposing (required)


type Folder
    = Folder
        { name : String
        , photoUrls : List String
        , subfolders : List Folder
        , expanded : Bool
        }
```

Folder is a custom type with a single variant, which is also named Folder.

```
type alias Model =
    { selectedPhotoUrl : Maybe String
    , photos : Dict String Photo                 ◁─────┐  A mapping from String
    , root : Folder                                    │  keys to Photo values
    }


initialModel : Model
initialModel =
    { selectedPhotoUrl = Nothing
    , photos = Dict.empty
    , root =
        Folder
            { name = "Loading..."
            , expanded = True
            , photoUrls = []
            , subfolders = []
            }
    }


init : () -> ( Model, Cmd Msg )
init _ =
    ( initialModel
    , Http.get
        { url = "http://elm-in-action.com/folders/list"
        , expect = Http.expectJson GotInitialModel modelDecoder
        }
    )
```

If both decoders succeed, run the
callback to get the final value.

```
modelDecoder : Decoder Model
modelDecoder =
    Decode.map2
        (\photos root ->
            { photos = photos, root = root, selectedPhotoUrl = Nothing }
        )
        modelPhotosDecoder
        folderDecoder


type Msg
    = ClickedPhoto String
    | GotInitialModel (Result Http.Error Model)
    | ClickedFolder FolderPath


update : Msg -> Model -> ( Model, Cmd Msg )
update msg model =
    case msg of
        ClickedFolder path ->
            ( { model | root = toggleExpanded path model.root }, Cmd.none )

        ClickedPhoto url ->
            ( { model | selectedPhotoUrl = Just url }, Cmd.none )
```

```
        GotInitialModel (Ok newModel) ->
            ( newModel, Cmd.none )

        GotInitialModel (Err _) ->
            ( model, Cmd.none )


view : Model -> Html Msg
view model =
    let
        photoByUrl : String -> Maybe Photo
        photoByUrl url =
            Dict.get url model.photos

        selectedPhoto : Html Msg
        selectedPhoto =
            case Maybe.andThen photoByUrl model.selectedPhotoUrl of      <──┐
                Just photo ->
                    viewSelectedPhoto photo
```
```
                Nothing ->
                    text ""
    in
    div [ class "content" ]
        [ div [ class "folders" ]
            [ h1 [] [ text "Folders" ]
            , viewFolder End model.root
            ]
        , div [ class "selected-photo" ] [ selectedPhoto ]
        ]


main : Program () Model Msg
main =
    Browser.element
        { init = init
        , view = view
        , update = update
        , subscriptions = \_ -> Sub.none
        }


type alias Photo =
    { title : String
    , size : Int
    , relatedUrls : List String
    , url : String
    }


viewPhoto : String -> Html Msg
viewPhoto url =
    div [ class "photo", onClick (ClickedPhoto url) ]
        [ text url ]
```

Maybe.andThen is like Maybe.map, except it can change the outcome to Nothing.

```
viewSelectedPhoto : Photo -> Html Msg
viewSelectedPhoto photo =
    div
        [ class "selected-photo" ]
        [ h2 [] [ text photo.title ]
        , img [ src (urlPrefix ++ "photos/" ++ photo.url ++ "/full") ] []
        , span [] [ text (String.fromInt photo.size ++ "KB") ]
        , h3 [] [ text "Related" ]
        , div [ class "related-photos" ]
            (List.map viewRelatedPhoto photo.relatedUrls)
        ]


viewRelatedPhoto : String -> Html Msg
viewRelatedPhoto url =
    img
        [ class "related-photo"
        , onClick (ClickedPhoto url)
        , src (urlPrefix ++ "photos/" ++ url ++ "/thumb")
        ]
        []


viewFolder : FolderPath -> Folder -> Html Msg
viewFolder path (Folder folder) =
    let
        viewSubfolder : Int -> Folder -> Html Msg
        viewSubfolder index subfolder =
            viewFolder (appendIndex index path) subfolder   <┐
                                                             │
        folderLabel =
            label [ onClick (ClickedFolder path) ] [ text folder.name ]
    in
    if folder.expanded then
        let
            contents =
                List.append
                    (List.indexedMap viewSubfolder folder.subfolders)   <┐
                    (List.map viewPhoto folder.photoUrls)                │
        in
        div [ class "folder expanded" ]
            [ folderLabel
            , div [ class "contents" ] contents
            ]

    else
        div [ class "folder collapsed" ] [ folderLabel ]


appendIndex : Int -> FolderPath -> FolderPath
appendIndex index path =
    case path of
        End ->
            Subfolder index End
```

viewFolder is a recursive function; it calls itself.

indexedMap is like map, but the callback also receives the current index as an argument.

```
          Subfolder subfolderIndex remainingPath ->
               Subfolder subfolderIndex (appendIndex index remainingPath)


urlPrefix : String
urlPrefix =
    "http://elm-in-action.com/"


type FolderPath
    = End
    | Subfolder Int FolderPath
```

FolderPath is a recursive custom type; it potentially contains other FolderPaths.

```
toggleExpanded : FolderPath -> Folder -> Folder
toggleExpanded path (Folder root) =
    case path of
        End ->
            Folder { root | expanded = not root.expanded }

        Subfolder targetIndex remainingPath ->
            let
                subfolders : List Folder
                subfolders =
                    List.indexedMap transform root.subfolders

                transform : Int -> Folder -> Folder
                transform currentIndex currentSubfolder =
                    if currentIndex == targetIndex then
                        toggleExpanded remainingPath currentSubfolder

                    else
                        currentSubfolder
            in
            Folder { root | subfolders = subfolders }


type alias JsonPhoto =
    { title : String
    , size : Int
    , relatedUrls : List String
    }


jsonPhotoDecoder : Decoder JsonPhoto
jsonPhotoDecoder =
    Decode.succeed JsonPhoto
        |> required "title" string
        |> required "size" int
        |> required "related_photos" (list string)


finishPhoto : ( String, JsonPhoto ) -> ( String, Photo )
finishPhoto ( url, json ) =
    ( url
```

```
      , { url = url
        , size = json.size
        , title = json.title
        , relatedUrls = json.relatedUrls
        }
      )


fromPairs : List ( String, JsonPhoto ) -> Dict String Photo
fromPairs pairs =
    pairs
        |> List.map finishPhoto
        |> Dict.fromList


photosDecoder : Decoder (Dict String Photo)
photosDecoder =
    Decode.keyValuePairs jsonPhotoDecoder
        |> Decode.map fromPairs
```

First decode the photos into key-value pairs; then finish turning them into a Dict of Photo records.

```
folderDecoder : Decoder Folder
folderDecoder =
    Decode.succeed folderFromJson
        |> required "name" string
        |> required "photos" photosDecoder
        |> required "subfolders" (Decode.lazy (\_  > list folderDecoder)) <┤
```

Decode.lazy prevents cyclic-definition error.

```
folderFromJson : String -> Dict String Photo -> List Folder -> Folder
folderFromJson name photos subfolders -
    Folder
        { name = name
        , expanded = True
        , subfolders = subfolders
        , photoUrls = Dict.keys photos
        }


modelPhotosDecoder : Decoder (Dict String Photo)
modelPhotosDecoder =
    Decode.succeed modelPhotosFromJson
        |> required "photos" photosDecoder
        |> required "subfolders" (Decode.lazy (\_ -> list
    modelPhotosDecoder))


modelPhotosFromJson :
    Dict String Photo
    -> List (Dict String Photo)
    -> Dict String Photo
modelPhotosFromJson folderPhotos subfolderPhotos =
    List.foldl Dict.union folderPhotos subfolderPhotos <┘
```

foldl starts with the folderPhoto dictionary, then traverses subfolderPhotos and unions each of those dictionaries with it.

Single-page applications

> **This chapter covers**
> - Working with multiple modules
> - Optimizing performance with `Html.Lazy`
> - Routing
> - Parsing URLs

Our manager adores the two pages we've built for Photo Groove, and has a visionary idea for where to go next: "Now that we have all these pages, we need a header across the top with links so users can get between them quickly. Oh! And make sure it doesn't do that unsightly flash of blank page when switching between them. That drives me bananas."

Indeed, two pages is a lot more than one; a header to switch between them sounds like just what the doctor ordered.

In this chapter, we'll build a navigation header that is shared between the two pages we've built in the previous chapters. We'll build the combined page by using a single-page application (SPA) architecture, so users can transition between the two pages without the browser performing a fresh page load.

The "single page" in "single-page application" refers to a *single page load*—the browser loads the page only once. From the user's perspective, all the usual features of multiple pages still appear to work as normal: the URL in the address bar changes when clicking links, the browser's Back button still returns to the previous URL, and so on. Let's build ourselves a single-page application!

8.1 Framing the page

The first step in our plan for building this single-page application is to create a fresh Elm program that renders our header. We've also been informed by Legal that we'll need a footer as well, although they still need to consult with Marketing on exactly what will go in it. Once we've finished the basic header and footer, we'll get our application to respond to URL changes. Finally, we'll render the appropriate page content between the header and footer.

8.1.1 Creating Main.elm

We'll kick things off with a new file, Main.elm, which will go in the src/directory next to PhotoGroove.elm and PhotoFolders.elm. The following listing shows what we'll put in it.

Listing 8.1 Main.elm

```
module Main exposing (main)

import Browser exposing (Document)
import Html exposing (Html, a, footer, h1, li, nav, text, ul)
import Html.Attributes exposing (classList, href)


type alias Model =        We'll add some
    {}                    fields to Model later.

                                        This view function returns
                                        Document, letting it
view : Model -> Document Msg      ◁──┘  specify a title.
view model =                                       The title of the page
    { title - "Photo Groove, SPA Style"      ◁──┘ in the browser
    , body = [ text "This isn't even my final form!" ]  ◁──┐ Notice that
    }                                                        body is a List.


type Msg                          We'll add some real
    = NothingYet                  variants to Msg later.


update : Msg -> Model -> ( Model, Cmd Msg )
update msg model =
    ( model, Cmd.none )
```

```
subscriptions : Model -> Sub Msg
subscriptions model =
    Sub.none


main : Program () Model Msg
main =
    Browser.document
        { init = \_ -> ( {}, Cmd.none )
        , subscriptions = subscriptions
        , update = update
        , view = view
        }
```

Browser.document supports view returning a Document.

A few things in this file are different from the way we've done things in previous chapters. Let's first look at main, which is now calling Browser.document instead of the trusty Browser.element we've been using up to this point.

The difference between the two is that in Browser.element, our view function must return Html Msg, whereas in Browser.document, our view function instead returns Document Msg. This gives our Elm application control over the entire page, whereas with Browser.element we were confined to a single DOM element on the page.

RETURNING DOCUMENT INSTEAD OF HTML

Let's turn our attention to this new view function:

```
view : Model -> Document Msg
view model =
    { title = "Photo Groove, SPA Style"
    , body = [ text "This isn't even my final form!" ]
    }
```

This Document Msg value we're returning is a record with two fields:

- title is a string that sets the page's title in the browser. Because we control the whole page now, we can do that.
- body is a List (Html Msg) that specifies the children of the page's <body> element. It's a List rather than a single Html Msg node because we're controlling <body>'s entire list of children—whereas with Browser.element, we controlled a single element on the page.

The rest of Main.elm is similar to what we've done before. We don't have interesting Model or Msg types yet, but we'll expand them as we progress through the chapter. For now, let's move on to trying out what we've built!

REVISING INDEX.HTML

To view our Main.elm, we'll need to tweak index.html once more. Similar to the change we made to it in chapter 7, we'll replace the final <script> tag in index.html (the one that starts off var app = …) with this:

```
<script>
    var app = Elm.Main.init({node: document.getElementById("app")});
</script>
```

VIEWING THE PAGE

With that in place, we can build our app.js file by using `elm make` like so:

```
elm make --output=app.js src/Main.elm
```

Open index.html in the browser, as shown in figure 8.1, and behold!

Figure 8.1 First confirmed sighting of the compiled Main.elm in the wild

Stunning! Glorious! A triumph!

Of note, check the title on the page. Even though index.html does not specify a `<title>`, the browser should now display "Photo Groove, SPA Style" as the page's title. A fine start!

8.1.2 Rendering the header and footer

Now that we have a basic page up and running, we're ready to dive headfirst into the header and footer. Our designers have mocked up a basic design, shown in figure 8.2.

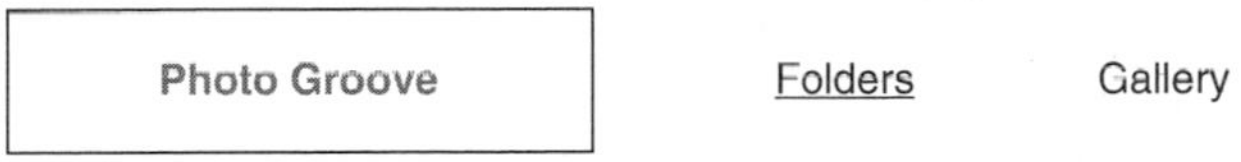

Figure 8.2 The design mockup for the header

We'll implement the design according to these rules:

- The words "Photo Groove" will go in an `<h1>` element.
- Folders and Gallery will be links.
- If the user is viewing the Folders page, the Folders link will be displayed as *active*, meaning it is underlined. Likewise with the Gallery page and the Gallery link. If the user is viewing neither of those pages, then neither link should be shown as active.

As for the footer, Legal and Marketing haven't yet agreed about exactly what should go in there, so for now we'll use a Douglas Adams quote as a placeholder. We assure ourselves that there's no chance we'll end up launching the final product before getting around to changing it.

ADDING PAGE STATE TO THE MODEL

We could render the static content by changing only `view`, but that third header requirement—displaying some links as active depending on the current page—requires a change to `Model`. We won't wire this up to the real URL until later in the chapter, but for now we can at least define a `Page` type to represent the different states we care about, and add it to `Model`.

Listing 8.2   Adding `Page` to `Model`

```
type alias Model =
    { page : Page }


type Page
    = Gallery
    | Folders
    | NotFound


view : Model -> Document Msg
view model =
    let
        content =
            text "This isn't even my final form!"
    in
    { title = "Photo Groove, SPA Style"
    , body =
        [ viewHeader model.page
        , content
        , viewFooter
        ]
    }


viewFooter : Html msg
viewFooter =
    footer [] [ text "One is never alone with a rubber duck. -Douglas Adams"
        ]
```

> **We'll define the viewHeader function in a moment.**

> **Later, we'll replace this with different content depending on your page.**

> **viewHeader is a function, but viewFooter is not; it takes no arguments.**

> **This type can be Html msg instead of Html Msg because viewFooter has no event handlers.**

Here's what we've done:

1. Introduced a `Page` type that represents the three page states we care about: the user is viewing the Gallery page, the user is viewing the Folders page, and the user is viewing a URL we don't recognize—meaning we'll show a Not Found page.
2. Stored the current `Page` value in the `Model` so that `view` can render things differently depending on the current page state.
3. Reorganized `view` to render three distinct sections: the header (`viewHeader model.page`), the main page content (`content`), and the footer (`view-Footer`). We've already implemented `viewFooter`, we'll implement `view-Header` next, and later in the chapter we'll take care of `content`.

Now that `Model` has a page field, we'll also need to change `init` to give it an initial value:

```
init = \_ -> ( { page = Gallery }, Cmd.none )
```

Lovely! Now let's turn to viewHeader.

IMPLEMENTING VIEWHEADER

For viewHeader, we'll use a mixture of techniques we've seen throughout the book, but combined in new and exciting ways! Let's start by sketching a basic outline:

```
viewHeader : Page -> Html Msg
viewHeader page =
    let
        logo =
            h1 [] [ text "Photo Groove" ]

        links =
            ul [] []
    in
    nav [] [ logo, links ]
```

The function accepts only the current Page as its argument, because our design specification tells us the only way viewHeader renders things differently is when the current page changes—at which point it might render a different link as active.

From scanning through the rest of the function, we can tell a few things:

- It's returning a <nav>, the semantically appropriate element for a navigation bar.
- The only two elements inside the <nav> are the logo and the links.
- The logo is a static <h1> that never changes.

Not a bad start! The links are pretty boring—empty <ul> elements—at the moment, though. Let's make them more interesting.

CREATING LINKS WITH NAVLINK

To implement the links, we'll define a helper function right below links in our let-expression, and then have links call it:

```
links =
    ul []
        [ navLink Folders { url = "/", caption = "Folders" }
        , navLink Gallery { url = "/gallery", caption = "Gallery" }
        ]


navLink : Page -> { url : String, caption : String } -> Html msg
navLink targetPage { url, caption } =
    li [ classList [ ( "active", page == targetPage ) ] ]
        [ a [ href url ] [ text caption ] ]
```

TIP As you can see with navLink here, you can add type annotations to declarations inside let-expressions.

DEFINING FUNCTIONS INSIDE LET-EXPRESSIONS

We've made helper functions before, but they haven't looked like this. Why is navLink defined inside a let-expression instead of at the top level like the rest of our functions? And why is it taking a record for its second argument?

The reason `navLink` is defined in the let-expression is so that it can use `page` in the expression `page == targetPage`. Because `page` is an argument to the `view-Header` function, if `navLink` were defined at the top level, it would need to accept `page : Page` as an additional argument, and that `page` value would have to be passed in every time.

> **NOTE** It is a completely reasonable design decision to go the other way—to make `navLink` a top-level function with an extra argument. This design decision could have gone either way, which made it a convenient chance to show the technique—but don't feel obliged to make the same choice in your own code. After all, top-level functions are by default nicer to maintain because their dependencies are more explicit.

PREVENTING ARGUMENT MIX-UPS

So why does `navLink` take a `{ url : String, caption : String }` record for its second argument? Well, let's suppose we didn't use a record here. Consider what `navLink`'s type would be:

```
navLink : Page -> String -> String -> Html msg
```

What happens if we accidentally mix up the order of the two `String` arguments? The types will still line up, so the compiler won't be able to help us . . . so how will we be able to look at a call site and tell if it's passing them in the right order? We'd pretty much have to go look up the implementation for `navLink` to find out.

PASSING "NAMED ARGUMENTS"

Anytime you have multiple arguments of the same type, and you're concerned about accidentally passing them in the wrong order, putting them into a record is a quick way to achieve "named arguments." I can tell at a glance that `{ url = "/", caption = "Folders" }` looks right, whereas something looks off about `{ url = "Folders", caption = "/" }`. The string `"Folders"` clearly isn't a URL, so why is `url` being set to that?

When using this pattern, it's common practice to destructure the arguments in the definition of the function:

```
navLink targetPage { url, caption } =
```

This way, they work and feel like normal arguments, but they are passed in with names instead of by position.

> **TIP** If you want to destructure these fields, but also want to be able to access the original record in its entirety, you can use the `as` keyword to name the original record. For example, this would give the name `config` to the record while destructuring its fields: `navLink targetPage ({ url, caption } as config) =`.

USING CLASSLIST

Notice that we're also using `classList` again, just as we did for `viewThumbnail` back in PhotoGroove.elm:

```
li [ classList [ ( "active", page == targetPage ) ] ]
    [ a [ href url ] [ text caption ] ]
```

This time, we're using it to add the `active` CSS class to our header link, but only when the page the link points to is the same as the page we're currently on. This will take care of the design requirement that the Folders link should be active when we're on the Folders page, and the same for the Gallery link.

TRYING IT OUT

To test that this all works, try running `elm make` and refreshing the browser. Then, to make sure it responds to different `page` values in the model, change `page` from `Gallery` to `Folders` inside `init`, like so:

```
init = \_ -> ( { page = Folders }, Cmd.none )
```

After running `elm make` again and refreshing the browser, the active header link should have changed from Gallery to Folders. Great success!

8.1.3 Skipping unnecessary renders with Html.Lazy

At this point, nothing is stopping us from moving ahead with our implementation of the header. However, one performance optimization technique is so cheap—we will ultimately be adding five *characters* to our view function's implementation—that it's commonly used on headers before there is any noticeable performance problem. Most important, the technique we'll use will be very useful in the future. Among all Elm performance problems that appear in the wild, this is by far the most common way they are solved.

> **NOTE** A notorious pitfall in software development is *premature optimization*—that is, spending time addressing performance problems that exist only in our minds. It's always worth asking the question: are we about to optimize prematurely? In this case, *we totally are*. But at least we're doing it for learning!

BUILDING AN HTML MSG VALUE

Back in chapter 2, I introduced The Elm Architecture, which is how every Elm program describes a user interface. By the end of chapter 5, we had a complete diagram of it. Here it is again in figure 8.3, with the `view` part highlighted.

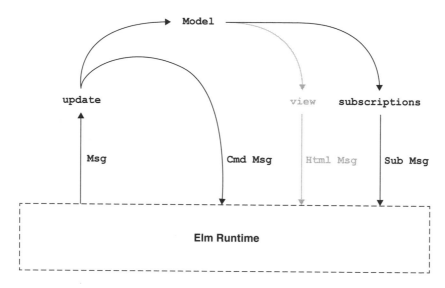

Figure 8.3   The Elm Architecture

Whenever the Elm Runtime calls our `view` function, it will return an `Html Msg` describing how we want the page to look. Building up this `Html Msg` representation usually doesn't take much of the computer's time, but if a `view` function gets large enough—and especially if it's running on an underpowered device like an old smartphone—it's possible (although rare) that assembling the `Html Msg` value itself can be the source of performance problems.

When this happens, the usual fix is to *avoid doing work*, by identifying sections of the `Html Msg` value that rarely change and avoiding having to rebuild them each time `view` is run.

PREMATURELY OPTIMIZING THE HEADER

We haven't observed any problems in Photo Groove, but we already know of one section of the page that will rarely change: the header. Nearly every time `viewHeader` is called, it will return the exact same `Html Msg` value as the previous time it was called. The only time it might possibly change is when `model.page` changes—because we navigated to a different page—in which case, it might return an `Html Msg` value with a different active link.

Happily, there's a quick way to tell the Elm Runtime to cache the previous return value of `viewHeader`, so `viewHeader` will get rerun only when `model.page` changes. If `model.page` is unchanged, that cached `Html Msg` value will be used, and `view-Header` won't rebuild it at all. We'll do this by using the `Html.Lazy` module.

CALLING LAZY ON VIEWHEADER

Let's import the `Html.Lazy` module, exposing its `lazy` function:

```
import Html.Lazy exposing (lazy)
```

Next, we'll introduce that `lazy` function right before our call to `viewHeader`:

```
{ title = "Photo Groove, SPA Style"
, body =
    [ lazy viewHeader model.page
```

Now instead of calling `viewHeader`, passing `model.page`, we're calling `lazy`, passing `viewHeader` and `model.page`. This compiles because `lazy` has this type:

```
lazy : (arg -> Html msg) -> arg -> Html msg
```

In other words, `lazy` expects a function that does the following:

- Takes a single argument (we'll refer to this argument's type as `arg`)
- Returns some `Html`

Our `viewHeader : Page -> Html Msg` function fits this description exactly! (Here, the `arg` type refers to `Page`.)

Besides this function that takes an `arg`, the other argument that `lazy` expects is a value of type `arg`. It has to be an `arg` too because `lazy` plans to pass it to the function.

> **TIP** If you want to use `lazy` with a function that takes multiple arguments, check out `lazy2` and `lazy3`.

TRYING THE FIRST RUN

The first time `lazy viewHeader model.page` gets run, `lazy` will not improve our performance. In fact, it'll be almost as if we hadn't added `lazy` at all; `lazy` will call `viewHeader`, passing `model.page`, and return whatever `viewHeader` returned. (How boring!) However, as it does this, `lazy` also quietly does something else: it stores the value of `model.page` as well as the value `viewHeader` returned.

The next time our program executes this line of code, `lazy` will first take a quick look at the `model.page` value we pass it. If it's the same `model.page` value that we passed last time, `lazy` won't bother calling `viewHeader` at all; instead, it will immediately return the result it stored previously.

> **NOTE** The `lazy` function is an interface to a particular feature of the Elm Runtime; there is no way we could have written it by using Elm code alone.

For details on how `lazy` decides whether a value has changed from one run to the next, see appendix C.

GUARANTEES THAT MAKE SKIPPING SAFE

It's safe for `lazy` to skip calling `viewHeader` like this, thanks to two important guarantees:

- As you learned in chapter 3, when you call an Elm function passing the same arguments, it's guaranteed to return the same value.
- As you learned in chapter 4, Elm functions are guaranteed not to have side effects.

Putting these together, if we already know what a function returned the last time we called it, then there's never any need to call that function again with those same arguments. Running the function again is guaranteed to do nothing more than return the value we already know.

Using lazy isn't free

It might seem that this ought to be the default behavior. Why not `lazy` everything? The answer is that `lazy` is not without its costs.

Remember, `lazy` relies on storing extra information about every function that gets passed to it. Each time we call `lazy`, our program takes up more memory and does a bit more work to store the value and compare the result. If we used `lazy` everywhere, we'd run the risk of ballooning our program's memory usage and doing a bunch of unnecessary comparisons. We might make our overall performance considerably worse by doing this.

This is why `lazy` is opt-in, and why it's best to use it only as needed.

VERIFYING THAT SKIPPING HAPPENED

At this point, we've added the call to `lazy`. Great!

Now how do we know it's doing anything? There's no visual indication that `lazy` did or did not choose to skip `viewHeader`—after all, `lazy` is designed to be a behind-the-scenes optimization rather than an in-your-face one—so how can we tell if it did anything differently? An easy way to tell is by using a function that's helpful in more ways than one: `Debug.log`.

UNDERSTANDING DEBUG.LOG

The `Debug.log` function is unusual among Elm functions in that it actually performs a side effect every time we call it. Specifically, whenever we call `Debug.log`, the Elm Runtime immediately sends a `String` to the browser's console—completely bypassing the typical Elm Architecture way of handling effects through returning `Cmd` values from `update`. It's harmless to do this, because all `Debug.log` does is write to the browser console for development purposes, and no other part of an Elm program can depend on that console.

Here is the type of this peculiar function:

```
Debug.log : String -> a -> a
```

We pass it a `String` to display in the console, as well as a value (of any type) to be displayed right after that `String`, and it returns the exact same value we gave it. The typical way we'd use this is by starting with something like this:

```
case msg of
```

. . . and then introducing a `Debug.log` like so:

```
case Debug.log "Processing this msg" msg of
```

If `msg` had the value `SlidHue 5`, this would log `"Processing this msg: SlidHue 5"` to the console, right when the `Debug.log` function was executed.

Because `Debug.log` returns its second argument—in this case, `msg`—adding `Debug.log` like this has no effect on the code's behavior. This `case` will still operate on `msg` just as before.

> **TIP** If you ever find yourself wanting to use `Debug.log` on your `msg` or `model`, you might instead try running `elm make` with the `--debug` flag. This will add an interactive time-traveling debugger to your compiled program, which makes it much easier to see how your `msg` and `model` are changing over time. Try it out!

USING DEBUG.LOG TO TELL WHEN A FUNCTION HAS BEEN RUN

The most common use for `Debug.log` is to engage in the age-old programming tradition of printing values to a console to see what they are at runtime. However, in our case, we can use it for a different purpose: as a way to tell when `viewHeader` has actually executed, and when `lazy` caused it to be skipped.

We'll modify the `navLink` function inside `viewHeader` to have its page value wrapped in a call to `Debug.log`, like so:

```
navLink route { url, caption } =
    li [ classList [ ( "active", isActive { link = route,
        page = Debug.log "Rendering nav link with" page
    } ) ] ] [ a [ href url ] [ text caption ] ]
```

> **NOTE** We don't need to import the Debug module because it's one of the modules Elm imports by default. Appendix B provides a complete list of Elm's default imports.

TRIGGERING RE-RENDERS

The Elm Runtime calls `view` only after a `Msg` gets sent to `update`, so to test this out, we'll need to introduce some sort of event handler. Our `Msg` type currently has one variant—called `NothingYet`—but for our purposes, that's enough. Let's add an `onMouseOver` to the last line of our `viewHeader` function like so:

```
nav [ onMouseOver NothingYet ] [ logo, links ]
```

We'll need to import `Html.Events` to access `onMouseOver`:

```
import Html.Events exposing (onMouseOver)
```

Now rerun `elm make` and refresh the page.

DETECTING RENDERS

Open the developer console in your browser and try moving the mouse around. Whenever one of our `"Running viewHeader with…"` messages gets logged to the console, that means `lazy` must have decided to run `viewHeader`. Notice that because `model.page` isn't changing, `lazy` isn't rerunning it.

Now try removing the call to `lazy` in our `view` function, run `elm make` again, and refresh the page. This time, watch how much more gets logged to the console when you move the mouse. It's a dramatic difference! `lazy` is often at its most helpful in Elm programs that respond to frequently firing events like `mousemove`.

CLEANING UP THE DEBUGGING CODE

Having now verified that `lazy` is working as intended, let's remove all of these from Main.elm:

- The call to `Debug.log` in `navLink`
- The call to `onMouseOver` at the end of `viewHeader`
- The `Html.Events` import

They were all helpful at the time, but we won't be needing them for the rest of the chapter. Now that we've optimized this into a Blazing Fast Header, complete with simulated awareness of URL changes, we're ready to start handling some *real* URL changes!

8.2   *Routing*

When the user visits a particular URL in the browser, our application will be notified about the URL they visited. Then it will inspect the URL and use its contents to decide which page to run. This process of determining which logic to run, based on the URL the user has visited, is called *routing*, and it's what we'll implement next for our single-page application.

8.2.1   *Handling the initial URL*

Before we start writing any Elm code, we'll need to make a small tweak to the way we're loading our compiled Elm code in the browser.

So far, we've been opening index.html directly in the browser, resulting in an address bar that always begins with *file://* and ends in *index.html.* If we want to start basing our application logic on different URLs in that address bar, we'll need a different setup—one that doesn't rely on always having the same fixed file:// URL in our address bar.

INSTALLING HTTP-SERVER-SPA

The `http-server-spa` package on npm will have us up and running in no time. (If you don't already have npm installed, head over to appendix A to get it.) Here's how to set it up:

1 Run `npm install -g http-server-spa`.
2 From the same directory as index.html, run `http-server-spa .` (Note the period at the end. It's important, and there must be a space before it.)
3 Leave this app running in the background for as long as you want to use it. (It's harmless to restart it, so you can stop it anytime and start it back up again later.)

The `http-server-spa` program is a static file server, which lets us visit http://local-host:8080 in the browser to view index.html. It will serve index.html whenever we visit *any* localhost:8080 URL—including localhost:8080/gallery and the like. Now our Elm code will always get run, no matter what localhost:8080 URL we visit.

LOADING /APP.JS INSTEAD OF APP.JS

Before we can successfully view our application in the browser, we'll need to tweak index.html one final time. It's a subtle change. We're going to add a single slash character just inside the string `"app.js"` in the `<script>` that imports it:

```
<script src="/app.js"></script>
```

Without that slash, the browser will try to load the app.js file from a location relative to whatever URL is currently in the address bar. This means if we visit localhost:8080/ gallery, the browser will try to load localhost:8080/gallery/app.js—but the file won't be there. It's actually hosted at localhost:8080/app.js (without the gallery/ part).

Fortunately, by loading the script from `"/app.js"` instead of `"app.js"`, the browser will fetch the file from the same (correct) location no matter what URL we're visiting. Try it out! You should now be able to visit localhost:8080 (or localhost:8080/gallery, for that matter) and see the same thing you do when opening index.html directly.

HANDLING DIFFERENT URL SCENARIOS

Onward to the URL handling! Our manager told us about three scenarios we'll need to support:

- When the user navigates to the base URL, with nothing after it—for instance, example.com rather than example.com/something—the application should display the Photo Folders page we built in chapter 7.
- When the user navigates to the base URL with /gallery after it—that is, example.com/gallery instead of example.com—we should show the Photo Groove page we built in the chapters leading up to chapter 7. Our manager says we're going to start calling this the "Gallery page," so we'll rename the module accordingly a bit later.
- When the user navigates to /photos/2turtles, things get trickier: the application should display the Photo Folders page once again, but this time the turtles.jpg photo should be selected. The idea is that users should be able to share links to specific photos, so this feature is supposed to work for any photo displayed in Photo Groove, not just turtles.jpg.

Currently, our application displays the same page no matter what URL the user has entered, so the first thing we'll need to do is to examine the URL and do something different depending on which one we find.

RECEIVING THE URL WITH BROWSER.APPLICATION

To examine the initial page URL, we'll need to upgrade `Browser.document` to `Browser.application`. As it turned out, that wasn't even our final form!

Let's replace our call to `Browser.document` with the following:

```
Browser.application
    { init = \_ _ _ -> ( { page = Folders }, Cmd.none )
    , onUrlRequest = \_ -> Debug.todo "handle URL requests"
    , onUrlChange = \_ -> Debug.todo "handle URL changes"
    , subscriptions = \_ -> Sub.none
    , update = update
    , view = view
    }
```

The changes that stand out the most here involve the two new fields: `onUrlChange` and `onUrlRequest`. They're both calling something called `Debug.todo`. What's that all about?

USING DEBUG.TODO

The `Debug.todo` function tells Elm's compiler, "I'm not ready to work on this part of my code base yet, so for now just pretend I put some valid code here, and I'll get back to it later." No matter where you put it, a call to `Debug.todo` will type-check, because this is its type:

```
Debug.todo : String -> a
```

> **TIP** One of the handiest uses for `Debug.todo` is to let you play around with the way certain types fit together. Try defining a few custom types and functions, and implement all the function bodies by using `Debug.todo`. Now you can use `elm repl` to see if calling those functions in the ways you'd like to compiles—based only on their types. Once you're happy with how the types fit together, you can go back and implement for real.

Now at this point, you might be wondering: it's fun to pretend and all, but what happens if that call to `Debug.todo` actually gets run? Elm will throw a runtime exception. That's right, a *runtime exception!* Remember those?

For this reason, although `Debug.todo` is a helpful tool for trying things out before everything is completely ready, it's also something we never want to leave around before deploying to production. Elm is designed to produce reliable applications, not ones that crash because we forgot to clean up some temporary code.

Thankfully, the compiler won't let us forget. When running `elm make` with the `--optimize` flag—a best practice for production builds, because it produces smaller compiled .js files—we'll see an error if any usages of the `Debug` module (like `Debug.todo` or `Debug.log`) are still hanging around our code base.

> **NOTE** `Debug.todo` is only one way to get Elm to throw a runtime exception. Another way is to run out of memory. Calling `modBy 0` on any number, using `==` on two values that contain functions, or trying to pass a malformed value into a port, all currently throw (self-explaining) runtime exceptions by design—although these behaviors could change in future Elm releases. It's also always possible that there is a bug in Elm's compiler or core libraries,

whose symptoms could be a crash. Programming languages are not immune to bugs, after all!

For now, Debug.todo will help us out by letting us wait until later to implement onUrlChange and onUrlRequest. We want to focus on handling the *initial* URL first.

EXTRACTING INIT

You may have noticed a subtle change between Browser.document and Browser.application: the init function receives three arguments instead of one. As it happens, this expanded argument set includes the page's initial URL.

Let's define a top-level named function for init and have Browser.application use it:

```
init : () -> Url -> Nav.Key -> ( Model, Cmd Msg )
init flags url key =
    ( { page = Folders }, Cmd.none )


main : Program () Model Msg
main =
    Browser.application
        { init = init
        ...
```

This init annotation includes two new types you haven't seen before: Url and Nav.Key. We'll need to add a couple of imports before those will compile:

```
import Browser.Navigation as Nav
import Url exposing (Url)
```

We'll use the Nav.Key value later, when we circle back to onUrlChange and onUrlRequest. For now, let's focus on that Url argument.

INSTALLING THE ELM/URL PACKAGE

A Url is a record representing different attributes about the URL such as its protocol (for example, "http" or "https"), host (for example, "elm-lang.org" or "elm-in-action.com"), and path (for example, "/gallery" or "/photos/2turtles "). When our application starts up, init will be passed a Url value representing the current URL in the user's address bar when the page loaded.

This Url type comes from the elm/url package, which includes lots of helpful functions for working with URLs. Let's install it by running this at the command line:

```
elm install elm/url
```

> **NOTE** Answer "Yes" when prompted to move elm/url from your *indirect* dependencies to your *direct* dependencies. For more on direct and indirect dependencies, see appendix B.

Besides the Url type, we'll be using some other goodies from the elm/url package shortly.

TIP   It's often helpful to have the documentation for a package open while working with it, for quick reference. Try searching for the elm/url package on the package.elm-lang.org website, so you can quickly reference the types and descriptions of these functions as I introduce them. Make sure you're looking at the documentation for the same version of the elm/url package as the one in your elm.json file.

INTERPRETING THE URL

Our Model already has a concept of which Page the user is viewing, so our goal at this point is to have init set that model.page value based on the Url it received. Let's have our initial translation from Url to Page work like this:

- If the URL is localhost:8080/gallery, we'll set model.page to be Gallery.
- If the URL is localhost:8080, we'll set it to Folders.
- If the URL is anything else, we'll default to NotFound.

Here's how we'll implement this:

```
init : () -> Url -> Nav.Key -> ( Model, Cmd Msg )
init flags url key =
    case url.path of
        "/gallery" ->
            ( { page = Gallery }, Cmd.none )

        "/" ->
            ( { page = Folders }, Cmd.none )

        _ ->
            ( { page = NotFound }, Cmd.none )
```

This revised init should mean we now see different active header links based on the URL of the page. Try it out! Open the browser and visit these URLs to see the different pages:

- http://localhost:8080
- http://localhost:8080/gallery
- http://localhost:8080/djent

Figure 8.4 shows the results—but beware! The Debug.todo we used earlier for onUrlRequest means that if you click either of the links, you'll get a runtime exception. We'll fix that later.

Figure 8.4   Viewing three different URLs

This is a great start! However, we still have yet to implement the final URL scenario our manager mentioned: handling URLs like /photos/sand. To implement that feature, we'll use a tool a bit more powerful than our current approach.

8.2.2 Parsing URL paths

Before we can parse a URL into a `Page` that stores the selected photo filename, we'll need to give `Page` the ability to store it. Let's add a new variant to the beginning of our `type Photo` declaration:

```
type Page
    = SelectedPhoto String
    | Gallery
    | Folders
    | NotFound
```

Now that we support this new `Page` type, we're all set up to parse some URLs into it.

UNDERSTANDING URL STRUCTURE

Single-page applications can get a lot of information out of a URL. Besides the path, there's the fragment, the query string, and more beyond that. Figure 8.5 diagrams some of the pieces of a URL that we might use in our SPA.

Figure 8.5   Anatomy of a URL

The `elm/url` package gives us three modules for working with the various pieces of a URL:

- `Url.Builder` helps us assemble URLs from these separate ingredients. We'll use it later in the chapter.
- `Url.Parser` and `Url.Parser.Query` help us translate the *path* and *query* portions of a URL into more helpful values. We'll be using `Url.Parser` ... soon. Really soon!

As foreshadowed in the previous bullet point, next we'll use `Url.Parser` to parse URLs like /photos/surf into information stored in our model.

DEFINING A PARSER

To use `Url.Parser`, we'll add this import to the top of Main.elm:

```
import Url.Parser as Parser exposing ((</>), Parser, s, string)
```

This will let us define the following `Parser` below our `init` declaration:

```
parser : Parser (Page -> a) a
parser =
    Parser.map SelectedPhoto (s "photos" </> Parser.string)
```

Similarly to the way a JSON `Decoder` value describes how to translate a JSON string into a different type, this `Parser` value describes how to translate a URL into a `Page`. Many of the concepts you've learned about JSON decoding in chapters 4 and 7 will apply here, but there are a few differences between `Decoder` and `Parser`.

> **NOTE**   One difference you might be wondering about is that type annotation. If we were decoding JSON into a `Page`, we would build a `Decoder Page`. However, our URL parser is not a `Parser Page`, but rather a `Parser (Page -> a) a`. The reason behind this has to do with the way parsers get built up internally, and is too long a detour for this chapter. To successfully build a single-page application, all we need to know is that `Parser (Route -> a) -> a` is the type of a `Parser` that translates a URL into a `Route`.

Let's break down the implementation of this parser:

```
Parser.map SelectedPhoto (s "photos" </> Parser.string)
```

The `(s "photos" </> Parser.string)` part says two things:

- This parser will succeed only if it is run on a URL whose path begins with the string `"/photos"` followed by a slash and then another string with a length of at least 1. (So the URL path `"/photos/"` would not match, but `"/photos/a"` would.)
- If it succeeds, the `Parser`'s final output will be the `String` following the `"photos/"` part of the URL path. (So it would succeed with `"puppy"` when parsing a path of `"/photos/puppy"`.)

> **TIP**   The `</>` operator expects a `Parser` value on each side, and the `Parser.s` function turns a hardcoded string into a parser for that string. For example, the parser `(s "photos" </> Parser.string </> s "other" </> s "things")` would match URLs like `"/photos/foo/other/things"`.

The `Parser.map SelectedPhoto` part works similarly to the `List.map`, `Result.map`, `Maybe.map`, and `Decode.map` functions we've seen so far: it transforms the value produced by the `Parser`. Without this call to `Parser.map`, our `Parser` would output a plain old `String` whenever it succeeds. Thanks to `Parser.map`, that `String` will instead be passed along to `SelectedPhoto`, so the resulting parser will output a `Page` we can store in our model.

RUNNING A PARSER

Just as we pass `Decoder` values to functions like `Json.Decode.decodeString` in order to run them on a JSON string, we pass `Parser` values to `Parser.parse` in order to run them on a particular URL. Calling `Parser.parse` with our `Page` parser will give us a Maybe Page value—Nothing if the parser did not match, and Just page if it did.

We could use this to sneak our parser into the default branch of init's case-expression:

```
init : () -> Url -> Nav.Key -> ( Model, Cmd Msg )
init flags url key =
    case url.path of
        …


        _ ->
            if String.startsWith "/photos/" url.path then
                case Parser.parse parser url of
                    Just page ->
                        ( { page = page }, Cmd.none )

                    Nothing ->
                        ( { page = NotFound }, Cmd.none )

            else
                ({ page = NotFound }, Cmd.none )
```

Unfortunately, doing this would introduce code duplication in two places:

- We call String.startsWith "/photos/" url.path and then, immediately after, we run a Parser that verifies that the path begins with "/photos/".
- This Nothing branch handles our "page not found" case, and then the else branch beneath it handles it again.

We can do better!

COMPOSING PARSERS WITH PARSER.ONEOF

Thankfully, just as with JSON decoders, we can compose Parser values together in a variety of ways. Let's replace our parser implementation with this slightly more capable one:

```
parser : Parser (Page -> a) a
parser =
    Parser.oneOf
        [ Parser.map Folders Parser.top
        , Parser.map Gallery (s "gallery")
        , Parser.map SelectedPhoto (s "photos" </> Parser.string)
        ]
```

Here we can see three new things:

- Parser.top, which matches the root path. Parser.map Folders Parser .top returns a Parser that succeeds on a path of "/" and outputs a Folders value.
- Parser.map Gallery (s "gallery"), which matches "/gallery" and outputs a Gallery value. Note that although we called the Parser.s function again, this time we did not need to use the </> operator.

- `Parser.oneOf`, which takes a `List` of parsers and tries them one at a time until it either finds a match or runs out.

TIP There's also a `Json.Decode.oneOf` that works similarly. It's useful for decoding JSON fields that situationally hold different types.

Believe it or not, this new `Parser` can replace every conditional branch in our `init` function except the `NotFound` one. Let's revise `init` like so:

```
init : () -> Url -> Nav.Key -> ( Model, Cmd Msg )
init flags url key =
    ( { page = urlToPage url }, Cmd.none )


urlToPage : Url -> Page
urlToPage url =
    Parser.parse parser url
        |> Maybe.withDefault NotFound
```

We've now isolated our logic for translating a `Url` into a `Page` into the `urlToPage` function.

Here's how that function works: Our `Parser` uses `Parser.oneOf` to try each of three `Parsers`—first, one that matches `"/"` and outputs `Folders`; then, one that matches `"/gallery"` and maps to `Gallery`; and finally, one that matches `"/photos/something"` and maps to `SelectedPhoto` with the string after `"/photos"` wrapped up inside it.

If this parser succeeds, then great! We have our `Page` and store it in the model. If it fails, then the path was unrecognized, and we return the `NotFound` page by default.

REVISING HEADER LINKS

We're almost done! The only missing puzzle piece is that our header logic doesn't account for our new `SelectedPhoto` variant. We'd like it to render the Folders link as active when the user is on any of the /photos/something URLs—after all, once we're finished implementing everything, the user will most definitely be looking at the Folders page.

We'll start by replacing our `page == targetPage` comparison with a call to a function called `isActive`, which we'll define next:

```
li [ classList [ ( "active", page == targetPage ) ] ]
li [ classList [ ( "active", isActive { link = targetPage, page = page } ) ]
    ]
```

We'll introduce `isActive` right below `viewHeader`, and implement it like so:

```
isActive : { link : Page, page : Page } -> Bool
isActive { link, page } =
    case ( link,            page            ) of
        --------------------------------------------
        ( Gallery,          Gallery         ) -> True
        ( Gallery,          _               ) -> False
```

```
( Folders,         Folders        ) -> True
( Folders,         SelectedPhoto _ ) -> True
( Folders,         _              ) -> False
( SelectedPhoto _, _              ) -> False
( NotFound,        _              ) -> False
```

Don't panic! This is a totally normal case-expression if you squint at it—we're using `case` on a tuple of (`link`, `page`) and then pattern matching on various combinations of tuples that it might match—but it's been laid out like a table for demonstration purposes. (You can feel free to format it normally in your code, and leave out the long `------` comment.)

USING THE TRUTH TABLE PATTERN

You can think of this case-expression as using tuples and pattern matching to describe a *truth table* of how we should handle these various combinations of links and current pages. The first "row" in the table—(`Gallery`, `Gallery`) -> `True`—says that if the `link` is to `Gallery`, and the current page is also `Gallery`, then `isActive` should be `True`. The next "row"—(`Gallery`, _) -> `False`—says that if the `link` is to `Gallery` and the current page is *anything else*, then `isActive` should be `False`.

This covers all the possible combinations of `Gallery` links, so we can move on to the more interesting `Folders` case. The `Folders` patterns look similar to the `Gallery` ones; we have (`Folders`, `Folders`) -> `True` and (`Folders`, _) -> `False`. The crucial difference is that between the two we have (`Folders`, `SelectedPhoto` _) -> `True`, meaning that if the current page is any `SelectedPhoto` variant, `isActive` will be `True`. That's exactly what we were missing!

The remaining (`SelectedPhoto` _, _) and (`NotFound`, _) patterns won't come up, because we don't have header links that point to those pages. We're including them instead of adding a default _ -> pattern only to benefit our future selves: so we can get those helpful missing-patterns errors if we introduce another new variant to `Page` and forget to consider its implications on `isActive`.

VIEWING THE SELECTED PHOTO PAGE

With all that in place, we should be able to view our "selected photo" route successfully. Try it out by visiting localhost:8080/photos/something (replacing "something" with various different words) and verify that the Folders link is indeed active.

Fantastic! Now that the initial URL is being handled gracefully, we're ready to circle back to those `Debug.todo` calls we made earlier, and make the links in the header work properly.

8.2.3 *Handing URL changes*

A common design goal of single-page applications is to maintain the URL bar's normal functionality. Ideally, it seems to the person using it as if they're using a multipage website, where links and the Back button work normally. The only noticeable difference is that things seem pleasantly snappier, because the SPA isn't doing a full page load for each new page.

ONURLREQUEST AND ONURLCHANGE

The onUrlRequest and onUrlChange functions in Browser.application give us the power to pull off this magic trick. Let's wire them up, replacing our placeholder Msg type with one that has two variants:

```
type Msg
    = ClickedLink Browser.UrlRequest
    | ChangedUrl Url
```

Now let's replace the Debug.todo calls we made in Browser.application with these variants:

```
Browser.application
    { init = init
    , onUrlRequest = ClickedLink
    , onUrlChange = ChangedUrl
    …
```

We'll walk through these one at a time.

OVERRIDING DEFAULT LINK BEHAVIOR

First we have onUrlRequest = ClickedLink. This says that whenever the user requests a new URL (by clicking a link), Elm's runtime will send a ClickedLink message to our update function. It's like a page-wide event handler, except that it goes a step further by overriding the default behavior of all links on the page.

With Browser.application, clicking links only sends this ClickedLink message—it doesn't automatically load a new page as the browser normally would. This gives us total control over what we want the application to do when the user clicks a link.

> **NOTE** Browser.application does not override the "open link in new tab" functionality. You can still right-click a link and select Open in New Tab, or use one of the various shortcuts for this such as middle-clicking, Command-clicking, or Ctrl-clicking, depending on your system. It also doesn't override the behavior of links with the download attribute set, because they're supposed to download things instead of navigating.

The onUrlChange = ChangedUrl setting also sends a message to update, except it triggers under different circumstances. We'll talk about those circumstances shortly.

HANDLING CLICKEDLINK

Next, let's incorporate the ClickedLink message into update like so:

```
update : Msg -> Model -> ( Model, Cmd Msg )
update msg model =
    case msg of
        ClickedLink urlRequest ->
            case urlRequest of
                Browser.External href ->
                    ( model, Nav.load href )
```

```
Browser.Internal url ->
    ( model, Nav.pushUrl model.key (Url.toString url) )
```

> **NOTE** We don't have a `model.key` field yet, but have no fear! We'll add it after we finish with `update`.

INTERNAL AND EXTERNAL URL REQUESTS

The `Browser.UrlRequest` value inside `ClickedLink` has two variants. It looks like this:

```
type UrlRequest
    = External String
    | Internal Url
```

Our `ClickedLink` message will contain an `External` request if the user clicked a link to a different domain. For example, if they're viewing any URL whose domain is `elm-in-action.com` and the user clicks a link to anywhere on `manning.com`, that would be an `External` request containing the exact string of the `href` attribute of the link they clicked.

As you may have guessed, `ClickedLink` will contain an `Internal` request if the user clicked a link to the same domain. So if they're viewing an elm-in-action.com URL and they click a link to /foo, or to elm-in-action.com/foo, that will be an `Internal` request containing a `Url` record like the one `init` receives.

NAV.LOAD

Let's take a closer look at what we're doing in the `Browser.External` branch:

```
Browser.External href ->
    ( model, Nav.load href )
```

This `Nav.load` performs a full page load, just as a traditional multipage app would do. This call essentially says, "If we get a request to a third-party page, load it as normal." We don't have to do it this way, though.

For example, if our manager later asks us to add a disclaimer like, "You are about to leave the comfort and safety of Photo Groove for the harsh wilderness of The Internet, an unfathomably complex series of tubes," we could implement that logic here instead of unconditionally calling `Nav.load` right away.

NAV.PUSHURL

The `Internal` variant is similar to the `External` one, but slightly more involved:

```
Browser.Internal url ->
    ( model, Nav.pushUrl model.key (Url.toString url) )
```

The `Url.toString` call converts the `Url` to a `String`, because `Nav.pushUrl` wants the URL in `String` form rather than in record form. We'll get to `model.key` soon, but first let's go over what `Nav.pushUrl` does differently from the `Nav.load` we used in the `External` case.

Whereas `Nav.load` does a full page load of an entirely new page, all `pushUrl` does is to push the given URL onto the browser's history stack. This has a few implications:

- The URL shown in the browser's address bar will become this one.
- `Browser.application` will send a `ChangedUrl` event to `update`, with this URL stored inside it. That's because we specified `ChangedUrl` for our `onUrl-Changed` handler when we set up our `Browser.application`.
- When the user clicks the Back button in the browser, this URL will now be one of the ones it goes back to. Also, when the user does that, `Browser.application` will send a `ChangedUrl` event to `update`.

This `Nav.pushUrl` function is how we give users the appearance of the address bar working as normal, without causing full page loads. Because it *only* manipulates the address bar, and does not directly request any page loads, we are free to display what *appears* to be a new page—without actually doing a real page load.

Because both `pushUrl` and the browser's Back button result in `UrlChanged` events being sent to `update`, we don't need separate handling code for the case where the user arrived at a given URL from `pushUrl` compared to using the browser's Back button. Once we implement handling code for the `ChangedUrl` message, we'll have covered both cases.

MODEL.KEY

Okay, so we have `Nav.load` to do full page loads, and `Nav.pushUrl` to push URLs onto the browser history and trigger a `ChangedUrl` message. What's the deal with that `model.key` argument to `Nav.pushUrl`? To understand what's happening there, let's go back to `init` and make a small addition to its implementation—setting `key = key` in the `Model` it returns:

```
init : () -> Url -> Nav.Key -> ( Model, Cmd Msg )
init flags url key =
    ( { page = urlToPage url, key = key }, Cmd.none )
```

Because the `key` argument to `init` has the type `Nav.Key`, we can infer that the type of `model.key` must also be `Nav.Key`, so let's add that to our `Model` type alias before moving on:

```
type alias Model =
    { page : Page, key : Nav.Key }
```

Let's recap what we know about `model.key`:

- It has the type `Nav.Key`, whatever that is.
- Our `init` function receives one from the Elm Runtime, and stores it in `Model`.
- Later, in `update`, we access the stored key via `model.key` and pass it to `Nav.pushUrl`.

This is precisely how `Nav.Key` is typically used: write it down in `init`, and then retrieve it later when `Nav.pushUrl` asks for it. Never change it!

The design of Nav.Key

The reason `Nav.Key` exists is to restrict `Nav.pushUrl` to being used only by Elm programs started up by using `Browser.application`. Because the only way to obtain a `Nav.Key` is by having `init` provide one, and because only `Browser.application` has an `init` function that provides one, it is impossible to call `Nav.pushUrl` unless you originally started up by using `Browser.application`. Clever, eh?

This restriction exists because Elm's navigation APIs are designed with the assumption that they have total control over the page. That's what makes it safe for them to do things like overriding the default behavior for all links on the page. If that assumption is violated—say, because we were using `Browser.element` to embed a small Elm application inside an existing single-page application written in JavaScript—then using `pushUrl` could result in some nasty bugs.

The sole purpose of the `Nav.Key` restriction on `pushUrl` is to make these bugs impossible. As such, the inner value of `Nav.Key` doesn't matter one bit. (In fact, if you look at the source code for `Browser.Navigation`, you'll see that it is literally defined as `type Key = Key`.) All that matters is that it's a token proving that the Elm Runtime has been started up by using `Browser.application`, and thus you can be confident it has full control over the page.

Now that we have the `ClickedLink` message fully handled in `update`, it's time to circle back to the `ChangedUrl` message. Here's the code we'll add to `update`. Ready? Drumroll, please. . . .

```
ChangedUrl url ->
    ( { model | page = urlToPage url }, Cmd.none )
```

That's it! Granted, we're choosing to do about the least interesting thing possible here: whenever the URL changes because of a history change (such as a call to `Nav.pushUrl`, or the user using the Back button to go back to one of those changes), we translate that URL into a `Page` and store it in our `Model`.

We could do a lot more, though. For example, if we wanted to animate transitions between pages—using a fade, a slide, or even a cinematic wipe—this would be the place to do it.

THE FULLY URL-ENABLED PAGE

If you recompile and bring up the page, you should see that URLs now fully work as expected:

- If you visit a URL, it renders the appropriate header links as active.
- Clicking either of the links in the header takes you to the appropriate URL, which results in the active link changing as appropriate.
- These behaviors continue to work as expected when using the browser's Back and Forward buttons.

Now that our URL handling is in place, we're ready to tie it all together—by rendering the real pages between the header and footer, instead of the placeholder text we've been using so far.

8.3   *Delegating pages*

At this point, we have all the ingredients necessary to make our single-page application work:

- A working Photo Folders page from chapter 7
- A working Photo Gallery page from the earlier chapters
- A working `Main` module that handles URLs and maintains a conceptual `Page`

Our next task will be to unite the three into a single application. To do this, we'll first change the `PhotoFolders` and `PhotoGroove` modules to expose their `init`, `view`, `update`, and `subscriptions` functions instead of having their own `Program` values. Then we'll configure `Main` to call those functions depending on which page the user is viewing. Let's get to it!

8.3.1   *Revising module structure*

Let's start by incorporating our `PhotoFolders` module. Ultimately, we'd like Main.elm to render the Photo Folders page between our header and footer. To do that, we'll need to call `PhotoFolders.view`. However, at the moment, our `Main` module can't possibly call `PhotoFolders.view`, because the `PhotoFolders` module does not publicly expose `view`. Until it's exposed, no other module can access that function.

EXPOSING VALUES IN THE PHOTOFOLDERS MODULE

Let's address this by editing the first line of PhotoFolders.elm to say the following:

```
module PhotoFolders exposing (Model, Msg, init, update, view)
```

This declaration is now saying these things:

- This module's name is `PhotoFolders`. (Big surprise!)
- It's exposing the `Model` type alias, so other modules can import that type alias.
- It's exposing the `Msg` type, but not its variants. (To expose its variants too, we would have written `Msg(..)` in the exposing list.)
- It's exposing the `init`, `update`, and `view` functions.

TIP   In general, it's best to have modules expose values only when absolutely necessary. This principle extends to custom types' variants as well; variants should be exposed only when absolutely necessary.

RENAMING PHOTOGROOVE.ELM

We'll give PhotoGroove.elm the same treatment—and while we're at it, we'll add `init` to its exposing list and rename it PhotoGallery.elm, since that's what our manager has started calling that page these days. We'll change the first line of the renamed PhotoGallery.elm to this:

```
port module PhotoGallery exposing (init, Model, Msg, init, update, view)
```

Now that we've exposed these values, let's import these modules into our `Main` module:

```
import PhotoFolders as Folders
import PhotoGallery as Gallery
```

Now `Main` can call the view functions inside the `PhotoFolders` and `Photo-Gallery` modules, by referring to them as `Folders.view`, and `Gallery.view`, respectively. Great!

> **NOTE** If you want to run the tests again, you'll need to find/replace `Photo-Groove` with `PhotoGallery` in PhotoGrooveTests.elm too.

STORING PHOTOFOLDERS.MODEL

Let's open up the `PhotoFolders` module and take a look at the type of `view`:

```
view : Model -> Html Msg
```

Hmm. How are we going to call that from `Main`? It says it wants a `Model`, but we're inside the `PhotoFolders` module—meaning it wants a `Folders.Model`, not a `Main.Model`. If we're calling this function from `Main`, how will we be able to provide this function with the `Folders.Model` it requires?

The answer is that we'll store a `Folders.Model` inside our `Main.Model`. Because we'll be calling `Folders.view` only when we're on the Photo Folders page—and, similarly, calling `Gallery.view` only when we're on the Gallery page—we can add these two models to our `Page` custom type instead of cramming both of them into the `Model` record.

Let's revise `Page` to look like this:

```
type Page
    = Gallery Gallery.Model
    | Folders Folders.Model
    | SelectedPhoto String Folders.Model
    | NotFound
```

Splendid! Now if our `Model` contains a `Page` that happens to be one of the two Photo Folders variants—that is, `Folders` or `SelectedPhoto`—we'll have access to a `Photo-Folders.Model` value, which we can pass to `PhotoFolders.view` to render the page.

MAIN.INIT AND PHOTOFOLDERS.INIT

Because we've changed the shape of our `Page` custom type, our code won't compile again until we populate those `Folders.Model` values in our `init` function. How can we obtain a `Folders.Model` value? By calling `Folders.init`.

Happily, `Folders.init` takes an argument we can easily provide. Here is its type:

```
Folders.init : () -> ( Folders.Model, Cmd Msg )
```

This means that by calling `Tuple.first (Folders.init ())`, we'll end up with the `Folders.Model` value we seek. No sweat, right?

PROBLEMS WITH PAGE

Unfortunately, this approach creates a bit of a problem for our URL parser. It's supposed to parse a `String` into a `Page`. If we wanted that to keep working, we'd have to modify it like so:

```
Parser.oneOf
    [ Parser.map (Folders (Folders.init ())) Parser.top
    , Parser.map (Gallery (Gallery.init ())) (s "gallery")
    , Parser.map (SelectedPhoto (Folders.init ()))
        (s "photos" </> Parser.string)
    ]
```

Yikes—now we're calling `init` functions *three times* just to define a URL parser? Something feels off. There's a similar situation in `viewHeader`, too. We can no longer pass `navLink` a standalone `Folders` value, because instantiating a `Folders` value now requires a `Folders.Model`. Instead, we'll have to do something like this:

```
ul []
    [ navLink (Folders (Folders.init ()))
        { url = "/", caption = "Folders" }
    , navLink (Gallery (Gallery.init ()))
        { url = "/gallery", caption = "Gallery" }
    ]
```

This is getting out of hand! What's the problem here? Why isn't `Page` working well everywhere it used to, now that we've expanded it to hold onto more information?

SIMILAR BUT NOT THE SAME

What we have here is a classic case of needing to revisit a data structure based on changing circumstances. We now have two needs that are similar but not quite the same:

- Storing either `Folders.Model` or `Gallery.Model`, depending on which page is being viewed. Here, our main goal is for the data structure to store different models.
- Representing a parsed route, such as `Folders` or `SelectedPhoto String`, as we were doing before. In this use case, we want the data structure to store no models, because we don't want `parser` or `navLink` to have to call `init` to do their jobs.

On closer inspection, these two goals are at odds. We need two different data structures!

Thankfully, there is no law against having two data structures that are *similar but not the same*. In fact, it is considered good practice in Elm to keep an eye out for situations like this. As we saw here, sometimes it's not obvious that a particular use case has outgrown a single data structure; we have to remember to revisit our assumptions as our program grows.

PAGE AND ROUTE

Table 8.1 shows the two new data structures we'll be using for our different use cases.

Table 8.1 Two data structures for use cases that are similar but not the same

Storing different models	Representing a parsed route
| ```
type Page
    = GalleryPage Gallery.Model
    | FoldersPage Folders.Model
    | NotFound
``` | ```
type Route
    = Gallery
    | Folders
    | SelectedPhoto String
``` |

After we separate these, a few more differences emerge:

- It doesn't actually make sense to have a Not Found route. After all, Not Found means our parser failed, and we couldn't recognize a route from the given URL.
- There is, however, a Not Found page; we want to store that in our `Model` so that we know to render a Not Found page to the viewer.
- For `Page`'s purposes, there's no longer any need to have separate variants for `Folders` and `SelectedPhoto`. The information of which photo is selected (if any) will be stored in the `Folders.Model` value we already have in the `FoldersPage` variant.

Now that we've built out our data model, we're ready to put these two new types to use as we initialize our different page states.

8.3.2 Initializing page states

First, let's alter `navLink` to use our new `Route` type:

```
navLink : Route -> { url : String, caption : String } -> Html msg
navLink route { url, caption } =
    li | classList | ( "active", isActive { link = route, page = page } ) | |
        [ a [ href url ] [ text caption ] ]
```

We don't need to change how `navLink` is being called, because we used the same names for the `Route` variants (`Folders` and `Gallery`) as what they were called before. For the same reason, we don't need to change the implementation of `parser`, although we will need to change `Page` to `Route` in its type annotation:

```
parser : Parser (Route -> a) a
```

We'll need to revise `isActive` too, although its new truth table is shorter and easier to read:

```
isActive : { link : Route, page : Page } -> Bool
isActive { link, page } =
    case ( link,          page           ) of
            -----------------------------------------
            ( Gallery,        GalleryPage _  ) -> True
            ( Gallery,          _            ) -> False
            ( Folders,        FoldersPage _  ) -> True
            ( Folders,          _            ) -> False
            ( SelectedPhoto _, _             ) -> False
```

This is a common benefit of separating one overloaded data structure into two: related code often ends up becoming clearer and more concise.

This new `Route` type has now resolved our previous problems with `init`. We still have page : Page in our `Model`, it still stores `Folders.Model` and `Gallery.Model` under the appropriate circumstances, and we no longer need to call `init` a bunch of times in `parser` or in `viewHeader`. Wonderful!

REVISING urlToPage

Next up: the `urlToPage` function. This is where we actually do want to call `Folders.init` and `Gallery.init`: when converting a `Url` to a `Page`. Here's a first draft that type-checks but doesn't quite do what we want yet:

```
urlToPage : Url -> Page
urlToPage url =
    case Parser.parse parser url of
        Just Gallery ->
            GalleryPage (Tuple.first (Gallery.init 1))

        Just Folders ->
            FoldersPage (Tuple.first (Folders.init ()))

        Just (SelectedPhoto filename) ->
            FoldersPage (Tuple.first (Folders.init ()))

        Nothing ->
            NotFound
```

This implementation has a lot going for it. It faithfully translates all the URL scenarios into a `Page` value, it never calls `init` functions unnecessarily, and it gives us `Model.Folders` and `Model.Gallery` values exactly in the places where we need them.

However, two problems stand out:

- `Gallery.init` takes a `Float` because, way back in chapter 5 (Remember chapter 5? We've come a long way since then!) we passed in the Pasta.js version number from index.html as a flag. Our current `Main` module isn't configured to accept any flags, so for now we're passing `Gallery.init` a hardcoded 1. We'll fix that soon.
- After going to all the trouble of parsing out the photo's filename from the /photos/thing URL in the `SelectedPhoto` branch, we then completely ignore that filename and call `Folders.init ()` just as we did in the `Folders` branch. In our defense, that's because at the moment `Folders.init` accepts only (). We haven't set it up to accept a filename yet, but we'll fix that too.

REVISING FOLDERS.INIT

The `Folders.init` fix is quick, so let's knock that one out. What we'd like to do is to pass `Folders.init` the filename when we have it, and nothing when we don't—and then let `Folders.init` decide what to do with that information.

Sounds like a good use case for `Maybe`. Over in PhotoFolders.elm, we'll revise the `init` function to accept a `Maybe String` for the selected filename, and then record it directly in its `model`:

```
init : Maybe String -> ( Model, Cmd Msg )
init selectedFilename =
    ( { initialModel | selectedPhotoUrl - selectedFilename }
    , Http.get …
    )
```

Piece of cake! This will mean `main` inside PhotoFolders.elm no longer type-checks, but we're done with it anyhow. It's safe to go ahead and delete it.

Now we can hop back to Main.elm and revise the `Folders` and `SelectedPhoto` branches in our `urlToPage` function to pass `Folders.init` the appropriate values depending on the route:

```
Just Folders ->
    FoldersPage (Tuple.first (Folders.init Nothing))

Just SelectedPhoto filename ->
    FoldersPage (Tuple.first (Folders.init (Just filename)))
```

The `Tuple.first` here extracts the `Model` portion of `Folders.init`'s return value, which has the type `( Folders.Model, Cmd.Msg )`—and `FoldersPage` wants the `Model` on its own.

REVISING urlToPage

The last thing to address is that hardcoded `Gallery.init 0`. To fix that, we'll need to make `urlToPage` accept the Pasta.js version number as an argument:

```
urlToPage : Float -> Url -> Page
urlToPage version url =
    case Parser.parse parser url of
        Just Gallery ->
            GalleryPage (Tuple.first (Gallery.init version))
```

Easy enough! Now that it accepts and uses a version number, we'll need to obtain the actual version number to pass it.

REVISING index.html

To obtain the version number from JavaScript, we'll need to edit index.html. Specifically, we'll adjust it to start passing in `Pasta.version` once again, as we first did back in chapter 5:

```
var app = Elm.Main.init({
    flags: Pasta.version,
    node: document.getElementById("app")
});
```

REVISING MAIN.INIT

With that in place, we can switch back to Main.elm and revise our declarations for `main` and `init` to reflect the flags they'll now be receiving. `main` will now have this type annotation:

```
main : Program Float Model Msg
```

The change to `Main.init` is a bit less obvious. We're going to not only receive the `Float` and pass it along to `urlToPage`, but also start storing it in our top-level `Model` record—for reasons that will become apparent momentarily:

```
init : Float -> Url -> Nav.Key -> ( Model, Cmd Msg )
init version url key =
    ( { page = urlToPage version url, key = key, version = version }
    , Cmd.none
    )
```

Why bother storing this in the `Model`? We already passed it to `urlToPage`, which is the only function that needs it.

That's very true, but we also call `urlToPage` at the end of `update`. If we want that code to continue working, we'll need to have it pass `version` to `urlToPage`, and the only way we can access `version` from within `update` is if `init` stores that value in the model while it still can. Here's the change we'll make to the last line of `update` to make this work:

```
ChangedUrl url ->
    ( { model | page = urlToPage model.version url }, Cmd.none )
```

> ## Why not store the version in GalleryPage instead?
>
> You may be wondering why we stored `version` in the top-level `Model` record instead of the `Page` variant for `Gallery`, because the Gallery page is the only one that uses the version number.
>
> The reason is that when we switch `Page` values from `GalleryPage Gallery`
> `.Model` to `FoldersPage Folders.Model`, we have discarded all data that was held in the `GalleryPage` variant. This means that if the user goes from the Gallery page to the Folders page and back again, we will be on the `FoldersPage` variant and no longer have access to any information we stored in the `GalleryPage` variant before we switched pages.
>
> Because the `version` is something we need to pass to `Gallery.init`, the only way we can be sure we'll have access to it every time we call `Gallery.init` is to store it in the top-level `Model`; that data is always available no matter which pages we transition between.

Finally, because we added a `version` field to `Model`, we'll need to update its type alias to match:

```
type alias Model =
    { page : Page, key : Nav.Key, version : Float }
```

Success! Our pages are now fully initialized, and we're ready for the final step: calling their `view` and `update` functions to render them between our header and footer.

8.3.3   Delegating page logic

As mentioned earlier, in order to call `Folders.view`, we need a `Folders.Model` to pass it. Fortunately, we now have one of those stored in our `Model`. Not only that, we also have a `Gallery.Model` to pass to `Gallery.view`.

Let's have the content declaration inside our `Main.view` function call these functions, depending on which page we currently have stored in the `model`:

```
content =
    case model.page of
        FoldersPage folders ->
            Folders.view folders

        GalleryPage gallery ->
            Gallery.view gallery

        NotFound ->
            text "Not Found"
```

Now we can rerun `elm make` and . . . huh? It didn't compile!

We have a subtle type mismatch here. `Main.view` wants to return an `Html Msg` value, but `Folders.view` returns an `Html Folders.Msg` value, and `Gallery.view` returns an `Html Gallery.Msg` value.

USING HTML.MAP

Just as a function that wants to return a `List Foo` can't return a `List Bar` instead, a function that wants to return an `Html Msg` can't return an `Html Gallery.Msg`. Fortunately, just as we could use `List.map` to convert a `List Foo` value into a `List Bar` value, we can use `Html.map` to convert an `Html Gallery.Msg` value into an `Html Msg` value.

Here's the type of `Html.map`. Spoiler alert: it's a lot like `List.map`, `Maybe.map`, and `Decode.map`:

```
Html.map : (before -> after) -> Html before -> Html after
```

This tells us that to convert `Html Gallery.Msg` into `Html Msg`, we need a `(Gallery.Msg -> Msg)` function. (Similarly, we'll also need a `(Folders.Msg -> Msg)` function to convert the value returned by `Folders.view`.) We can get both of those by adding two new variants to our `Msg` type:

```
type Msg
    = ClickedLink Browser.UrlRequest
    | ChangedUrl Url
    | GotFoldersMsg Folders.Msg
    | GotGalleryMsg Gallery.Msg
```

DELEGATING VIEW

Conveniently, the type of `GotFoldersMsg` is `(Folders.Msg -> Msg)`, and the type of `GotGalleryMsg` is `(Gallery.Msg -> Msg)` —exactly what we needed to pass to `Html.map`. That means we can do this:

```
FoldersPage folders ->
    Folders.view folders
        |> Html.map GotFoldersMsg

GalleryPage gallery ->
    Gallery.view gallery
        |> Html.map GotGalleryMsg
```

Conceptually, what `Html.map` is doing for us here is wrapping a `Folders.Msg` or `Gallery.Msg` in a `Main.Msg`, because `Main.update` knows how to deal with only `Main.Msg` values. Those wrapped messages will prove useful later when we handle these new messages inside `update`.

DELEGATING SUBSCRIPTIONS

You may recall from chapter 5 that the Gallery page also has some relevant subscriptions that we'll need to incorporate by using a similar trick. The only difference is that we'll use `Sub.map` instead of `Html.map`, to translate a `Sub  Gallery.Msg` into a `Sub Msg`:

```
subscriptions : Model -> Sub Msg
subscriptions model =
    case model.page of
        GalleryPage gallery ->
            Gallery.subscriptions gallery
                |> Sub.map GotGalleryMsg

        _ ->
            Sub.none
```

No need to add any new variants to `Msg` this time. `GotGalleryMsg` has us covered already. However, we're currently referencing a `subscriptions` function from the Gallery module . . . but that module exposes no such function.

The last thing we need to do is to expose it. Add `subscriptions` to the list of exposed values in `module PhotoGallery exposing` at the top of PhotoGallery.elm, and we're all set.

DELEGATING UPDATE

Now we have `view` delegating to `Folders.view` and `Gallery.view`, and subscriptions delegating to `Gallery.subscriptions`. All those functions compile just fine, but we'll get a missing-patterns error if we try to compile `Main.elm`, because our case-expression inside `update` doesn't account for the two new variants we just added to `Msg`. Let's handle those new `Msg` variants one at a time, starting with `GotFoldersMsg`.

Listing 8.3 Delegating `update`

```
update msg model =
    case msg of
        ...

        GotFoldersMsg foldersMsg ->                              Delegates to Folders.update,
            case model.page of                                  then converts its output
                FoldersPage folders ->                          to ( Model, Cmd Msg )
                    toFolders model (Folders.update foldersMsg folders)   ◁

                _ ->                         If we aren't on the Folders page,
                    ( model, Cmd.none )      ignore Folders messages.


    toFolders : Model -> ( Folders.Model, Cmd Folders.Msg ) -> ( Model, Cmd Msg )
    toFolders model ( folders, cmd ) =
        ( { model | page = FoldersPage folders }    ◁        Stores the Folders.Model
        , Cmd.map GotFoldersMsg cmd           ◁              in FoldersPage
        )
```

Destructures the tuple inline

Cmd.map works just like
Html.map and Sub.map.

This requires a few more steps than those we did with `view` and `subscriptions`, but fundamentally we're doing the same delegation as we did there. Let's walk through the steps this is taking:

1. When `update` receives a `GetFoldersMsg`, first it checks `model.page` to see if we're actually on the Folders page. (We might not be! For example, the user might do something on the Folders page that sends an HTTP request, and then switch to a different page before the server responds. That response would arrive as a `Folders.Msg`, but `model.page` would no longer be `FoldersPage`.)

2. If we're not on `FoldersPage`, ignore the message. We could do some error logging here if we wanted to, but in this case, we'll assume the user no longer cares about the message (because they transitioned away from that page) and ignore the message.

3. Now that we have in scope `foldersMsg : Folders.Msg` (the value held in our `GotFoldersMsg`) as well as `folders : Folders.Model` (the value held in `FoldersPage`, our current `model.page` value), we can pass them both to

Folders.update. It will return a (Folders.Model, Cmd Folders.Msg) tuple.

4 We call toFolders to convert this (Folders.Model, Cmd Folders.Msg) tuple into the (Model, Cmd Msg) tuple that update wants to return. We do this by using Cmd.map, which works just like Html.map and Sub.map.

The code for the GotGalleryMsg branch and its corresponding toGallery function will follow the same recipe, except everywhere this code says Folders, that code will say Gallery instead. Try implementing it on your own. (If you get stuck, you can sneak a peek at the final code listing at the end of the chapter.)

TRYING THE PAGE

Everything compiles! Wonderful! Figure 8.6 shows how it looks.

Figure 8.6   First confirmed sighting of the compiled Main.elm in the wild

Hmm, that doesn't quite look right. Upon closer inspection, the problem is that we only partially delegated init. We have it calling Tuple.first on the result of the init functions it calls. This compiles, but it means we're keeping the Model portion of the tuple and chucking the Cmd down a garbage chute.

KEEPING BOTH MODEL AND CMD FOR INIT

Without having their init commands run, our pages' initial HTTP requests aren't being sent to the server to load the pages' initial data. Whoops!

We'll fix that by deleting urlToPage (including from the module's exposing list) and replacing it with a more helpful updateUrl function like so:

```
init version url key =
    updateUrl url { page = NotFound, key = key, version = version }


updateUrl : Url -> Model -> ( Model, Cmd Msg )
updateUrl url model =
    case Parser.parse parser url of
        Just Gallery ->
            Gallery.init model.version
                |> toGallery model

        Just Folders ->
            Folders.init Nothing
                |> toFolders model
```

```
Just (SelectedPhoto filename) ->
    Folders.init (Just filename)
        |> toFolders model

Nothing ->
    ( { model | page = NotFound }, Cmd.none )
```

Because the `ChangedUrl` branch inside `update` also relied on `urlToPage`, we'll want to change it to use our shiny new `updateUrl` function instead:

```
ChangedUrl url ->
    updateUrl url model
```

Lovely! Let's try it out; see figure 8.7.

Figure 8.7   The final pages

REMOVING DUPLICATION

Nice! We do have a bit of header duplication going on, though. `Main.viewHeader` puts `<h1>` in the upper left, and then each of the pages also puts its own competing `<h1>` in there below it—but that's easy enough to fix:

- In PhotoGallery.elm, delete the call to `h1` at the top of `viewLoaded`.
- In PhotoFolders.elm, delete the call to `h1` near the end of `view`.

With that cosmetic fix in the bank, we're ready for the final feature of the book. Thankfully, this one is extremely quick: we're going to change a grand total of *three* lines of code.

LINKING TO /PHOTOS/FILENAME

We're going to turn the file buttons on the Folders page into links, so when the user clicks them, the URL bar will update to /photos/filename—meaning the user will be able to share it, bookmark it, and use the browser's Back button to return to it.

To make this work, we're going to replace our `<div class="photo">` buttons with `<a>` links that will change the URL to /photos/whatever. When the user clicks one of those links, it will trigger a `UrlChange` in Main.elm, which in turn will cause it to invoke `Folders.init`, passing the newly selected value.

We will need to make one change before this will work, specifically to Photo-Folders.update. It currently resets the selected photo every time it receives a new list of them from the server (which will now happen every time we click a photo link, thanks to `Folders.init` being run again).

Instead, we'll make it preserve the currently selected photo by making this change:

```
update : Msg -> Model -> ( Model, Cmd Msg )
update msg model =
    …

    GotInitialModel (Ok newModel) ->
        ( { newModel | selectedPhotoUrl = model.selectedPhotoUrl }, Cmd.none
        )
```

With that adjustment in place, all that remains is to introduce the link.

MAKING THE FINAL CHANGE

This is it! This is the final touch before Photo Groove is complete. Are you excited? You deserve to be—you've come so far and learned so much!

Here's the change: inside PhotoFolders.elm, replace the `<div>` in `viewPhoto` with an `<a>` whose `href` is set to the appropriate /photos/ URL:

```
viewPhoto : String -> Html Msg
viewPhoto url =
    a [ href ("/photos/" ++ url), class "photo", …
```

The third and final change will be exposing `href`, because `PhotoFolders` wasn't using it before:

```
import Html.Attributes exposing (class, href, src)
```

That's it! Now when you click the different photos, the URL changes, and you can use the browser's Back button to reselect the previous photo. And with that, Photo Groove is complete, as shown in figure 8.8.

You did it! You built an entire Elm single-page application from start to finish! Give yourself a round of applause; you have 100% earned it. Congratulations, and seriously, well done!

WHAT IF I WANT TO KEEP THIS PHOTO GROOVE GOING?

If you'd like to keep tinkering with Photo Groove, here are some ideas for things to try:

- Change the page's title depending on which page the user is viewing.
- There's a bit of code duplication between the `PhotoFolders` and `Photo-Gallery` modules: they both have identical `urlPrefix` constants. Try replacing those two with a single `urlPrefix` constant that they both import and reference. (Spoiler: Moving it into `Main` and having them both import it won't work.)

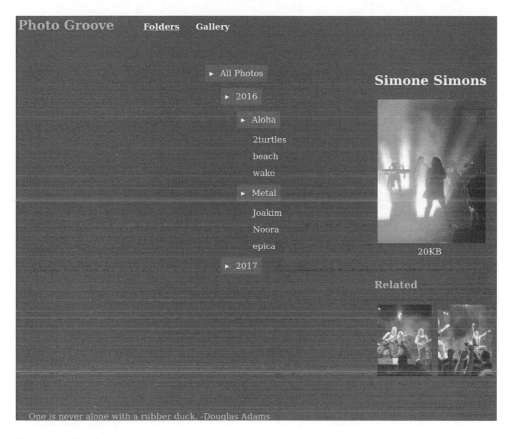

Figure 8.8   The final pages

- Theoretically, we shouldn't need the `SelectedPhotoUrl` variant in `Photo-Folders.Msg` because we switched to linking directly to the photo URLs. However, it's still in use in one place. See if you can think of a good change that would make it obsolete, and then drop it.

- Here's a more involved one, if you really want to roll up your sleeves. If you click quickly between photos on the Folders page, you briefly see a Loading message. This is because the URL is now changing, causing `Folders.init` to be rerun, which in turn triggers a new HTTP request. See if you can figure out a way to avoid doing this HTTP request when clicking between photos to change which one is selected, without causing any regressions anywhere else.

These are some ideas for ways to polish Photo Groove, but you can learn even more from exploring on your own. Think up a new feature to add and try adding it. You might be surprised at what you can do!

Summary

Here are some of the new concepts you used in the course of building your single-page application:

- Coordinating between multiple modules in a single Elm project
- Rendering pages with custom titles by using `Browser.document` and having `view` return a `Document` record
- Giving the Elm Runtime control of the entire page by using `Browser.application`
- Using `Debug.todo` as a temporary placeholder that always type-checks, but crashes at runtime if you actually reach the code that calls it
- Using the `onUrlRequest` and `onUrlChanged` events to respond to users clicking links and interacting with the browser's address bar
- Stashing `Nav.Key` in `Model` during `init`, for later use with `Nav.pushUrl` in `update`
- Parsing URLs in `Browser.application`'s init function by using `Url.Parser`
- Identifying when two data structures are similar but not the same, and splitting them up as we did with `Page` and `Route`
- Delegating to other pages's `init`, `view`, `subscriptions`, and `update` functions by using `Html.map`, `Sub.map`, and `Cmd.map`

Here is the final Main.elm file.

Listing 8.4   Final Main.elm

```
module Main exposing (main)

import Browser exposing (Document)
import Browser.Navigation as Nav
import Html exposing (Html, a, footer, h1, li, nav, text, ul)
import Html.Attributes exposing (classList, href)
import Html.Lazy exposing (lazy)
import PhotoFolders as Folders
import PhotoGroove as Gallery
import Url exposing (Url)
import Url.Parser as Parser exposing ((</>), Parser, s, string)


type alias Model =
    { page : Page
    , key : Nav.Key
    , version : Float
    }


type Page
    = FoldersPage Folders.Model
    | GalleryPage Gallery.Model
```

Stores the Folders model only when we're on the Folders page, and the same for Gallery

```
    | NotFound


type Route
    = Gallery
    | Folders
    | SelectedPhoto String
```

These correspond to URL routes like /gallery and /photos/foo.

```
view : Model -> Document Msg
view model =
    let
        content =
            case model.page of
                FoldersPage folders ->
                    Folders.view folders
                        |> Html.map GotFoldersMsg

                GalleryPage gallery ->
                    Gallery.view gallery
                        |> Html.map GotGalleryMsg

                NotFound ->
                    text "Not Found"
    in
    { title = "Photo Groove, SPA Style"
    , body =
        [ lazy viewHeader model.page
        , content
        , viewFooter
        ]
    }
```

Delegates view based on which page we're viewing

lazy means viewHeader reruns only when model.page changes.

```
viewHeader : Page -> Html Msg
viewHeader page =
    let
        logo =
            h1 [] [ text "Photo Groove" ]

        links =
            ul []
                [ navLink Folders { url = "/", caption = "Folders" }
                , navLink Gallery { url = "/gallery", caption = "Gallery" }
                ]

        navLink : Route -> { url : String, caption : String } -> Html msg
        navLink route { url, caption } =
            li
                [ classList
                    [ ( "active"
                      , isActive { link = route, page = page }
                      )
                    ]
                ]
```

```
                       [ a [ href url ] [ text caption ] ]
        in
        nav [] [ logo, links ]
```

Parses a Route based on whichever of these parsers passes first

```
parser : Parser (Route -> a) a
parser =
    Parser.oneOf
        [ Parser.map Folders Parser.top
        , Parser.map Gallery (s "gallery")
        , Parser.map SelectedPhoto (s "photos" </> Parser.string)
        ]
```

```
isActive : { link : Route, page : Page } -> Bool
isActive { link, page } =
    case ( link, page ) of
        ( Gallery       , GalleryPage _ ) -> True
        ( Gallery       , _             ) -> False
        ( Folders       , FoldersPage _ ) -> True
        ( Folders       , _             ) -> False
        ( SelectedPhoto _, _            ) -> False
```

Destructures "named arguments" immediately

A "truth table" determining whether a link should be shown as "active"

```
viewFooter : Html msg
viewFooter =
    footer []
        [ text "One is never alone with a rubber duck. -Douglas Adams" ]
```

```
type Msg
    = ClickedLink Browser.UrlRequest
    | ChangedUrl Url
    | GotFoldersMsg Folders.Msg
    | GotGalleryMsg Gallery.Msg
```

Wrapper messages for the Folders and Gallery pages

```
update : Msg -> Model -> ( Model, Cmd Msg )
update msg model =
    case msg of
        ClickedLink urlRequest ->
            case urlRequest of
                Browser.External href ->
                    ( model, Nav.load href )

                Browser.Internal url ->
                    ( model, Nav.pushUrl model.key (Url.toString url) )

        ChangedUrl url ->
            updateUrl url model

        GotFoldersMsg foldersMsg ->
            case model.page of
                FoldersPage folders ->
                    toFolders model (Folders.update foldersMsg folders)
```

Handles requests to our same domain by doing a pushUrl— which will trigger a ChangedUrl message

Handles requests to external domains by doing a full page load

Delegates wrapped messages for the Folders page to Folders.update

```
                    _ ->                      If we're on the Folders page,
                        ( model, Cmd.none )   ignore non-Folders messages.

            GotGalleryMsg galleryMsg ->           case model.page of
                    GalleryPage gallery ->
                        toGallery model (Gallery.update galleryMsg gallery)


                    _ ->
                        ( model, Cmd.none )


toFolders : Model -> ( Folders.Model, Cmd Folders.Msg ) -> ( Model, Cmd Msg )
toFolders model ( folders, cmd ) =
    ( { model | page = FoldersPage folders }      Converts a ( Model, Cmd
    , Cmd.map GotFoldersMsg cmd                   Msg ) from the Folders page
    )                                             to Main's equivalent


toGallery : Model -> ( Gallery.Model, Cmd Gallery.Msg ) -> ( Model, Cmd Msg )
toGallery model ( gallery, cmd ) =
    ( { model | page = GalleryPage gallery }
    , Cmd.map GotGalleryMsg cmd
    )


main : Program Float Model Msg
main =
    Browser.application
        { init = init
        , onUrlChange = ChangedUrl
        , onUrlRequest = ClickedLink
        , subscriptions = subscriptions
        , update = update
        , view = view
        }


init : Float -> Url -> Nav.Key -> ( Model, Cmd Msg )
init version url key =
    updateUrl url { page = NotFound, key = key, version = version }


subscriptions : Model -> Sub Msg
subscriptions model =
    case model.page of
        GalleryPage gallery ->
            Gallery.subscriptions gallery
                |> Sub.map GotGalleryMsg


        _ ->
            Sub.none


updateUrl : Url -> Model -> ( Model, Cmd Msg )
updateUrl url model =
```

```
case Parser.parse parser url of
    Just Gallery ->
        toGallery model (Gallery.init model.version)

    Just Folders ->
        toFolders model (Folders.init Nothing)

    Just (SelectedPhoto filename) ->
        toFolders model (Folders.init (Just filename))

    Nothing ->
        ( { model | page = NotFound }, Cmd.none )
```

When the URL changes, parse it into a Route and init a new Model and Cmd Msg.

appendix A
Getting set up

This appendix covers installing the following

- Node.js (10.0.0 or higher) and NPM (6.0.0 or higher)
- Required command-line tools
- The *Elm in Action* repository
- Recommended optional tools

A.1 Installing Node.js and NPM

In addition to having the Elm Platform installed, the examples in this book require having Node.js 10.0.0 or higher and NPM 6.0.0 or higher installed as well. If you haven't already, visit https://nodejs.org and follow the instructions to download and install them.

> **NOTE** The Node.js installer at https://nodejs.org also installs NPM for you, so if you install Node that way, you will not need to install NPM separately.

To confirm that you have Node.js 10.0.0 or higher and NPM 6.0.0 or higher installed, you should be able to run these commands in your terminal and see similar output:

```
$ node --version
v10.0.0

$ npm --version
6.0.0
```

If you have Node installed but not NPM, then your installation of Node is probably not the one from https://nodejs.org. Please make sure you have NPM installed before continuing.

A.2   *Installing command-line tools*

Now that you have NPM installed, you can use it to get the Elm Platform along with the `elm-test` and `http-server-spa` command-line tools. (You'll need `elm-test` in chapter 6 and `http-server-spa` in chapter 8.) Here's the command:

```
npm install -g elm elm-test http-server-spa@1.3.0
```

> **TIP**   If npm gives you a lengthy error involving the word EACCES, visit https://docs.npmjs.com/getting-started/fixing-npm-permissions for how to resolve it. If you are unable to resolve this error, you can fall back on installing the Elm Platform directly from http://elm-lang.org/install, but this will get you through only chapters 1 through 5. Starting in chapter 6, being able to run `npm install -g` will be required to run the examples.

Let's verify that the Elm platform was installed properly:

```
elm --version
0.19.1
```

If you see a version higher than `0.19.1`, then as of this writing, you are living in the future! Hello from the past, where `0.19.1` is the latest release.

> **NOTE**   Any version that starts with `0.19` should work fine with this book, but according to semantic versioning, a version number beginning with `0.20` or higher indicates breaking changes. In such a case, there's a good chance your examples will not compile. Try `npm install -g elm@latest-0.19.1` to get a compatible version.

A.3   *Obtaining the Elm in Action repository*

This book does not require using Git or any Git knowledge. If you are not a Git user, you can download and extract a zip archive of the repository at https://github.com/rtfeldman/elm-in-action/archive/master.zip and proceed directly to the next section.

Git users can download the repository by running this:

```
git clone https://github.com/rtfeldman/elm-in-action.git
```

The repository has been tagged with various checkpoints. Suppose you are about to read chapter 2, section 2.2.1. You can visit this URL to obtain all the code necessary to work through the examples in section 2.2.1:

```
https://github.com/rtfeldman/elm-in-action/tree/2.2.1
```

You can replace the `2.2.1` in that URL with a different section number to view the code at the start of that section. For example, if you want to peek ahead and see where things stand at the end of section 2.2.1, you can bring up the `2.2.2` tag by visiting https://github.com/rtfeldman/elm-in-action/tree/2.2.2 in a browser. Alternatively, you can run `git checkout 2.2.2` from a terminal if you ran `git clone` on the repository earlier.

A.4 Installing recommended optional tools

To get syntax highlighting and other niceties, visit http://elm-lang.org/install#syntax-highlighting and select your editor of choice to find an appropriate Elm plugin. Make sure your editor is configured to convert tabs to spaces, as tab characters are syntax errors in Elm.

I also strongly recommend installing `elm-format`: https://github.com/avh4/elm-format. I absolutely love `elm-format`. It automatically formats Elm code according to a nice, consistent standard.

I use it for personal projects, my whole team at work uses it, and I have my editor configured to run it whenever I save. (Several editors enable this by default, but if not, there are easy instructions in the preceding link for how to enable format-on-save.) All of the examples in this book are formatted with `elm-format`, so using it will make life easier as you work through them.

appendix B
Installing Elm packages

This appendix elaborates on these concepts first introduced in chapter 3

- Direct and indirect dependencies
- Default imports
- Elm's semantic versioning
- Installation of Elm packages

Whenever we run `elm install` to add a new dependency, it modifies our elm.json file. Here is the elm.json file we'll have at the beginning of the book's final chapter, chapter 8.

Listing B.1   Photo Groove's elm.json

```
{
    "type": "application",
    "source-directories": [
        "src"
    ],
```

We'd replace "application" with "package" if we were building a package.

Elm will look in our src/ directory only for source code.

```
"elm-version": "0.19.1",
"dependencies": {                              We can import modules
    "direct": {                                from direct dependencies.
        "NoRedInk/elm-json-decode-pipeline": "1.0.0",
        "elm/browser": "1.0.1",
        "elm/core": "1.0.2",                   New releases mean you may
        "elm/html": "1.0.0",                      see different version
        "elm/http": "2.0.0",                   numbers in your elm.json.
        "elm/json": "1.1.2",
        "elm/random": "1.0.0"
    },
    "indirect": {                              We cannot import modules
        "elm/bytes": "1.0.7",                  from indirect dependencies.
        "elm/file": "1.0.1",
        "elm/time": "1.0.0",
        "elm/virtual-dom": "1.0.2"
    }
},
"test-dependencies": {                         test-dependencies are available
    "direct": {                                only when running elm-test.
        "elm-explorations/test": "1.2.0"
    },
    "indirect": {}
}
}
```

B.1 *Direct and indirect dependencies*

As mentioned in chapter 3, section 3.3.1, an Elm package is a collection of modules, and packages can depend on other packages. These break down into direct and indirect dependencies:

- *Direct dependencies*—Packages we've installed using the `elm install` command. Our application code can reference anything these packages expose.
- *Indirect dependencies*—Packages our direct dependencies depend on. Our application code cannot directly reference anything in these packages. (If we want to use something they expose, we can always move them from *indirect* to *direct*.)

NOTE The reason indirect dependencies are listed explicitly, along with their version numbers, is so that teams working on the same Elm application can be confident everyone is using the exact same versions of all dependencies.

The reason `elm/core`, `elm/browser`, and `elm/html` were all installed by the `elm init` command we ran in chapter 2 is that they are the minimum requirements for building an Elm user interface in the browser:

- `elm/html` houses `Html` and related modules.
- `elm/browser` gives us the `Program` type that we use for `main`.

- `elm/core` has foundational modules like `List`, `String`, and `Cmd`. It also contains a module called `Basics`, which provides bread-and-butter stuff like arithmetic operations and the `not` function.

Default imports

Certain frequently used `core` modules are imported by default. For example, there is an implicit `import List` at the top of each file, even if you don't manually write one. That's why you can write `List.reverse` even if you haven't explicitly imported the `List` module. Here are the default imports for every Elm file:

```
Basics, List, Maybe, Result, String, Tuple, Debug, Platform,
Platform.Cmd as Cmd, Platform.Sub as Sub
```

In addition to these modules, many of the types and type constructors in `core` are exposed by default. For example, the `Maybe` type as well as its `Just` and `Nothing` variants are all exposed by default. This means you can always write `Nothing` instead of `Maybe.Nothing`. Check out the README for the `elm/core` package for an up-to-date list.

B.2 Semantic versioning in packages

Packages have *version numbers* that are specified in a three-digit format, like so:

```
"elm/core": "1.0.1",
"elm/http": "2.0.0"
```

All packages are initially released at version 1.0.0. Each of these three numbers has a specific meaning, according to certain *semantic versioning* rules, which in Elm are defined as follows:

- *Major version* number (the 3 in 3.2.1)—This number increments whenever a package makes a change to any public-facing values. For example, changing the type of a function that is publicly accessible, or removing the function altogether, would demand a major version number increase.
- *Minor version number* (the 2 in 3.2.1)—This increments whenever a package introduces a new public-facing value. You'd see a minor version number bump in a release that introduced new publicly accessible values without altering or removing any existing ones.
- *Patch version number* (the 1 in 3.2.1)—This increments whenever a release neither introduces nor alters any publicly accessible values. It might modify documentation or internal implementations, though; for example, to fix a bug discovered in a previous release.

When any of these numbers increments, the numbers after it become zero. As such, releasing a package updated from version 3.2.1 would change the version number as shown in table B.1.

Table B.1   Incrementing a package version from 3.2.1

Current version	Type of change	Next version
3.2.1	*Major change*	4.0.0
3.2.1	*Minor change*	3.3.0
3.2.1	*Patch change*	3.2.2

B.2.1   *Semantic versioning enforced*

All packages in Elm's ecosystem are guaranteed to respect these semantic versioning rules. If a package author makes a breaking change to a publicly accessible value, and attempts to publish the package while increasing only the minor or patch version numbers, the package repository will detect this and refuse to publish. The author will see an error message explaining that this breaking change requires a major version number bump.

B.2.2   *Browsing package documentation*

Published packages are also required to document their publicly exposed values and to provide a link to their source code. You can view documentation and links to source code for any package in the Elm ecosystem by visiting http://package.elm-lang.org. This site lists the modules in each package and the values they expose.

B.3   *Example: Installing elm/url*

Let's say we were to run `elm install elm/url`. After it completes, this command will have done the following:

1   Edited elm.json to include the latest version of `elm/url` as a direct dependency
2   Downloaded the code for the `elm/url` package to a directory called .elm inside our home directory
3   Downloaded any code necessary for `elm/url`'s dependencies into that same .elm directory, and listed them as indirect dependencies in our elm.json file

TIP   `elm make` looks in that .elm directory for all downloaded packages, which means after `elm install` has downloaded a package, it will never bother downloading it again unless your .elm directory gets deleted. This also means you can use `elm init` and `elm install` when you're offline; as long as the versions of all the packages you want to use have already been downloaded, you'll be all set!

Ahh, the internet. Shout-out to any programmers who remember what sharing code was like before the internet. Personally, I liked to wrap a printout around the ankle of my pterodactyl.

appendix C
Html.Lazy's change check

> **This appendix adds details about the** `Html.Lazy`
> **function first used in chapter 8**
>
> - How `lazy` works with strings and numbers
> - How it works for other values
> - How it works when memory locations change

In chapter 8, we used the `Html.Lazy.lazy` function to skip running view code if certain values did not change on repeated calls. How does `lazy` decide whether a value has changed? The answer to this question involves two important design goals:

- `lazy` must never skip calling the function if there is any chance the function could return a different value. At worst, `lazy` should be an ineffective performance optimization; it should never cause bugs under any circumstances.
- Because it's a tool for making things run faster, `lazy` should perform the "Is it safe to skip?" check as quickly as possible.

To balance these goals, `lazy` does the fastest check it can to determine whether the argument it receives is *possibly different* from the last time it was called. This check compiles down to using JavaScript's === operator, which often gives different results from Elm's == operator. Let's zoom in on some of those differences.

C.1 *lazy's check for strings and numbers*

When it comes to strings and numbers, lazy's check works the same way as plain old == checks do in Elm. If two strings or two numbers are equal according to Elm's == operator, then lazy considers them the same.

C.2 *lazy's check for everything else*

For every other type in Elm, lazy checks whether the value has the same location in memory as it did before. Values other than strings and numbers get assigned a unique location in memory when they are initially defined, and they retain this memory location when they get passed around or returned from functions. For example, here are two values with the same content but different locations in memory:

```
jess =
    [ "dev", "dot", "to" ]

ben =
    [ "dev", "dot", "to" ]
```

Here, jess == ben evaluates to True, but jess and ben have different memory locations because they were initially defined separately. Table C.1 summarizes this relationship.

Table C.1 Equality relationships between jess and ben

First value	Second value	==	Memory locations
jess	jess	True	Same
ben	ben	True	Same
jess	ben	True	Different
ben	jess	True	Different

> **TIP** In Elm, memory location is a detail that matters only for performance optimization, not application logic. The only consequence of changes that affect memory locations is that things might run faster or slower.

C.3 *When memory locations stay the same*

Custom type variants that don't hold data—for example, the values True, False, and Nothing—always have the same memory location. They work the same way with lazy as strings and numbers do. (In contrast, values created with `Just` might not have the same memory locations, because `Just` holds data.)

Other values keep the same memory location when they are passed around. Table C.2 shows some ways to get a value with the same memory location as another value.

Table C.2   Ways to get a value with the same memory location as another value

Operation yielding same memory location	Examples
Assigning it to another constant	`sameMemory = oldValue`
Reading it from a record field	`sameMemory = record.oldValue`

Reading it by destructuring	`{ sameMemory } = record`
	`( sameMemory, _ ) = tuple`
	
	In a case-expression:
	`SomeVariant sameMemory ->`

Passing it to a function	`myFunction sameMemory =`
Returning it from a function	`sameMemory = Tuple.first ( oldVal, [] )`

C.3.1   *Memory locations for collections*

When creating a new collection based on an old collection, it's common to end up with the *content* of the new collection having the same memory location as before, but the *collection itself* having a different memory location. Table C.3 shows some ways to create such collections.

Table C.3   Collections with different memory locations whose contents are the same

Operation yielding different memory location	Examples
Updating a record	`newMemory = { oldRec	x = oldRec.x }`

Rewrapping a record or tuple	`newMemory =`
	`    ( Tuple.first oldTuple`
	`    , Tuple.second oldTuple`
	`    )`

Rewrapping a custom type variant	`newMemory =`
	`    case someResult of`
	`        Ok oldValue ->`
	`            Ok oldValue`
	
	`        Err oldValue ->`
	`            Err oldValue`

Mapping over a collection	`newMemory = List.map identity oldList`

C.3.2 Memory locations across updates

In practice, model values are most often either records or custom types. According to the preceding rules, the only way for such a model to keep the same memory location after an update is if update returns unchanged the same model it receives as an argument. Consider this code:

```
update : Msg -> Model -> ( Model, Cmd Msg )
update msg model =
    case msg of
        Search ->
            ( model, runSearch model.query )

        SetQuery query ->
            ( { model | query = query }, Cmd.none )


view : Model -> Html Msg
view model =
    lazy viewEverything model
```

When update receives a Search message, it returns model unchanged. This means model will have the same memory location as before, and the lazy call inside view will skip running viewEverything.

However, when update receives a SetQuery message, it returns a record update of model, which will have a different memory location. This means the lazy call inside view will rerun viewEverything, passing the updated model.

> **TIP** To get the most out of lazy, use it on functions that take only the subset of the Model they need.

C.3.3 Memory locations for functions

Functions are first-class values in Elm, and their memory locations are relevant to lazy. This is true for any function passed to lazy, including the viewSidebar function we want to skip. lazy will skip calling viewSidebar only if the viewSidebar function we pass has the same memory location as the previous one we passed.

For this reason, it's never useful to pass lazy a function that was defined inside another function; there's no chance its memory location will be the same from one call to the next, so lazy can't possibly improve performance.

```
Possibly beneficial:    lazy          viewSidebar      model.user
No possible benefit:    lazy (\arg -> viewSidebar arg) model.user
```

This is true not only of anonymous functions inside view, but also of named functions defined in a let-expression inside view.

C.3.4   *Named top-level functions always keep the same memory location*

Conveniently, named functions defined at a module's top level always keep the same memory location. The following listing shows a `viewSidebar` function that will always work the way we want it to with `lazy`, and a `badViewSidebar` function that will never work right with `lazy` because it's defined inside another function.

Listing C.1   Defining functions in a lazy-friendly way

```
module MyModule exposing (view)


viewSidebar : User -> Html Msg          Named functions defined at the
viewSidebar = …                         top level always work with lazy.


view : Model -> Html Msg
view =
    let
        badViewSidebar : User -> Html Msg        Functions defined inside other
        badViewSidebar =                         functions never work with lazy.
            …
    in
    lazy viewSidebar model.user    ◁───   If we passed badViewSidebar
                                          instead, it would never get skipped.
```

As long as we always pass only named top-level functions to `lazy`, we'll be all set!

index